ExpressWays

ENGLISH FOR COMMUNICATION

3

Steven J. Molinsky · Bill Bliss

Prentice-Hall, Englewood Cliffs, NJ 07632

Library of Congress Cataloging in Publication Data

Molinsky, Steven J.
  ExpressWays: English for communication.

  Includes index.
  1. English language—Text-books for foreign speakers.
I. Bliss, Bill. II. Title.
PE1128.M674 1986   428.3'4   85-30059
ISBN 0-13-298274-9 (set)
ISBN 0-13-298282-X (3A)
ISBN 0-13-298316-8 (3B)

Editorial/production supervision and interior design: Sylvia Moore
Development: Ellen Lehrburger
Notes and Commentary section: Carla Meskill
Cover design: Lundgren Graphics Ltd.
Manufacturing buyer: Harry P. Baisley
Page layout: Diane Koromhas

Illustrations and Cover Drawing by Gabriel Polonsky

Printed in the United States of America

10 9 8 7 6 5 4 3 2

ISBN 0-13-298274-9

Prentice-Hall International, Inc., *London*
Prentice-Hall of Australia Pty. Limited, *Sydney*
Editora Prentice-Hall do Brasil, Ltda., *Rio de Janeiro*
Prentice-Hall Canada Inc., *Toronto*
Prentice-Hall Hispanoamericana, S.A., *Mexico*
Prentice-Hall of India Private Limited, *New Delhi*
Prentice-Hall of Japan, Inc., *Tokyo*
Prentice-Hall of Southeast Asia Pte. Ltd., *Singapore*
Whitehall Books Limited, *Wellington, New Zealand*

Contents

TO THE TEACHER

ExpressWays is a functional English program for adult and young-adult learners of English. The program consists of the following components:

Student Course Books—offering intensive conversational practice;
Companion Workbooks—offering grammar, reading, writing, and listening comprehension practice fully coordinated with the student course books;
Guide Books—providing background notes and expansion activities for all lessons and step-by-step instructions for teachers;
Audio Program—offering realistic presentation of dialogs in the texts;
Placement and Achievement Testing Program—providing tools for the evaluation of student levels and progress.

ExpressWays—Book 3 is intended for students who have been exposed to the essentials of intermediate-level grammar and who have already mastered the usage of English for everyday life situations. The text builds upon and reinforces this foundation and prepares students for higher level language skills required for effective interpersonal communication. *ExpressWays—Book 3* is organized functionally, while incorporating integrated coverage of grammar and topics.

THE DIMENSIONS OF COMMUNICATION: FUNCTION, FORM, AND CONTENT

A number of texts present the functional syllabus by describing language use and listing sets of functional phrases. The exercises and activities that normally accompany these descriptions and lists usually occur in isolation, rather than being totally integrated into active conversational practice. In addition, traditional functional approaches usually do not give students intensive communicative practice using the correct grammatical forms that are required by particular functional language choices.

ExpressWays, essentially, does not seek to provide students with background knowledge about language use. Rather, it provides dynamic, communicative practice that involves students in lively interactions based on the content of real-life contexts and situations. The functional syllabus is fully integrated into a complete conversational course in which students not only learn the various ways to express each function, but also intensively practice the grammatical forms required to turn functional expressions into lines of effective communication in English.

Every lesson in the program offers students simultaneous practice with one or more functions, the grammatical forms needed to express those functions competently, and the contexts and situations in which the functions and grammar are used. This "tri-dimensional clustering" of function, form, and content is the organizing principle behind each lesson and the cornerstone of the *ExpressWays* approach to functional syllabus design.

ExpressWays aims to offer students broad exposure to uses of language in a variety of relevant contexts: in community, academic, employment, home, and social settings.

The characters portrayed are people of different ages, ethnic groups, and occupations, interacting in real-life situations.

While some texts make a point of giving students a range of ways of expressing a function, from extremely polite to very impolite, we have chosen to "take the middle ground" and concentrate on those expressions that would most frequently occur in normal polite conversation between people in various settings. *ExpressWays* does offer a variety of registers, from the formal language someone might use in a job interview, with a customer, or when speaking with an authority figure, to the informal language someone would use when talking with family members, co-workers, or friends. When appropriate, the text also presents students with alternative degrees of expressing a function, such as strength of disagreement and certainty or the directness of requests and advice.

A special feature of the program is the treatment of discourse strategies. Students actively practice initiating conversations and topics, interrupting, hesitating, asking for clarification, and other conversation skills.

AN OVERVIEW

Guided Conversations

Guided Conversations are the dialogs and exercises that are the central learning devices in the program. Each lesson begins with a model guided conversation that illustrates the use of one or more functions and the structures they require, all in the context of a meaningful exchange of communication. Key functional expressions in the models are in bold-face type and are footnoted, referring students to short lists of alternative expressions for accomplishing the functions. In the exercises that follow, students create new conversations by placing new contexts, content, or characters into the framework of the model, and by using any of the alternative functional expressions.

"Now Present Your Own Conversations"

Each lesson ends with this open-ended exercise which offers students the opportunity to create and present original conversations based on the model and any of the alternative expressions. Students contribute content based on their experiences, ideas, and imaginations, while staying within the framework of the model.

We should emphasize that the objective of each lesson is to provide a measure of controlled practice with a dialog and guided conversation exercises so that students can competently use functional expressions in creating their own original conversations.

Interchange

This end-of-chapter activity offers students the opportunity to create and to present "guided role plays." Each activity consists of a model that students can practice and then use as a basis for their original presentations. Students should be encouraged to be inventive and to use new vocabulary in these presentations and should feel free to adapt and expand the model any way they wish.

Scenes & Improvisations

These "free role plays" appear after every third chapter, offering review and synthesis of functions and conversation strategies in the three preceding chapters. Students are presented with eight scenes depicting conversations between people in various situations. They use the information in the scenes to determine who the people are and what they are talking about. Then, students improvise based on their perceptions of the scenes' characters, contexts, and situations.

The purpose of these improvisations is to offer recombination practice that promotes students' absorption of the preceding chapters' functions and strategies into their repertoire of active language use.

Support and Reference Sections

ExpressWays offers a number of support and reference sections:

- *Chapter Opening Pages* provide an overview of functions and conversation strategies highlighted in each chapter.
- *End-of-Chapter Summaries* provide complete lists of expressions for the functions and conversation strategies appearing in each chapter.
- An *Inventory of Functions and Conversation Strategies* in the Appendix offers a comprehensive display of all expressions for the functions and conversation strategies in the text, and indicates the chapters in which the expressions appear.
- A *Notes and Commentary* section in the Appendix provides background information for each lesson, including notes on language usage, grammar, and culture; commentaries on the characters, contexts, and situations; and explanations of idiomatic and colloquial expressions.
- An *Index of Functions and Conversation Strategies* and an *Index of Grammatical Structures* provide a convenient reference for locating coverage of functions and grammar in the text.

THE TOTAL *ExpressWays* PROGRAM

The *ExpressWays Student Course Books* are essentially designed to offer intensive communicative practice with functional language. These texts may be used independently or in conjunction with the *ExpressWays Companion Workbooks*, which offer practice in the other skill areas of reading, writing, and listening, as well as focused practice with particular grammar structures as they occur in the program. Each exercise in the Companion Workbook indicates the specific Student Course Book page that it corresponds to.

The *ExpressWays Guide Books* provide step-by-step instructions for coverage of each lesson, background notes, sample answers to guided conversation exercises, and answer keys and listening-activity scripts for exercises in the Companion Workbooks. Perhaps the most important feature of the Guide Books is the expansion exercise that is recommended for each lesson. These exercises offer students free, spontaneous practice with the functional content that is treated in a more systematic manner in the text itself. Activities include improvisations, "information gap" role plays, problem-solving, and topics for discussion and debate. We encourage teachers to use these activities or similar ones as springboards to help their students "break away" from the text and incorporate lesson content into their everyday use of English.

The *ExpressWays Audio Program* includes a set of tapes providing realistic presentation of all model dialogs and selected guided conversation exercises in the Student Course Books. The tapes are designed to be used interactively, so that the recorded voice serves as the student's speaking partner, making conversation practice possible even when the student is studying alone. The Audio Program also includes a set of tapes for the listening comprehension exercises in the Companion Workbooks.

The *ExpressWays Testing Program* includes a Placement Testing Kit for initial evaluation and leveling of students, and sets of Mid-Term and Final Examinations to measure students' achievement at each level of the program. All tests in the program include both oral and written evaluation components.

In using *ExpressWays*, we encourage you to develop approaches and strategies that are compatible with your own teaching style and the needs and abilities of your students. While the program does not require any specific method or technique in order to be used effectively, you may find it helpful to review and try out some of the following suggestions. (Specific step-by-step instructions may be found in the Guide Book.)

Guided Conversations

1. *Listening.* With books closed, have students listen to the model conversation—presented by you, a pair of students, or on the audio tape.

2. *Discussion.* Have students discuss the model conversation: Who are the people? What is the situation?

   (At this point, you may want to call students' attention to any related language or culture notes, which can be found in the Appendix to the Student Course Book and in the Guide Book.)

3. *Reading.* With books open, have students follow along as two students present the model.

4. *Practice.* In pairs, small groups, or as a class, have students practice the model conversation.

5. *Alternative Expressions.* Present to the class each sentence of the dialog containing a footnoted expression. Call on different students to present the same sentence, but replacing the footnoted expression with its alternatives. (You can cue students to do this quickly by asking, "What's another way of saying that?" or "How else could he/she/you say that?")

6. *Pair Practice.* (optional) Have pairs of students simultaneously practice all the exercises, using the footnoted expressions or any of their alternatives.

7. *Presentation.* Call on pairs of students to present the exercises, using the footnoted expressions or any of their alternatives. Before students present, "set the scene" by describing the characters and the context or have the students do this themselves.

   (Discuss any language or culture notes related to the exercises, as indicated in the Student Course Book Appendix and the Guide Book.)

"Now Present Your Own Conversations"

In these activities that follow the guided conversations at the end of each lesson, have pairs of students create and present original conversations based on the model and any of the alternative expressions. Encourage students to be inventive as they create their characters and situations. (You may want to assign this exercise as homework, having students prepare their original conversations, practice them the next day with another student, and then present them to the class. In this way, students can review the previous day's lesson without actually having to repeat the specific exercises already covered.)

Expansion

We encourage you to use the expansion activity for each lesson suggested in the Guide Book or a similar activity that provides students with free, spontaneous practice while synthesizing the content of the lesson.

Interchange

Have students practice the model using the same steps listed above for guided conversations. Then have pairs of students create and present original conversations using the model dialog as a guide. Encourage students to be inventive and to use new vocabulary. (You may want to assign this exercise as homework, having students prepare their conversations, practice them the next day with another student, and then present them to the class.) Students should present their conversations without referring to the written text, but they should also not memorize them. Rather, they should feel free to adapt and expand them any way they wish.

Scenes & Improvisations

Have students talk about the people and the situations, and then present role plays based on the scenes. Students may refer back to previous lessons as a resource, but they should not simply re-use specific conversations. (You may want to assign these exercises as written homework, having students prepare their conversations, practice them the next day with another student, and then present them to the class.)

Review

You will notice that most functions and conversation strategies occur at several different points in the text. We have built a system of spiraling into the design of the program, so that content is reviewed and expanded upon at regular intervals. We encourage you to provide continual review practice based on your students' needs. Students may find it especially helpful to have frequent focused reviews of many of the alternative expressions for specific functions and conversation strategies. One useful technique is to have a pair of students present a model conversation from a previous lesson while other students listen with books closed. Stop the presentation after any line that contains a footnoted expression and ask different students to present the same line, but replacing the footnoted expression with its alternatives. (You can cue students to do this quickly by asking, "What's another way of saying that?" or "How else could he/she/you say that?")

In conclusion, we have attempted to offer students a communicative, meaningful, and lively way of practicing the functions of English, along with the grammar structures needed to express them competently. While conveying to you the substance of our textbook, we hope that we have also conveyed the spirit: that learning to communicate in English can be genuinely interactive . . . truly relevant to our students' lives . . . and fun!

Steven J. Molinsky
Bill Bliss

A NOTE ABOUT USING THE FOOTNOTES

Here are the conventions that you will need to know in order to use the footnotes containing alternative expressions in each lesson.

1. In the model conversation, a bold-faced footnoted expression indicates that there are alternative ways of expressing this function. Sometimes this expression is an entire sentence, and sometimes it is only a portion of a sentence.

2. (   ) indicates that the word or words are optional. For example, the footnote:

   I'm (very) sorry to hear (about) that. = I'm sorry to hear that.
   I'm very sorry to hear that.
   I'm sorry to hear about that.
   I'm very sorry to hear about that.

3. / indicates that the words on either side of the / mark are interchangeable. For example, the footnote:

   I don't/can't believe it! = I don't believe it!
   I can't believe it!

4. Sometimes the (   ) and / symbols appear together. For example, the footnote:

   I'm not (completely/absolutely) positive. = I'm not positive.
   I'm not completely positive.
   I'm not absolutely positive.

5. Sometimes the footnote indicates that an alternative expression requires a change in the grammar of the sentence. For example, the footnote:

   How about _____ing?   How about going shopping?
   Let's _____.   =   Let's go shopping.
   What if we _____ed?   What if we went shopping?

Components of an ExpressWays Lesson

A **model conversation** offers initial practice with the functions and structures of the lesson.

Key **functional expressions** are in bold-face type and are footnoted, referring students to a box containing alternative expressions for accomplishing the functions.

I'd Much Rather See a Movie

A. **Would you like to**[1] stay home or see a movie?
B. I think **I'd prefer to**[2] stay home. How about you?
A. Well, to be honest, **I really don't feel like** staying home.[3] I'd much rather see a movie. Is that okay with you?
B. Sure. We haven't seen a movie in a long time anyway.

[1] Would you like to
Would you prefer to
Would you rather
Do you want to

[2] I'd prefer to
I'd rather
I'd like to

[3] I (really) don't feel like _____ing.
I'm not (really) in the mood to _____.
I'd (really) prefer not to _____.

1. eat at home or at a restaurant?
2. swim at the beach or in the pool?
3. walk home or take a taxi?
4. watch the game on TV or go to the stadium?
5. put Rover in the kennel or take him on vacation with us?

"I'D MUCH RATHER SEE A MOVIE"

Now present your own conversations.

In the **exercises,** students create conversations by placing new contexts, content, or characters into the model, and by using any of the alternative functional expressions.

The **open-ended exercise** at the end of each lesson asks students to create and present original conversations based on the model and any of the alternative expressions.

For example:

Exercise 1 might be completed by placing the new exercise content into the existing model:

A. Would you like to eat at home or at a restaurant?
B. I think I'd prefer to eat at home. How about you?
A. Well, to be honest, I really don't feel like eating at home. I'd much rather eat at a restaurant. Is that okay with you?
B. Sure. We haven't eaten at a restaurant in a long time anyway.

Exercise 2 might be completed by using the new exercise content *and* some of the alternative functional expressions:

A. Would you prefer to swim at the beach or in the pool?
B. I think I'd like to swim at the beach. How about you?
A. Well, to be honest, I'm not really in the mood to swim at the beach. I'd much rather swim in the pool. Is that okay with you?
B. Sure. We haven't swum in the pool in a long time anyway.

Greeting People
Introductions
Identifying
Asking for and Reporting
  Information

Initiating Conversations
Initiating a Topic

I Don't Think We've Met
Let Me Introduce . . .
Don't I Know You from Somewhere?
Guess Who I Saw Yesterday!

• Negative Questions • One/Ones • Relative Clauses
with Who/Whose • Used to/Would • WH-Questions

I Don't Think We've Met

⁽¹⁾ My name is
I'm

⁽²⁾ Hello.

[less formal]
Hi.

[more formal]
How do you do?

⁽³⁾ (It's) nice to meet you.
(It's) nice meeting you.
(I'm) happy to meet you.
(I'm) glad to meet you.
(I'm) pleased to meet you.

⁽⁴⁾ How about you?
What about you?
And you?

Carmen   Kenji

A. I don't think we've met. **My name is**⁽¹⁾ Carmen.
B. **Hello.**⁽²⁾ **I'm**⁽¹⁾ Kenji. **Nice to meet you.**⁽³⁾
A. **Nice meeting you,**⁽³⁾ too. Where are you from?
B. Japan. **How about you?**⁽⁴⁾
A. Venezuela.

Tom   Carol

1. dancer
English teacher

Arlene   Betty

2. 2C
4D

Pedro   Nick

3. two months
one year

Ted   Carl

4. Dr. Murphy
Dr. Gold

5. Accounting
Shipping

6. History
Chemistry

7. the morning shift
the night shift

8. the bride's
the groom's

9. a lawyer
a journalist

10. rock
jazz

11. next month
any day now

Now present your own conversations.

Let Me Introduce . . .

(1) How are you?
How have you been?

[less formal]
How are you doing?
How are things?
How's it going?

(2) Fine (thank you/thanks).
Good.
All right.
Okay.
Not bad.

(3) Let me introduce (you to)
I'd like to introduce (you to)
I'd like you to meet

[less formal]
Meet
This is

A. Hi! **How are you?**(1)
B. **Fine.**(2) And you?
A. **Fine, thanks.**(2) **Let me introduce you to**(3) my friend Paul.
B. Nice to meet you.

1. my brother Tom

2. my sister Kate

3. my roommate, Peter

4. my English teacher, Mrs. Simon

5. my fiancé, Steve Smith

Now present your own conversations.

4

Don't I Know You from Somewhere?

A. **Excuse me,**[1] but don't I know you from somewhere?
B. No, I don't think so.
A. **Sure.**[2] Don't you work at the bank on Main Street?
B. No, I'm afraid not. You must have me **confused**[3] with somebody else.
A. Oh, **I'm sorry.**[4] I guess I made a mistake.

[1] Excuse me.
Pardon me.

[2] Sure.
Of course.

[3] confused
mixed up

[4] I'm sorry.
Excuse me.

1.

2.

3.

4.

5.

Now present your own conversations.

*Federal Bureau of Investigation

Guess Who I Saw Yesterday!

Kathy Wilson
She saved my life when
I almost drowned at
the beach last year.

The Bradley twins
Their parents used to dress
them alike all the time.

A. **Guess**[1] who I **saw**[2] yesterday!
B. Who?
A. Kathy Wilson!
B. Kathy Wilson? I don't think I remember her.
A. Oh, sure you do! She's the one who saved my life when I almost drowned at the beach last year.
B. Oh, of course. Now I remember her. How IS she?
A. **Pretty good.**[3]
B. Did she have anything to say?
A. Not really. We just talked **for a minute.**[4] But it was really good to see her again.

A. **You won't believe**[1] who I **ran into**[2] yesterday!
B. Who?
A. The Bradley twins!
B. The Bradley twins? I don't think I remember them.
A. Oh, sure you do. They're the ones whose parents used to dress them alike all the time.
B. Oh, of course. Now I remember them. How ARE they?
A. **Fine.**[3]
B. Did they have anything to say?
A. Not really. We just talked **for a moment.**[4] But it was really good to see them again.

[1] Guess	[2] saw	[3] Pretty good.	[4] for a minute
You won't believe	ran into	Fine.	for a moment
	bumped into	She looks terrific/	for a few minutes
		great/fine.	for a few seconds

1. Professor Kingston
   He taught Economic Theory at Business School.

2. Mr. and Mrs. Larson
   They used to live next door to us when we lived across town.

3. Miss Hubbard
   Her car would always break down in front of our house.

4. The Bennetts
   Their daughter baby-sits for us every once in a while.

5. Lucy Crawford
   She's the head of the Board of Education.

6. Patty Taylor
   She had a crush on me in the sixth grade.

7. Mr. and Mrs. Miller
   They're retired and living in Florida now.

8. Eddie Long
   He was my high school sweetheart.

9. Butch Baker
   His dog would always get loose and scare all the children in the neighborhood.

Now present your own conversations.

Functions

Greeting People

Hello.
[less formal]
Hi.
[more formal]
How do you do?

(It's) nice to meet you.
(It's) nice meeting you.
(I'm) happy to meet you.
(I'm) glad to meet you.
(I'm) pleased to meet you.

How are you?
How have you been?
[less formal]
How are you doing?
How are things?
How's it going?
  Fine (thank you/thanks).
  Good.
  All right.
  Okay.
  Not bad.

Introductions

Introducing Oneself

My name is _____.
I'm _____.

Introducing Others

Let me introduce (you to) _____.
I'd like to introduce (you to) _____.
I'd like you to meet _____.
[less formal]
Meet _____.
This is _____.

Identifying

My friend *Paul,* my brother *Tom,* . . .

She's the one who _____.

Apologizing

I'm sorry.
Excuse me.

Asking for and Reporting Information

Where are you from?
  Japan.
What do you do?
  I'm an *English teacher.*
Which *apartment do you live in?*
How long *have you been studying here?*
Who *is your doctor?*
Whose *family are you in?*
What kind of *music do you play?*
When *are you due?*

How about you?
What about you?
And you?

Don't you work at the bank on Main Street?

How is she?
  Pretty good.
  Fine.
  She looks terrific/great/fine.

Did _____ have anything to say?

Conversation Strategies

Initiating Conversations

I don't think we've met.

Excuse me, but . . .
Pardon me, but . . .

Don't I know you from somewhere?

Initiating a Topic

Guess _____!
You won't believe _____!

Asking for and Reporting
   Information
Asking for and Reporting
   Additional Information
Describing
Congratulating
Sympathizing

Good News!
Bad News!
Have You Heard from . . .?
What Do They Look Like?
What Are They Like?
Tell Me a Little About Yourself

• Adjectives • Must • Passives • Possessive Adjectives
• Pronouns • Simple Present Tense • Tense Review

Good News!

A. I have some good news.
B. Really? What is it?
A. I was just promoted to assistant manager!
B. Assistant manager?! **That's fantastic!**[1]
    You must be **thrilled.**[2]
A. I am.
B. Well, congratulations! **I'm very happy to hear that.**[3]
A. Thanks.

1. given a twenty percent raise

2. accepted at Oxford University

3. awarded the Nobel Prize for Physics

4. named "Outstanding Employee of the Year"

5. offered a movie contract by a major Hollywood studio

Now present your own conversations.

Bad News!

A. I have some bad news.
B. Oh? What is it?
A. My husband just lost his job.
B. He did?
A. I'm afraid so.
B. Oh, **that's too bad!**[1] You must be very upset.
A. I am.
B. **I'm very sorry to hear about that.**[2]

[1] That's too bad!
That's a shame/a pity!
What a shame/a pity!

[2] I'm (very) sorry to hear (about) that.
I'm (very/so) sorry.

1. My dog was run over by a car.

2. The factory where I work is going to shut down next month.

3. My son and his wife have decided to get a divorce.

4. I have to stay home all weekend and take care of my little brother.

5. I was rejected by every medical school I applied to.

Now present your own conversations.

Have You Heard from . . . ?

A. Have you **heard from**[1] your granddaughter lately?
B. As a matter of fact, I have. I **heard from**[1] her just the other day.
A. **How's she doing?**[2]
B. **Fine.**[3] She's getting straight A's in school.
A. She is? That's fantastic!
B. I think so, too.
A. Next time you see her, please **give her my regards.**[4]
B. I'll be sure to do that.

A. Have you **run into**[1] your cousin Ralph lately?
B. As a matter of fact, I have. I **ran into**[1] him just the other day.
A. **How's he doing?**[2]
B. **Not too well.**[5] He had to have four teeth pulled last week.
A. He did? That's too bad!
B. I think so, too.
A. Next time you see him, please **tell him I'm thinking of him.**[4]
B. I'll be sure to do that.

[1] heard from run into talked to seen spoken to been in touch with	[2] How's she doing? How is she? How has she been?	[3] Fine. Great. Wonderful.	[4] give her my regards tell her I say/said hello tell her I'm thinking of her
	[5] Not too well. Not so well. Not very well.		

1. your parents

2. your neighbors across the street

3. your son

4. your cousins in Detroit

5. George and Irene

6. Janet

7. your friend Elizabeth

8. your grandfather

9. The President

Now present your own conversations.

*Parent Teacher Association

What Do They Look Like?

A. Could you please take these reports over to Charlie Jones in Accounting?
B. Sure. I'd be happy to. But I'm afraid I don't remember what he looks like.
A. Oh, you can't miss him. He's **about your height, sort of heavy,** with **curly dark** hair.
B. Okay. I think I'll be able to find him.
A. Thanks very much. I appreciate it.

height	weight	hair		additional features
about your height	sort of	curly	dark	and (wears) glasses
about average height	kind of } heavy/thin	wavy	light	and (has) a beard/
about ____ feet tall	very	straight	brown	mustache
(very) tall	a little on the		black	
(very) short	heavy side		blond(e)	
a little taller/shorter			red	
than you/me			gray	

Complete these conversations using the information above.

1. Could you please take these boxes over to Stella in Shipping?

2. Would you be willing to pick up my brother at the airport?

3. Could you possibly get some chalk from Ms. Crenshaw in the principal's office?

4. Could I possibly ask you to meet my sister at the train station?

5. Could I possibly ask you to take another picture of my Uncle Charlie?

"WHAT DO THEY LOOK LIKE?"

Now present your own conversations.

What Are They Like?

A. **Have you heard anything**[1] about our new English teacher?
B. Yes. **People say**[2] she's very intelligent.
A. Hmm. **What else have you heard?**[3]
B. Well, they also say she's very patient.
A. Really? That's interesting.

[1] Have you heard anything
    Do you know anything

[2] People say
    They say
    People/They tell me
    Everybody says
    Everybody tells me
    I've heard
    Word has it (that)

[3] What else have you heard?
    Have you heard anything else?
    Do you know anything else?

1. the new boss
   bright
   strict

2. the new superintendent
   friendly
   helpful

3. the new student in our class
   nice
   outgoing

4. our new senator
   articulate
   honest

5. the new supervisor
   unfriendly
   short-tempered

"WHAT ARE THEY LIKE?"

Now present your own conversations.

Tell Me a Little About Yourself

(1) I don't know where to begin.
I don't know where to start.
I don't know what to say.

(2) What do you want to know?
What would you like to know?
What can I tell you?

(3) exciting
interesting
challenging
difficult
important
creative
.
.
.

A. So, tell me a little about yourself.
B. Gee - uh . . . **I don't know where to begin.**(1) **What do you want to know?**(2)
A. Well, let's see . . . What do you do?
B. I'm a civil engineer.
A. A civil engineer. Hmm. That's interesting. Do you enjoy your work?
B. Yes. I like it a lot.
A. Tell me, what exactly do you do as a civil engineer?
B. Well, I design roads and bridges for the city.
A. Oh. That sounds like a very **exciting**(3) job.
B. It is.

1. I'm a criminal lawyer.
I defend people accused of crimes.

2. I'm a political speech writer.
I write speeches for a congressman.

3. I'm an administrative assistant.
I handle all the business communication
for the president of my company.

4. I'm an emergency medical technician.
I drive an ambulance and assist
people with medical emergencies.

5. I'm a real estate agent.
I help people who want to buy or sell
a house.

6. I'm an anthropologist.
I study about people from different
cultures all over the world.

7. I'm a computer programmer.
I design computer programs for
business and industry.

8. I'm a meteorologist.
I report the weather on TV.

9. I'm a forest ranger.
I watch out for fires and protect all
the animals in the forest.

"TELL ME A LITTLE ABOUT YOURSELF"

Now present your own conversations.

Functions

Asking for and Reporting Information

Have you { heard from / run into / talked to / seen / spoken to / been in touch with } ___ lately?

How's ___ doing?
How is ___?
How has ___ been?
  Fine.
  Great.
  Wonderful.
  Not too well.
  Not so well.
  Not very well.

Have you heard anything about ___?
Do you know anything about ___?

People say . . .
They say . . .
People/They tell me . . .
Everybody says . . .
Everybody tells me . . .
I've heard . . .
Word has it (that) . . .

Tell me a little about yourself.

What do you want to know?
What would you like to know?
What can I tell you?

Asking for and Reporting Additional Information

What else have you heard?
Have you heard anything else?
Do you know anything else?

Describing

He's about your height, sort of heavy, with curly dark hair.

He's/She's very ___.

Congratulating

That's fantastic!
That's great/wonderful/exciting/ marvelous!

Congratulations!

I'm very happy to hear that.
I'm very happy for you.

Sympathizing

That's too bad!
That's a shame/a pity!
What a shame/a pity!

I'm (very) sorry to hear (about) that.
I'm (very/so) sorry.

Requests

Direct, More Polite

Could you please ___?
Could you possibly ___?
Could I possibly ask you to ___?
Would you be willing to ___?

Surprise-Disbelief

Assistant manager?!

Deduction

You must be ___.

Conversation Strategies

Hesitating

Gee-uh . . .

I don't know where to begin.
I don't know where to start.
I don't know what to say.

Well, let's see . . .

Initiating a Topic

I have some good/bad news.

Asking for and Reporting
   Information
Asking for and Reporting
   Additional Information
Describing
Identifying
Certainty/Uncertainty
Remembering/Forgetting

Which One?
What's It Like There?
As Far As I Know . . .
Did You Remember?
Did You Hear?
Have You Heard the News?
What Happened?

• Adjectives • Declarative Sentences with Question
Intonation • Embedded Questions • Indirect Objects
• One/Ones • Passives • Past Continuous Tense • Past
Tense • Sequence of Tenses • Superlatives • Tag
Questions

Which One?

> You should wear your new tie with that jacket.

⁽¹⁾ You should wear _____.
Why don't you wear _____?
How about wearing _____?

> The children gave you a *blue* tie *with gray and yellow stripes.*

A. **You should wear**[1] your new tie with that jacket.
B. Which one?
A. The one the children gave you.
B. Hmm. Which one is that?
A. You remember. It's the *blue* one *with gray and yellow stripes.*
B. Oh, that one. I know where it is. I'll get it.

> Why don't you wear your new bathing suit to the beach?

1. I gave you a *purple* bathing suit *with yellow polka dots.*

> How about wearing your new sweater this evening?

2. Aunt Margaret sent you a *wool* sweater *made in Scotland.*

> You should wear that pretty scarf of yours.

3. The people at the office gave you a *red* scarf *made of silk.*

> Let's take the camera with us!

4. Uncle Harry gave us a *pocket-size* camera *in a brown leather case.*

> Why don't you play with your new doll?

5. Grandma sent you a *cute* doll *that cries when you pull the string.*

"WHICH ONE?"

Now present your own conversations.

What's It Like There?

A. Have you by any chance ever been to Hong Kong?
B. Yes, I have. Why?
A. I'm going there with my family for a vacation next month. Can you tell me what it's like there?
B. Well, it's a very *exciting* place. **As a matter of fact,**(1) it's probably one of the *most exciting* places I know.
A. Really? That's good to hear. **Can you tell me anything else?**(2)
B. Well-uh . . . what else would you like to know?
A. How about the weather . . . and the people?
B. The weather at this time of year is usually *cool,* and **in my opinion,**(3) the people there are very *interesting.*
A. It sounds like a wonderful place.
B. It is. I'm sure you'll have a good time there.

(1) ·As a matter of fact,
In fact,

(2) Can you tell me anything else?
Can you tell me anything more?
What else can you tell me?

(3) in my opinion,
if you ask me,
as far as I'm concerned,

1. dynamic
warm
nice

2. nice
pleasant
easygoing

3. pretty
delightful
pleasant

4. charming
cool
helpful

5. lively
comfortable
friendly

Now present your own conversations.

As Far As I Know . . .

When is the President going to arrive?

A. **Do you by any chance know**(1) when the President is going to arrive?
B. Yes. As far as I know, he's going to arrive at 2:30.
A. Hmm. Somehow I thought he was going to arrive earlier than that.
B. **I don't think so.**(2)
A. **Are you sure?**(3)
B. Yes, **I'm positive.**(4) He arrives at 2:30.

When does the post office open?

1. at 9

What time does the bank close?

2. at 4

What time does the movie begin?

3. at 7:45

When is Nancy due?

4. late next month

When is your mother planning to leave?

5. two weeks from Sunday

"AS FAR AS I KNOW..."

Now present your own conversations.

Did You Remember?

A. Uh-oh! **Did you remember to**[1] feed the dog?
B. No, I didn't. I thought YOU were going to feed him!
A. Hmm. I guess I WAS . . . but **I forgot all about it.**[2]
B. Well, since the dog hasn't been fed yet, I guess one of us should go and do it.
A. Okay. I'll do it.

[1] Did you (happen to) remember to ____?
You didn't (by any chance) remember to ____, did you?

[2] I forgot (all about it).
I completely forgot.
It (completely) slipped my mind.

1. take the garbage out

2. set the table

3. turn the downstairs lights off

4. do the laundry

5. change the baby's diaper

Now present your own conversations.

Did You Hear?

School is going to be closed tomorrow!

A. Did you hear (that) school is going to be closed tomorrow?
B. **You're kidding!**(1) School isn't really going to be closed tomorrow, is it?
A. Yes, it is.
B. Are you sure?
A. I'm absolutely positive! I heard it on the radio.

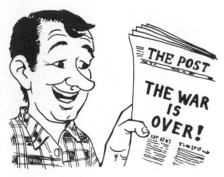

1. I saw it in the paper.

They predict a hurricane for tomorrow!

2. I heard it on TV.

We won five gold medals at the Olympics today!

3. I heard it on the radio.

4. I read it in the morning paper.

The Americans and the Russians have just signed a nuclear arms treaty!

5. I heard it on the 7 o'clock news.

"DID YOU HEAR?"

Now present your own conversations.

Have You Heard the News?

A. Have you heard the news?
B. No, what?
A. They're going to make the park across the street into a parking lot.
B. They're going to make the park across the street into a parking lot?! I don't believe it! **Where did you hear that?**[1]
A. All the neighbors are talking about it.
B. Do you think it's true?
A. I think so, but **I don't know for sure.**[2]
B. Well, personally, I doubt it.

[1]
Where did you hear that?
How do you know (that)?
Who told you (that)?

[2]
I don't know for sure.
I'm not (completely/absolutely) positive.
I'm not a hundred percent positive.

1. It's a rumor going around town.

2. I heard it from some people at the supermarket.

3. I overheard some people talking on the bus.

4. It's a rumor going around the office.

5. Some kids in my class were talking about it.

Now present your own conversations.

25

INTERCHANGE
What Happened?

A. What happened?
B. Well, I was lying on the beach listening to the radio, when suddenly I heard someone shouting for help.
A. So what did you do?
B. I jumped up, looked out toward the ocean, and saw a little boy waving his arms in the air.
A. **What did you do next?**[1]
B. I took off my shirt and my watch and jumped into the water.
A. **And THEN what did you do?**[1]
B. I swam out to the little boy, held him so his head stayed above water, and brought him back to shore.
A. Well, that sounds like it was quite an experience!
B. It sure was!

A. What happened?
B. Well, I was _____ing, when suddenly _____.
A. So what did you do?
B. _____.
A. **What did you do next?**[1]
B. _____.
A. **And THEN what did you do?**[1]
B. _____.
A. Well, that sounds like it was quite an experience!
B. It sure was!

---

[1] What did you do next?   And then what did you do?
     What did you do after that?   What was the next thing you did?

1.

2.

You're telling somebody about something that happened. Create an original conversation using the model dialog on p. 26 as a guide. Feel free to adapt and expand the model any way you wish.

Functions

Asking for and Reporting Information

Which one is that?

Have you by any chance ever _____ed?

Can you tell me what it's like?

Do you/Would you (by any chance) know _____?
Do you/Would you (by any chance) happen to know _____?

Did you hear (that) _____?

What happened?

Where did you hear that?
How do you know (that)?
Who told you (that)?

I heard it on the radio/on TV/on the news.
I saw/read it in the paper.

School isn't really going to be closed tomorrow, is it?

Asking for and Reporting Additional Information

Can you tell me anything else?
Can you tell me anything more?
What else can you tell me?

What did you do next?
What did you do after that?
And then what did you do?
What was the next thing you did?

What else would you like to know?

As a matter of fact, . . .
In fact, . . .

Describing

It's the _____ one with the _____

It's a (very) _____ _____.

It's one of the _____est _____s I know.

Identifying

The one *the children gave you.*

Certainty/Uncertainty

Inquiring about . . .

Are you positive/certain/sure (about that)?

Expressing Certainty

I'm positive/certain/sure.
I'm absolutely positive/certain/sure.
I'm a hundred percent sure.
There's no doubt about it.
I'm absolutely positive.

Expressing Uncertainty

I don't know for sure.
I'm not (completely/absolutely) positive.
I'm not a hundred percent positive.

I don't think so.
Not as far as I know.

I doubt it.

Remembering/Forgetting

Inquiring about . . .

Did you (happen to) remember to _____?
You didn't (by any chance) remember to _____, did you?

Indicating . . .

I forgot (all about it).
I completely forgot.
It (completely) slipped my mind.

You remember.

Oh, that one.

Surprise-Disbelief

School isn't really going to be closed tomorrow, is it?

They're going to make the park across the street into a parking lot?!

You're kidding!
No kidding!
You're joking!
I don't/can't believe it!
Oh, come on!
No!
That can't be!
You've got to be kidding!

Advice-Suggestions

Offering . . .

You should _____.
Why don't you _____?
How about _____ing?

Conversation Strategies

Focusing Attention

As a matter of fact, . . .
In fact, . . .

In my opinion, . . .
If you ask me, . . .
As far as I'm concerned, . . .

Initiating a Topic

Have you heard the news?

SCENES & IMPROVISATIONS
Chapters 1, 2, 3

Who do you think these people are?
What do you think they're talking about?
Create conversations based on these scenes and act them out.

1.

2.

3.

4.

5.

6.

7.

8.

What Did You Say?
I'm Sorry. I Didn't Hear You
Have You Got It?
Are You With Me So Far?

• Embedded Questions • Gerunds • Imperatives
• Partitives • Question Formation • Sequence of Tenses

What Did You Say?

A. Would you mind playing your radio someplace else?
B. I'm sorry. **I didn't hear you.**(1) **What did you say?**(2)
A. I asked you if you'd play your radio someplace else.
B. Sure. I'd be happy to.
A. Thanks.

1.

2.

3.

4.

5.

Now present your own conversations.

I'm Sorry. I Didn't Hear You

(1) WHEN do you want me to
WHEN should I
WHEN did you tell me to

A. Please report for work tomorrow at 7:45.
B. I'm sorry. I didn't hear you.
WHEN do you want me to(1) report for work tomorrow?
A. At 7:45.
B. Oh, okay.

1. Please give these packages to Tom.

2. Please get a loaf of bread and a dozen eggs at the supermarket.

3. Put three slices of tomato on each salad.

4. Take these pills four times a day.

5. Put the money in a brown paper bag.

Now present your own conversations.

Have You Got It?

- • Go to the corner and turn right.
- • Walk two blocks to Main Street.
- • Turn left, walk two more blocks, and you'll see the post office next to the bank.

A. **Could you please tell me**[1] how to get to the post office?

B. Sure. Go to the corner and turn right. Walk two blocks to Main Street. Turn left, walk two more blocks, and you'll see the post office next to the bank. **Have you got it?**[2]

A. I think so. **Let me see.**[3] First, I go to the corner and turn right.

B. **Uh-húh.**[4]

A. Then I walk two blocks to Main Street. Right?

B. **Um-hḿm.**[4]

A. And then I . . . Hmm. I forgot the last part. What do I do after that?

B. You turn left, walk two more blocks, and you'll see the post office next to the bank.

A. Okay.

B. Do you think you've got it now?

A. I think so. Thanks very much.

---

[1] Could you (please/possibly) tell me
Do you/Would you (by any chance) know
Can you (please) tell me
Would you (possibly/by any chance) be able to tell me

[2] (Have you) got it?
Do you follow me?
Okay?

[3] Let me see.
Let me see if I understand.
Let me see if I've got that (right).

[4] Uh-húh.
Um-hḿm.
Yes.
(That's) right.

A. **Could you please tell me**[1] how to _____?
B. Sure. _____.
_____.
_____.

Have you got it?[2]
A. I think so. **Let me see.**[3]
First, I _____.
B. **Uh-húh.**[4]
A. Then I _____. Right?
B. **Um-hḿm.**[4]
A. And then I . . . Hmm. I forgot the last part. What do I do after that?
B. You _____
A. Okay.
B. Do you think you've got it now?
A. I think so. Thanks very much.

• Pick up the receiver.

• Put in the money.

• Wait for the dial tone and dial.

1. use this telephone

• Pick up the nozzle.

• Put the nozzle in the gas tank.

• Press the handle to start the gas flowing.

2. work the gas pump

• Use the jack to raise up the car.

• Unscrew the bolts and take off the flat tire.

• Put on the new tire, put the bolts on tight, and lower the car.

3. change a flat tire

• Turn around and drive down this road until you get to a big intersection.

• Take a left and drive about three miles until you get to the entrance of the interstate.

• Take the interstate north to exit 27.

4. get to the airport

"HAVE YOU GOT IT?"

Now present your own conversations.

INTERCHANGE
Are You With Me So Far?

A. Could you tell me your recipe for chocolate chip cookies?
B. Sure. I'll be happy to. But it's pretty complicated. You might want to write this down.
A. I'm afraid I don't have a pencil on me. But go ahead anyway.
B. Okay. First, mix together 2 cups of flour and a teaspoon of baking soda. Then, add a teaspoon of salt. After that, mix together a cup of butter and a cup of sugar in a separate bowl. **Are you with me so far?**[1]
A. Yes, I'm with you.
B. Okay. Then, add 2 eggs. Next, combine all the ingredients into a large bowl. And then . . .
A. Wait a minute! **I didn't get that.**[2] Could you repeat the last two **instructions?**[3]
B. Sure. Add 2 eggs. And combine all the ingredients into a large bowl.
A. Okay. **Now I've got it.**[4]
B. Good. Now, let's see. Where was I? Oh, yes. Slowly mix in a cup of chocolate chips and a cup of nuts. Then, form little cookies from the mixture and place them on a cookie sheet. And finally, bake for 8 minutes at 375 degrees Fahrenheit. Have you got all that?
A. I think so. But let me repeat that back to make sure. First, I . . .

[1] Are you with me (so far)? Okay (so far)? Are you following me (so far)?	[2] I didn't get that. I'm lost. I'm not following you.	[3] instructions directions steps things you said
	[4] Now I've got it. I understand. I see. I'm with you.	

A. Could you tell me _____?
B. Sure. I'll be happy to. But it's pretty complicated. You might want to write this down.
A. I'm afraid I don't have a pencil on me. But go ahead anyway.
B. Okay. First, _____.
   Then, _____.
   After that, _____.
   Are you with me so far?[1]
A. Yes, I'm with you.
B. Okay. Then, _____.
   Next, _____.
   And then . . .
A. Wait a minute! **I didn't get that.**[2] Could you repeat the last two **instructions**?[3]
B. Sure. _____.
   And _____.
A. Okay. **Now I've got it.**[4]
B. Good. Now, let's see. Where was I? Oh, yes.
   _____
   Then, _____.
   And finally, _____.
   Have you got all that?
A. I think so. But let me repeat that back to make sure.
   First, I . . .

Write out a list of 8 steps to do something. (For example, directions to a place, how to make or repair something, or a recipe.)

1. _____

2. _____

3. _____

4. _____

5. _____

6. _____

7. _____

8. _____

Create an original conversation using your list of instructions and the model dialog above as a guide. (Be sure to have the other person repeat back your instructions to make sure he or she understands you.) Feel free to adapt and expand the model any way you wish.

Functions

Instructing

(Please) _____

First, . . .
Then, . . .
After that, . . .
Next, . . .
And finally, . . .

Directions-Location

Giving Directions

Go to _____.
Turn _____.
Walk _____ blocks.

Asking for and Reporting Information

Could you (please/possibly) tell me
_____?
Do you/Would you (by any chance)
know _____?
Can you (please) tell me _____?
Would you (possibly/by any chance)
be able to tell me_____?

Requests

Direct, Polite

Please _____.

Direct, More Polite

Would you mind _____ing?

Conversation Strategies

Asking for Repetition

I didn't hear you.
I didn't (quite) catch that.
I didn't get that.
I missed that.
I'm lost.
I'm not following you.

What did you say?
Could/Would you (please) repeat
   that?
Could/Would you say that again?
Would you mind saying that again?
Would you mind repeating that?

Could you repeat the last two { instructions?
directions?
steps?
things you said?

WHEN do you want me to _____?
WHEN should I _____?
WHEN did you tell me to _____?

I forgot the last part.

Checking and Indicating Understanding

Checking Another Person's Understanding

(Have you) got it?
Do you follow me?
Okay?

Are you with me (so far)?
Okay (so far)?
Are you following me (so far)?

Do you think you've got it now?
Have you got all that?

Checking One's Own Understanding

Let me see.
Let me see if I understand.
Let me see if I've got that (right).
Let me repeat that back.

Indicating Understanding

Now I've got it.
I understand.
I see.
I'm with you.

Uh-húh.
Um-hḿm.
Yes.
(That's) right.

Thanks for Saying So
You're Just Saying That!
Just What I Had in Mind!
I'd Like a Refund, Please
I Was a Little Disappointed
I'm Really Annoyed
Would You Like to Get Together This Weekend?

• Adjectives • Comparatives • Gerunds • Infinitives
• Negative Questions • Present Continuous Tense to
Express Habitual Action • Singular/Plural • Superlatives
• Too/Enough • Would

Thanks for Saying So

A. That was **a very good**(1) performance!
B. Did you really like it?
A. **Yes.**(2) I thought it was **excellent.**(3)
B. **Thanks for saying so.**(4)

1. dinner

2. lecture

3. presentation

4. party

5. speech

Now present your own
conversations.

You're Just Saying That!

<table>
<tr><td>(1)</td><td>(really) like
love</td></tr>
<tr><td>(2)</td><td>very
so</td></tr>
<tr><td>(3)</td><td>Oh/Aw, go on!
Oh/Aw, come on!
Oh!</td></tr>
<tr><td>(4)</td><td>I mean it!
I'm (really) serious.
I'm being honest with you.</td></tr>
</table>

A. I **really like**[1] your apartment. It's **very**[2] spacious.
B. **Oh, go on!**[3] You're just saying that!
A. No. **I mean it!**[4] It's one of the most spacious apartments I've ever seen.
B. Well, thanks for saying so. I'm glad you like it.

1. tie
attractive

2. dress
pretty

3. painting
interesting

4. blouse
colorful

5. haircut
nice

Now present your own
conversations.

41

Just What I Had in Mind!

(1) How do you like
What do you think of

(2) fine
very nice
perfect

(3) satisfied
happy
pleased

(4) Very.
Very much.
Yes.

(5) just what I
had in mind/
wanted/was
looking for

A. **How do you like**(1) the bicycle?
B. It's **fine.**(2)
A. It isn't too heavy?
B. No, not at all.
A. Is it large enough?
B. Oh, yes. I wouldn't want it any larger.
A. So you're **satisfied**(3) with it?
B. **Very.**(4) It's **just what I had in mind!**(5)

1. mattress
   short
   firm

2. tennis racket
   big
   light

3. wedding dress
   plain
   fancy

4. pants
   tight
   long

5. gloves
   bulky
   warm

Now present your own
conversations.

I'd Like a Refund, Please

A. I'd like to return this hat.
B. **What seems to be the problem with it?**[1]
A. It's too old-fashioned.
B. Would you like to exchange it for one that's more modern?
A. **I don't think so.**[2] I'd just like a refund, please.
B. I'm sorry. We don't give refunds. **However,**[3] we'll be happy to offer you credit toward another purchase in our store.
A. No refunds??
B. I'm afraid not.
A. Oh. Thanks anyway.

[1] What seems to be the problem (with it)?
What seems to be the matter (with it)?
What's the problem/the matter/wrong (with it)?

[2] I don't think so.
Not really.
Probably not.

[3] However,
But

1. coat
   long
   short

2. sport shirt
   flashy
   conservative

3. Home Repair book
   complicated
   simple

4. video game
   easy
   challenging

5. parrot
   talkative
   quiet

Now present your own conversations.

I Was a Little Disappointed

(1) to tell (you) the truth,
honestly,
to be honest (with you),

(2) I was (a little) disappointed.
I wasn't very pleased with it.
It was (a little) disappointing.

(3) Why?
How come?

(4) expected it to be
thought it would be
hoped it would be

A. How did you like the play?
B. Well, **to tell the truth,**(1) **I was a little disappointed.**(2)
A. **Why?**(3)
B. It wasn't as funny as I thought it would be.
I really **expected it to be**(4) a lot funnier.
A. That's too bad.

1. your vacation
relaxing

2. the game
exciting

3. the steak
juicy

4. your date with Ted last night
enjoyable

5. English class today
good

Now present your own conversations.

I'm Really Annoyed

A. I'm really **annoyed with**[1] my landlord.
B. Why?
A. **He's always**[2] forgetting to fix things.
B. Have you spoken to him about it?
A. Well, actually not.
B. I don't understand. If his forgetting to fix things **bothers**[3] you so much, why don't you **mention it to him?**[4]
A. I guess I should. But I don't like to complain.

1. My secretary is always making spelling mistakes.

2. My neighbors are always playing their stereo past midnight.

3. My teacher is always giving us homework over the weekend.

4. My roommate is always snoring at night.

5. My parents are always treating me like a baby.

Now present your own conversations.

INTERCHANGE
Would You Like to Get Together This Weekend?

A. Would you like to get together this weekend?

B. Sure. What would you like to do?

A. Well, how about seeing a movie?

B. That sounds good. Did you have any particular movie in mind?

A. Well, they say that "A Man and His Horse" is very good. It's playing at the Rialto Theater.

B. "A Man and His Horse"? That's a **western,**[1] isn't it?

A. I think so.

B. Well, to tell the truth, **I don't like westerns**[1] **very much.**[2]

A. Oh. Well, is there any particular movie you'd like to see?

B. How about "The Return of the Monster"? It's playing at the Shopping Mall Cinema, and I hear it's excellent.

A. "Return of the Monster"? Hmm. Isn't that a **science fiction movie?**[1]

B. Yes. Don't you like **science fiction movies?**[1]

A. No, not really. Maybe we shouldn't see a movie. Maybe we should do something else.

B. Okay. Would you be interested in doing something outdoors?

A. Sure. Any suggestions?

B. Well, we could go ice skating.

A. Oh. I'm afraid **I don't really enjoy**[2] going ice skating. How about going hiking?

B. Well, to tell the truth, I've gone hiking several times in the past few weeks.

A. Really? Then I guess you must be pretty **tired of**[3] hiking.

B. I am. Let's do something else.

A. Why don't we just have dinner together somewhere this Saturday?

B. That sounds like a good idea. Where would you like to go?

A. Well, one of my favorite places to eat is "The Captain's Table."

B. Hmm. "The Captain's Table"? What kind of food do they serve there?

A. **Seafood.**[4] But if you don't like **seafood,**[4] we can go someplace else.

B. No. On the contrary, I LOVE **seafood!**[4]

A. You do?! Great!

B. Then **it's settled.**[5] "The Captain's Table" for dinner on Saturday. What time?

A. How about 7 o'clock?

B. Is 8 okay?

A. Fine.

A. Would you like to get together this weekend?
B. Sure. What would you like to do?
A. Well, how about seeing a movie?
B. That sounds good. Did you have any particular movie in mind?
A. Well, they say that "_____" is very good. It's playing at the _____.
B. "_____"? That's a _____,(1) isn't it?
A. I think so.
B. Well, to tell the truth, **I don't like** _____s(1) **very much.**(2)
A. Oh. Well, is there any particular movie you'd like to see?
B. How about "_____"? It's playing at the _____, and I hear it's excellent.
A. "_____"? Hmm. Isn't that a _____?(1)
B. Yes. Don't you like _____s?(1)
A. No, not really. Maybe we shouldn't see a movie. Maybe we should do something else.
B. Okay. Would you be interested in doing something outdoors?
A. Sure. Any suggestions?
B. Well, we could go _____ing.
A. Oh. I'm afraid **I don't really enjoy**(2) going _____ing. How about going _____ing?
B. Well, to tell the truth, I've gone _____ing several times in the past few weeks.
A. Really? Then I guess you must be pretty **tired of**(3) _____ing.
B. I am. Let's do something else.
A. Why don't we just have dinner together somewhere this Saturday?
B. That sounds like a good idea. Where would you like to go?
A. Well, one of my favorite places to eat is "_____."
B. Hmm. "_____"? What kind of food do they serve there?
A. _____.(4) But if you don't like _____,(4) we can go someplace else.
B. No. On the contrary, I LOVE _____!(4)
A. You do?! Great!
B. Then **it's settled.**(5) "_____" for dinner on Saturday. What time?
A. How about _____ o'clock?
B. Is _____ okay?
A. Fine.

Create an original conversation using the model dialog above as a guide. In your conversation, use the names of movies, theaters, and restaurants where you live, and refer to outdoor activities you enjoy doing on the weekend. Feel free to adapt and expand the model any way you wish.

Functions

Satisfaction/Dissatisfaction

Inquiring about . . .

How do you like _____?
What do you think of _____?

How did you like _____?

Did you (really) like it?

Are you { satisfied / happy / pleased } with it?

Is it _____ enough?

What seems to be the problem (with it)?
What seems to be the matter (with it)?
What's the problem/the matter/wrong (with it)?

Expressing Satisfaction

It's { fine. / very nice. / perfect. }

It's just what I { had in mind. / wanted. / was looking for. }

I wouldn't want it any _____er.

Expressing Dissatisfaction

It's too _____.

I really { expected it to be / thought it would be / hoped it would be } _____er.

It wasn't as _____ as I thought it would be.

Gratitude

Expressing . . .

Thanks/Thank you (for saying so).
It's nice of you to say so/that.

Persuading-Insisting

I mean it!
I'm (really) serious.
I'm being honest with you.

Likes/Dislikes

Inquiring about . . .

How do you like _____?
What do you think of _____?

How did you like _____?

Did you like _____?

Don't you like _____?

Expressing Likes

I like _____.
I love _____.

Expressing Dislikes

I don't (really) like/enjoy _____ very much.
I don't (particularly) care for _____.
I'm not (really) crazy about _____.
[stronger]
I hate _____.

Complimenting

Expressing Compliments

That was { a very good / quite a / [less formal] / some } _____!

I thought it was { excellent. / wonderful. / terrific. / magnificent. / fabulous. / superb. }

I (really) like _____.
I love _____.

It's very _____.
It's so _____.

It's one of the _____est _____s I've ever _____ed.

Responding to Compliments

Thanks/Thank you (for saying so).
It's nice of you to say so/that.
I'm glad you like it.

Oh/Aw, go on!
Oh/Aw, come on!
Oh!

You're just saying that.

Disappointment

I was (a little) disappointed.
I wasn't very pleased with it.
It was (a little) disappointing.

Complaining

It's too _____.

I was (a little) disappointed.
I wasn't very pleased with it.
It was (a little) disappointing.

I'm { annoyed with / upset with / [stronger] / mad at / angry at / furious with } _____.

He's always / He's constantly / He keeps on _____ing.

His _____ing { bothers / annoys / upsets } me.

I'm tired of _____(ing).
I'm sick of _____(ing).
I'm sick and tired of _____(ing).

Advice-Suggestions

Asking for . . .

Any suggestions?

Offering . . .

How about _____?
How about _____ing?
Would you be interested in _____?
We could _____.
Why don't we _____?
Let's _____.

Why don't you _____?

Have you _____ed?

Maybe we should _____.
Maybe we shouldn't _____.

They say that _____ is very good.
One of my favorite _____s is _____.

Is _____ okay?

6

I'd Prefer a Baked Potato
I'd Much Rather See a Movie
A Serious Disagreement
It Doesn't Make Any Difference
It's Entirely Up to You
The International Gourmet

• Gerunds • Infinitives • Partitives • Present Perfect Tense
• Sequence of Tenses • Want + Object + Infinitive
• Whether • WH-ever Words • Would

I'd Prefer a Baked Potato

(1) I'd like
I'll have
I want

(2) prefer
rather have
like

A. May I help you?
B. Yes, **I'd like**(1) a steak.
A. How would you like it?
B. Rare.
A. Okay. And would you **prefer**(2) a baked potato or rice with that?
B. I'd **prefer**(2) a baked potato.
A. Anything to drink?
B. How about a cup of coffee, please?
A. Okay. That's a rare steak with a baked potato and a cup of coffee.

*a hamburger
well-done
french fries
a Coke*

1. french fries or potato chips?

*the chicken
baked
a salad
a glass of white wine*

2. a salad or a vegetable?

*an order of eggs
scrambled
toast
a glass of milk*

3. toast or a muffin?

*a cheese sandwich
grilled
potato salad
a glass of lemonade*

4. potato salad or cole slaw?

*the fish
fried
noodles
a diet soda*

5. noodles or mashed potatoes?

Now present your own conversations.

I'd Much Rather See a Movie

A. **Would you like to**[1] stay home or see a movie?
B. I think **I'd prefer to**[2] stay home. How about you?
A. Well, to be honest, **I really don't feel like** staying home.[3]
   I'd much rather see a movie. Is that okay with you?
B. Sure. We haven't seen a movie in a long time anyway.

[1] Would you like to
    Would you prefer to
    Would you rather
    Do you want to

[2] I'd prefer to
    I'd rather
    I'd like to

[3] I (really) don't feel like
    _____ing.
    I'm not (really) in the mood
    to _____.
    I'd (really) prefer not to
    _____.

1. eat at home or at a restaurant?

2. swim at the beach or in the pool?

3. walk home or take a taxi?

4. watch the game on TV or go to the stadium?

5. put Rover in the kennel or take him on vacation with us?

Now present your own conversations.

A Serious Disagreement

I want you to switch to the night shift.

I'd rather stay on the day shift.

(1) You've seemed troubled
You've seemed upset
You've seemed preoccupied
You haven't been yourself

(2) wrong
the matter
going on

(3) resolve it
settle it
work it out

A. **You've seemed troubled**(1) for the past few days. Is anything **wrong?**(2)
B. Well, to tell the truth, I've been having a disagreement with my boss.
A. Oh? What's it all about?
B. Well, to make a long story short, my boss wants me to switch to the night shift, but I'd rather stay on the day shift.
A. Does he feel strongly about your switching to the night shift?
B. Yes, he does. And I feel just as strongly about staying on the day shift.
A. Well, it sounds like a serious disagreement. I hope you can **resolve it**(3) soon.
B. So do I.

I want you to get a haircut.

I'd rather leave my hair long.

1. my mother

I'd like to start a family now.

I'd rather wait until we have a little more money in the bank.

2. my wife

3. my parents

5. my family

7. the people in my parish

9. some members of my labor union

4. my business partner

6. my husband

8. my economic advisor

Now present your own conversations.

It Doesn't Make Any Difference

(1)
have any strong feelings
  about it
have any feelings about it
  one way or another
care one way or the other
have a preference/any
  preferences

A. When do you want to leave?
B. Oh. I don't know. Whenever you'd like to leave is fine with me.
A. You don't **have any strong feelings about it?**(1)
B. No, not really. **It doesn't make any difference.**(2)

(2)
It doesn't make any
  difference (to me).
It doesn't matter (to me).
It's all the same to me.
I don't care.
I don't feel strongly about it
  one way or the other.

1. Who would you like to invite to the party?

2. What would you like to do this weekend?

3. Which movie would you rather see?

4. How would you like me to cut your hair?

5. Where do you want us to put the couch?

Now present your own conversations.

It's Entirely Up to You

A. **Would you mind**[(1)] if I went home early?
B. No. I wouldn't mind.
A. Are you sure? I mean if you'd rather I didn't I won't.
B. No. Honestly. It doesn't matter to me whether you go home early or not. **It's entirely up to you.**[(2)]

[(1)] Would you mind
Would it bother you
Would it disturb you

[(2)] It's (entirely) up to you.
It's (entirely) your decision.
It's for you to decide.

1. smoke

2. invite my boss for dinner

3. drop something off at the post office

4. have a date with someone else

5. take away your "security blanket"

"IT'S ENTIRELY UP TO YOU"

Now present your own conversations.

INTERCHANGE
The International Gourmet

A. Welcome to "The International Gourmet." My name is Walter, and I'll be your waiter this evening. Would you like to see the menu, or would you care to order our special complete dinner of the day?

B. What's the special today?

A. Leg of lamb . . . and I highly recommend it.

B. Well . . . Let me see . . . Okay. I think I'll have the special.

A. All right. Now, as an appetizer, you have a choice of fruit salad or tomato juice.

B. Hmm. I think I'd like the fruit salad.

A. All right. And the soups we're offering today are split pea or French onion.

B. Split pea or French onion? Hmm. That's a difficult choice. I guess I'd rather have the split pea.

A. And what kind of dressing would you like on your salad?

B. What do you have?

A. Well, let's see. We have Italian, French, Russian, and blue cheese.

B. I'd prefer Italian.

A. Italian. Fine. Now, with your leg of lamb, you can have your choice of two of our side dishes. Today we're featuring brown rice, baked potato, string beans in a cream sauce, and . . . Hmm . . . Let me see if I can remember them all . . . Oh, yes . . . And we also have fresh squash and marinated mushrooms.

B. That's quite a selection! Let's see . . . uh . . . hmmm. Let me have brown rice and fresh squash.

A. Okay. I think that's it. Oh! I almost forgot. What would you like to drink with your meal?

B. I'll have a glass of red wine.

A. All right. I'll put this order in right away, and I'll be back in a moment with some rolls and butter.

B. Thank you.

A. Welcome to "_____." My name is _____, and I'll be your waiter/waitress this evening. Would you like to see the menu, or would you care to order our special complete dinner of the day?

B. What's the special today?

A. _____ . . . and I highly recommend it.

B. Well . . . Let me see . . . Okay. I think I'll have the special.

A. All right. Now, as an appetizer, you have a choice of _____ or _____.

B. Hmm. I think I'd like the _____.

A. All right. And the soups we're offering today are _____ or _____.

B. _____ or _____? Hmm. That's a difficult choice. I guess I'd rather have the _____.

A. And what kind of dressing would you like on your salad?

B. What do you have?

A. Well, let's see. We have _____, _____, _____, and _____.

B. I'd prefer _____.

A. _____. Fine. Now, with your _____, you can have your choice of two of our side dishes. Today we're featuring _____, _____, _____, and . . . Hmm . . . Let me see if I can remember them all . . . Oh, yes . . . And we also have _____ and _____.

B. That's quite a selection! Let's see . . . uh . . . hmmm. Let me have _____ and _____.

A. Okay. I think that's it. Oh! I almost forgot. What would you like to drink with your meal?

B. I'll have _____.

A. All right. I'll put this order in right away, and I'll be back in a moment with some rolls and butter.

B. Thank you.

You're a waiter or waitress in a restaurant. Give your restaurant a name, design a "special of the day," and then create an original conversation using the model dialog above as a guide. Feel free to adapt and expand the model any way you wish.

(Use the "memo" below to design your "special of the day.")

MEMO TO ALL WAITERS AND WAITRESSES

Please let your customers know that today's special is as follows:

Special of the Day: _____

Appetizers: _____ Soups: _____

_____ _____

Salad Dressings: Side Dishes:

_____ _____ _____ _____

_____ _____ _____ _____

_____

CHAPTER 6 SUMMARY

Functions

Preference

Inquiring about . . .

Would you { prefer _____?
rather have _____?
like _____? }

Would you like to
Would you prefer to
Would you rather   } _____ (or
Do you want to   _____)?
Would you care to

How would you like it?

Do you have any strong feelings
about it?
Do you have any feelings about it
one way or another?
Do you care one way or the other?
Do you have a preference/any
preferences?

Expressing . . .

I'd prefer _____.
I'd rather have _____.
I'd like _____.

I'd prefer to _____.
I'd rather _____.
I'd like to _____.
I'd much rather _____.

I'd prefer not to _____.

I feel strongly about _____ing.

If you'd rather I didn't _____ I
won't.

Want-Desire

Inquiring about . . .

When do you want to _____?
Who would you like to _____?
What would you like to do?
How would you like me
to _____?
Which _____ would you rather
_____?
Where do you want _____ to
_____?

Expressing . . .

I'd like _____.
I'll have _____.
I want _____.

I (really) don't feel like _____ing.
I'm not (really) in the mood to
_____.
I'd (really) prefer not to _____.

_____ wants me to _____.

Requests

Direct, More Polite

Would you mind
Would it bother you   } if I _____ed?
Would it disturb you

Indifference

Whenever _____ is fine with me.
(Whoever . . . . Whatever . . . .
However . . . . Whichever . . . .
Wherever . . . .)

It doesn't make any difference (to
me).
It doesn't matter (to me).
It's all the same to me.
I don't care.
I don't feel strongly about it one way
or the other.

It doesn't matter to me whether you
_____ or not.

It's (entirely) up to you.
It's (entirely) your decision.
It's for you to decide.

Conversation Strategy

Hesitating

Well . . .
Let me see . . .
Let's see . . .
Hmm . . .
Okay . . .
Uh . . .
I think . . .
I guess . . .

SCENES & IMPROVISATIONS
Chapters 4, 5, 6

Who do you think these people are?
What do you think they're talking about?
Create conversations based on these scenes and act them out.

1.

2.

3.

4.

5.

6.

7.

8.

7

I Promise
I Won't Let You Down
He Gave Me His Word
I've Made a Decision
I'll Probably Stay Home and Read a Book
I Haven't Made Up My Mind Yet
I Was Planning to Do Room 407 a Little Later
I Changed My Mind

• Embedded Questions • Future: Going to • Future: Will
• Gerunds • Infinitives • Might • Past Continuous
to Express Future Intention • Present Perfect Tense
• Sequence of Tenses • Two-Word Verbs

I Promise

(1) rely on
depend on
count on

(2) I promise I'll
I promise to

A. Can I **rely on**(1) you to turn off the lights when you leave?
B. Yes. **I promise I'll**(2) turn them off.
A. You won't forget? It's really important.
B. Don't worry. You can **rely on**(1) me.

1. pick up the soda for the party tonight

2. bring back my typewriter tomorrow

3. drop off my suit at the cleaner's on the way to school

4. put away your toys before our guests arrive

5. clean up the kitchen before the health inspector gets here

"I PROMISE"

Now present your own conversations.

I Won't Let You Down

A. Will the car be ready by five?
B. Yes, it will.
A. Really? Can I **depend on**[1] that?
B. **Absolutely!**[2] **I promise**[3] it'll be ready by five.
A. Okay. Now remember, I'm **counting**[4] on you.
B. Don't worry! I won't **let you down.**[5]

[1] depend on
     count on
     rely on
     be sure of

[2] Absolutely!
     Definitely!
     Positively!

[3] I promise (you)
     I guarantee (you)
     I assure you
     I give you my word
     You can be sure

[4] counting
     depending
     relying

[5] let you down
     disappoint you

1. Will you write to me often?

2. Will we get to the airport in time for my 3:00 flight?

3. Will there be enough food for all our customers tonight?

4. Will this tooth extraction be painless?

5. Will you behave yourself for the baby-sitter tonight?

Now present your own conversations.

He Gave Me His Word

A. I'm very **disappointed with**[1] the salesman who sold me this watch.
B. How come?
A. He guaranteed me this watch was waterproof, . . . but it isn't!
B. **That's too bad.**[2] Are you going to talk to him about it? After all, he DID give you his word.
A. **Maybe I should.**[3]

A. I'm very **disappointed with**[1] my next-door neighbor.
B. How come?
A. She gave me her word she would keep her dog off my lawn, . . . but she hasn't!
B. **That's a shame.**[2] Are you going to talk to her about it? After all, she DID give you her word.
A. **Maybe I should.**[3]

| [1] disappointed with
disappointed in | [2] That's too bad.
That's/What a shame. | [3] Maybe I should.
I guess I will.
I suppose I will. |

1. my upstairs neighbor

2. my landlord

3. my daughter

4. my boss

5. my employees

6. the photographer

7. my agent in Hollywood

Now present your own conversations.

I've Made a Decision

A. You know, . . . I've made a decision.
B. What?
A. **I'm going to**(1) join the army.
B. **Gee!**(2) Joining the army! That's a big decision!
A. I know. It is. But **I've thought about it for a long time**(3) and decided it's time to do it.
B. Well, good luck!

1. get married

2. give up smoking

3. sell my house

4. quit my job

5. apply to business school

Now present your own conversations.

I'll Probably Stay Home and Read a Book

A. Hi! It's me!
B. Oh, hi! How are you?
A. Fine. Tell me, what are you doing this afternoon?
B. **I'm not sure.**[1] I'll **probably**[2] stay home and read a book. How about you?
A. Well, I'm planning to go fishing. **Would you like to join me?**[3]
B. Sure. **I'd be happy to.**[4] Going fishing sounds a lot more **exciting**[5] than staying home and reading a book.
A. Good! I'll pick you up at around one o'clock.
B. See you then.

[1] I'm not sure.
I'm not certain.
I don't know yet.

[2] probably
most likely

[3] Would you like to join me?
Do you want to join me?
Would you be interested in joining me?

[4] I'd be happy to.
I'd love to.
I'd like that.

[5] exciting
enjoyable
interesting

1. work in the garden
   play tennis

2. work on my car
   go swimming

3. do some chores around
   the house
   see the new exhibit at
   the museum

4. work on my term paper
   see a movie

5. catch up on some work at
   the office
   play a few rounds of golf

Now present your own
conversations.

I Haven't Made Up My Mind Yet

(1)
I've been thinking of
I'm thinking of
I've been thinking about
I'm thinking about

(2)
I thought I might
I thought I'd
I might
I may

A. Have you decided who you're going to ask to the prom?
B. No. I haven't made up my mind yet. **I've been thinking of**(1) asking Susan, but **I** also **thought I might**(2) ask Elizabeth.
A. Sounds like a difficult decision. I'll be curious to know what you decide.
B. I'll let you know.
A. Promise?
B. Promise.

1. Chemistry
   Music

2. to Florida
   to Arizona

3. right away
   when business gets better

4. on our next date
   in a long letter

5. an IBM
   an Apple

Now present your own conversations.

I Was Planning to Do Room 407 a Little Later

A. Have you done Room 407 yet?
B. No, I haven't. **I was planning to**[1] do it **a little later.**[2]
A. Would you mind doing it soon?
B. No, not at all. I'll do it **right away.**[3]

[1] I was planning to
I was going to
I intended to
I thought I would

[2] a little later
in a little while

[3] right away
right now
as soon as I can
the first chance I get

1. write the monthly report

2. copy my memo

3. distribute the mail

4. make my hotel reservations in Chicago

5. give out the paychecks

Now present your own conversations.

INTERCHANGE
I Changed My Mind

A. Well, if it isn't David Johnson!

B. Richard Peters! It's nice to see you again!

A. You know, David, I've been meaning to call you for a long time.

B. Me, too. How have you been?

A. Fine. How about yourself?

B. Pretty good.

A. Tell me, David. The last time I saw you, you were planning to go to law school, weren't you?

B. Yes, I guess I was. But as it turned out, I changed my mind.

A. Oh, really? But **if I remember correctly,**[1] you were intent on going to law school. Whatever made you change your mind?

B. Well, it's a long story, and I don't want to bore you with all the details. But **what it boils down to is that**[2] I decided that going to law school wasn't a very good idea. I decided to go to medical school instead.

A. Medical school? That's very interesting.

B. And how about you? The last time we talked, didn't you tell me you were going to open your own real estate business?

A. That's right. I was. But things turned out differently.

B. But you seemed so determined to do that. What happened?

A. Well, it's very complicated, and I'm sure you don't want to know all the details. But **as it turned out,**[2] I decided that opening my own real estate company just wasn't for me. So I decided to stay at my old job instead.

B. Well, **a lot sure has happened**[3] since we last saw each other.

A. **I'll say!**[4] You know, we should try to stay in touch.

B. Yes, we should. Let's have lunch together sometime soon.

A. Good idea.

B. Take care now.

A. You, too.

A. Well, if it isn't _____ _____!

B. _____ _____! It's nice to see you again!

A. You know, _____, I've been meaning to call you for a long time.

B. Me, too. How have you been?

A. Fine. How about yourself?

B. Pretty good.

A. Tell me, _____. The last time I saw you, you were planning to _____, weren't you?

B. Yes, I guess I was. But as it turned out, I changed my mind.

A. Oh, really? But **if I remember correctly,**(1) you were intent on _____ing. Whatever made you change your mind?

B. Well, it's a long story, and I don't want to bore you with all the details. But **what it boils down to is that**(2) I decided that _____ing wasn't a very good idea. I decided to _____ instead.

A. _____? That's very interesting.

B. And how about you? The last time we talked, didn't you tell me you were going to _____?

A. That's right. I was. But things turned out differently.

B. But you seemed so determined to do that. What happened?

A. Well, it's very complicated, and I'm sure you don't want to know all the details. But **as it turned out,**(2) I decided that _____ing just wasn't for me. So I decided to _____ instead.

B. Well, **a lot sure has happened**(3) since we last saw each other.

A. **I'll say!**(4) You know, we should try to stay in touch.

B. Yes, we should. Let's have lunch together sometime soon.

A. Good idea.

B. Take care now.

A. You, too.

You've just "bumped into" somebody you haven't seen in a while. Create an original conversation using the model dialog above as a guide. Feel free to adapt and expand the model any way you wish.

Functions

Intention

Inquiring about . . .

Have you decided _____?

What are you doing *this afternoon*?

Expressing . . .

I'm going to _____.
I'm planning to _____.
I plan to _____.
I intend to _____.
I've decided to _____.

I'll _____ {
 right away.
 right now.
 as soon as I can.
 the first chance I get.
}

I've been thinking of _____ing.
I'm thinking of _____ing.
I've been thinking about
 _____ing.
I'm thinking about _____ing.

I've been meaning to _____
 (for a long time).

I've thought about it for a long time.
I've given it a lot of thought.
I've given it a lot of serious
 consideration.

I've decided it's time to do it.

I haven't made up my mind yet.

I was planning to _____.
I was going to _____.
I intended to _____.
I thought I would _____.

I was intent on _____ing.
I was determined to _____.

Promising

Asking for a Promise

Can I {
 rely on
 depend on
 count on
} you to _____?

Can I {
 depend on
 count on
 rely on
 be sure of
} that?

Promise?

Offering a Promise

Promise.
I promise I'll _____.
I promise to _____.

I promise (you) _____.
I guarantee (you) _____.
I assure you _____.
I give you my word _____.
You can be sure _____.

Absolutely.
Definitely.
Positively.

You can {
 rely on
 depend on
 count on
} me.

I won't let you down.
I won't disappoint you.

Invitations

Extending . . .

Would you like to join me?
Do you want to join me?
Would you be interested in joining
 me?

Accepting . . .

I'd be happy to.
I'd love to.
I'd like that.

Disappointment

I'm (very) disappointed with/in
_____.

Sympathizing

That's too bad.
That's a/What a shame.

Surprise-Disbelief

Gee!
Boy!
Wow!

Certainty/Uncertainty

Expressing Uncertainty

I'm not sure.
I'm not certain.
I don't know yet.

Probability/Improbability

Expressing Probability

I'll probably _____.
I'll most likely _____.

Possibility/Impossibility

Expressing Possibility

I might _____.
I may _____.
I thought I might _____.
I thought I'd _____.

Agreement/Disagreement

Expressing Agreement

I agree.
You're right.
I'll say.
You can say that again!

Conversation Strategies

Initiating Conversations

Hi! It's me!

Well, if it isn't _____!

Initiating a Topic

You know, . . .

Focusing Attention

What it boils down to is that . . .
The fact of the matter is that . . .
As it turned out, . . .

Offering to Do Something
Offering to Help
Gratitude
Appreciation
Persuading-Insisting

Initiating a Topic

Do You Want Me to Wash the Dishes?
Want Any Help?
Let Me Give You a Hand
May I Help You?
Can I Do Anything to Help?
I'm Very Grateful to You
Words Can't Express . . .

• Can • Demonstrative Adjectives • Gerunds • Indirect
Objects • Passives • Relative Clauses with Who
• Should • Singular/Plural • Want + Object + Infinitive

Do You Want Me to Wash the Dishes?

(1) Do you want me to _____?
Would you like me to _____?
I'll _____, if you'd like.
I'll/I'd be happy/glad to _____, if you'd like.

(2) Don't worry about it.
That's okay/all right.

(3) No, really!
Listen!
(Oh,) come on!

(4) for a change
for once

(5) I appreciate it/that.
I'd appreciate it/that.
It's nice/kind of you to offer.
That's (very) nice/kind of you.
That would be nice.

A. **Do you want me to**(1) wash the dishes?
B. No. **Don't worry about it.**(2) I don't mind washing the dishes.
A. **No, really!**(3) You're always the one who washes the dishes. Let me, **for a change.**(4)
B. Okay. Thanks. **I appreciate it.**(5)

1. water the plants

2. mow the lawn

3. take out the garbage

4. defrost the refrigerator

5. feed the hamster

Now present your own conversations.

Want Any Help?

A. I see you're changing the oil.
B. Yes. It hasn't been changed in a long time.
A. **Want any help?**[1]
B. Sure. **If you don't mind.**[2]
A. No, not at all. **I'd be happy to give you a hand.**[3]
B. Thanks. I appreciate it.

[1] (Do you) want any help?
(Do you) need any help?
(Do you) want a hand?
(Do you) need a hand?
Can I help?
Can I give you a hand?

[2] If you don't mind.
If you wouldn't mind.
If it's no trouble.

[3] I'd be happy/glad to give
you a hand.
I'd be happy/glad to lend a
hand.
I'd be happy/glad to help.

1. clean the garage

2. wash the windows

3. paint the fence

4. sweep out the barn

5. shampoo Rover

"WANT ANY HELP?"

Now present your own
conversations.

Let Me Give You a Hand

⁽¹⁾ Would you like me to help you _____?

Do you want me to help you _____?

I'd be happy/glad to help you _____, (if you'd like).

Let me help you _____.

Would you like any help _____ing?

Would you like me to give you a hand _____ing?

⁽²⁾ There's no sense in your _____ing

There's no reason (for you) to _____

You don't have to _____

You shouldn't have to _____

⁽³⁾ it's nice of you to offer

thanks for offering

I appreciate your offering

⁽⁴⁾ Look!

Listen!

Come on!

⁽⁵⁾ trouble you

bother you

inconvenience you

put you to any trouble

put you out

A. **Would you like me to help you**⁽¹⁾ move that desk?

B. No, that's okay. I can move it myself.

A. Oh, come on! Let me give you a hand. **There's no sense in your**⁽²⁾ moving it yourself if I'm here to help.

B. Really, **it's nice of you to offer,**⁽³⁾ but . . .

A. **Look!**⁽⁴⁾ I insist! You're not moving that desk by yourself!

B. Well, okay. But I really don't want to **trouble you.**⁽⁵⁾

A. No trouble at all! Honestly! I'm happy to lend a hand.

1. lift that motor

2. carry those boxes

3. take down that sign

4. unload that truck

5. set those chairs up

6. cut that tree down

7. adjust that TV antenna

8. change that tire

9. alphabetize those index cards

"LET ME GIVE YOU A HAND"

Now present your own conversations.

May I Help You?

A. **May I help you?**(1)
B. Not right now, thanks. I'm just looking.
A. **Is there anything in particular I can help you find?**(2)
B. Well, actually, I'm looking for a digital watch.
A. Oh, I'm afraid **we're out of**(3) digital watches, but we expect some in very soon. Is there anything else I can help you with?
B. I guess not. But thanks anyway.
A. Well, **please let me know if I can be of any further assistance.**(4)
B. Thanks very much.

1. a size 40 jacket

2. a convertible sofa-bed

3. size 34 underwear

4. a remote-control video cassette recorder

5. sugar-free chewing gum

Now present your own conversations.

Can I Do Anything to Help?

A. Excuse me. Are you **okay?**[1]
B. Well, uh . . . I'm not sure.
A. What happened?
B. I was knocked down by someone on roller skates.
A. Oh, no! **Can I do anything to help?**[2]
B. **Huh?**[3]
A. Can I help? Should I **call an ambulance?**[4]
B. No, that's okay. I think I'll be all right.
A. Well, here. **Let me**[5] help you up.
B. Thanks. **You're very kind.**[6]
A. **Don't mention it.**[7]

1. I was just mugged.

2. I think I sprained my ankle.

3. I was just hit by a car.

4. I fell off my bicycle.

5. I must have fainted.

Now present your own conversations.

I'm Very Grateful to You

(1) it was nothing (at all)
don't mention it

(2) No, I mean it!
No, really!
No, honestly!

(3) I'm very grateful (to you).
I really appreciate it.
I appreciate it very much.

(4) I'm glad I could do it/
help/be of help.
(It was) my pleasure.
Any time.

A. You know, I keep forgetting to thank you for lending me your calculator.
B. Oh, **it was nothing.**[1]
A. **No, I mean it!**[2] It was very nice of you to lend it to me. **I'm very grateful to you.**[3]
B. **I'm glad I could do it.**[4]

1. loan me your car

2. give me a promotion

3. send me flowers when I was in the hospital

4. create a new position at the company for my daughter

5. fix my son up with your niece

Now present your own conversations.

INTERCHANGE
Words Can't Express . . .

I'm very grateful to receive this award for "Best Actress."
I can't begin to tell you how much I appreciate this honor.
There are many people I'd like to thank.

First of all,[1] I want to thank my parents for bringing me into this world.

I also want to express my gratitude to all of my teachers over the years, but especially to my acting teacher, Vincent Lewis, who taught me everything I know.

And finally, I want to express my appreciation to all of my friends for their **support,**[2] especially to Katherine Miller, for being there when I needed her.

This award means a great deal to me. Words can't express how **honored**[3] I feel at this moment. Thank you very much.

[1] First of all,	[2] support	assistance	[3] honored
First and foremost,	encouragement	guidance	thrilled
Most of all,	help	inspiration	excited
Above all,	advice		proud
			overwhelmed

I'm very grateful to receive this award for "_____."
I can't begin to tell you how much I appreciate this honor.
There are many people I'd like to thank.

First of all,[1] I want to thank my parents for _____.

I also want to express my gratitude to all of my teachers over the years, but especially to _____, who _____.

And finally, I want to express my appreciation to all of my friends for their _____,[2] especially to _____, for _____.

This award means a great deal to me. Words can't express how _____[3] I feel at this moment. Thank you very much.

You have just received an award. Make your acceptance speech using the model above as a guide. Feel free to adapt and expand the model any way you wish.

Functions

Offering to Do Something

Do you want me to _____?
Would you like me to _____?
I'll _____, if you'd like.
I'll/I'd be happy/glad to _____, if you'd like.

Let me (_____).

Offering to Help

Making an Offer

(Do you) want any help?
(Do you) need any help?
(Do you) want a hand?
(Do you) need a hand?
Can I help?
Can I give you a hand?

Would you like me to help you _____?
Do you want me to help you _____?
I'd be glad/happy to help you _____, (if you'd like).
Let me help you _____.
Would you like any help _____ing?
Would you like me to give you a hand _____ing?

Can I do anything to help?
Is there anything I can do to help?
Can I help?

I'd be happy/glad to give you a hand.
I'd be happy/glad to lend a hand.
I'd be happy/glad to help.

Let me give you a hand.
I'm happy to lend a hand.

Let me _____.
Allow me to _____.
I'll _____.

May/Can I help you?
May/Can I assist you?

Is there anything/something in particular I can help you find?
Is there anything/something you're looking for in particular?

Is there anything else I can help you with?

Please let me know if I can be of any further assistance.
Please feel free to call on me if I can be of any further assistance.
If I can be of any further assistance, please don't hesitate to ask/let me know.

Responding to an Offer

If you don't mind.
If you wouldn't mind.
If it's no trouble.

I don't want to $\begin{cases} \text{trouble you.} \\ \text{bother you.} \\ \text{inconvenience you.} \\ \text{put you to any trouble.} \\ \text{put you out.} \end{cases}$

Don't worry about it.
That's okay/all right.

Gratitude

Expressing . . .

Thanks (very much).
Thank you (very much).

I'm very grateful (to _____).

I want to thank _____.
I want to express my gratitude to _____.

I keep forgetting to thank you for _____.

Responding to . . .

You're welcome.
Don't mention it.
No problem.
Glad to be of help.
It was nothing (at all).

I'm glad I could do it/help/be of help.
(It was) my pleasure.
Any time.

Appreciation

I appreciate it/that.
I'd appreciate it/that.
It's nice/kind of you to offer.
Thanks for offering.
I appreciate your offering.
That's (very) nice/kind of you.
That would be nice.

You're very kind/nice.

I'm very grateful (to _____).

I really appreciate it.
I appreciate it very much.

It was very nice of you (to _____).

I can't begin to tell you how much I appreciate _____.

I want to express my appreciation to _____.

Persuading-Insisting

Listen!
Look!
(No,) really!
(No,) I mean it!
(No,) honestly!
(Oh,) come on!

I insist.

Let me, for a change.
Let me, for once.

There's no sense in your _____ing.
There's no reason (for you) to _____.
You don't have to _____.
You shouldn't have to _____.

Attracting Attention

Excuse me.

Conversation Strategy

Initiating a Topic

You know, . . .

9

Is Smoking Allowed Here?
Please Don't Pick the Flowers
Can I Possibly Have the Car Tonight?
Would You Mind If I Served Leftovers for Dinner?
I'd Rather You Didn't
I Can't Do That Without an Authorization
You Mustn't Under Any Circumstances

• Can/Could • Gerunds • Imperatives • Infinitives • May
• Must • Sequence of Tenses • Short Answers • Would

Is Smoking Allowed Here?

A. **Is** smoking **allowed**[1] here?
B. **Yes, it is.**[2]
A. Thanks.

A. **Are you permitted to** take pictures[1] here?
B. **No, you aren't.**[3]
A. Oh, okay. Thanks.

A. **Are people allowed to** park[1] here?
B. **Yes, they are.**[2]
A. Thanks.

A. **Do they permit** surfing[1] here?
B. **Not as far as I know.**[3]
A. Oh, okay. Thanks.

[1]	[2]	[3]
Is _____ing allowed/ permitted? Is it okay to _____?	Yes, it is. Yes, it is.	No, it isn't. No, it isn't.
Are you allowed/permitted to _____? Are people allowed to _____?	Yes, you are. Yes, they are.	No, you aren't. No, they aren't.
Do they allow/permit _____ing? Do they allow people to _____?	Yes, they do. Yes, they do.	No, they don't. No, they don't.
	[less certain] I think so. I believe so. Yes, as far as I know.	[less certain] I don't think so. I don't believe so. Not as far as I know.

1. swim

2. camp

3. ice skate

4. feed the animals

5. dive

6. picnic

7. play a radio

8. play frisbee

9. sunbathe in the nude

"IS SMOKING ALLOWED HERE?"

Now present your own conversations.

Please Don't Pick the Flowers

A. **Excuse me,**[1] but **I don't think** picking the flowers **is allowed.**[2]
B. Oh?
A. Yes. There's a sign here that says so.
B. Hmm. "Please Don't Pick the Flowers." **How about that!**[3] I never even noticed it. Thanks for telling me.
A. You're welcome.

1.

2.

3.

4.

5.

Now present your own conversations.

Can I Possibly Have the Car Tonight?

Check with your mother.

A. Could I ask you a favor?
B. Sure. What?
A. **Can I possibly**[1] have the car tonight?
B. Hmm. **Let me think for a minute.**[2] Well, **I guess so.**[3] But maybe you should also check with your mother. I'm sure she won't **object to**[4] your having the car tonight, but it wouldn't hurt to ask.
A. Okay. Thanks. I'll check with her right away.

---

[1] Can/Could I (possibly) _____?
Can/Could I please _____?
May I (please) _____?
Is it all right/okay (with you) if I _____?
Would it be possible for me to _____?
I'd like to _____, if that's all right/okay (with you).

[2] Let me think (for a minute).
Let me see.
Let's see now.

[3] I guess so.
I suppose so.
I don't see (any reason) why not.

[4] object to
have any objection to
mind

Check with Mrs. Fleming.

1. go home an hour early today

Check with your father.

2. stay over at Lucy's house tonight

Check with my roommate.

3. borrow your TV until tomorrow

Check with our manager, Mr. Larson.

4. stay in my room a few hours past check-out time

Check with the owners of the building.

5. put a hot tub on my balcony

"CAN I POSSIBLY HAVE THE CAR TONIGHT?"

Now present your own conversations.

Would You Mind If I Served Leftovers for Dinner?

serve leftovers for dinner?

A. **Would you mind if I** served leftovers for dinner?[1]
B. **No, I wouldn't mind.**[2]
A. Are you sure? I mean if you'd rather I didn't I won't.
B. **Honestly.**[3] If you want to serve leftovers for dinner, it's **fine**[4] with me. **Go right ahead.**[5]

turn up the heat?

A. **Is it all right with you if I** turn up the heat?[1]
B. **Certainly.**[2]
A. Are you sure? I mean if you'd rather I didn't I won't.
B. **Honestly.**[3] If you want to turn up the heat, it's **fine**[4] with me. **Go right ahead.**[5]

---

[1] Would you mind/object if I _____ed?
Would it bother you if I _____ed?
Do you mind if I _____?

→

[2] No, I wouldn't mind.
No, I don't mind.
No, of course not.
No, not at all.
No, it's all right/fine/okay with me.
No.

Is it all right/okay (with you) if I _____?
Would it be all right/okay (with you) if I _____ed?
I'd like to _____, if that's all right/okay (with you).

→

Certainly.
Sure.
Of course.
By all means.
It's all right/okay with me.
Yes.

- -

[3] Honestly.
Really.

[4] fine
all right
okay

[5] Go (right) ahead.
Be my guest.

1. Would you mind . . .?

2. Is it all right you with you . . .?

3. Would it bother you . . .?

4. I'd like to . . .

5. Do you mind . . .?

6. Would you object . . .?

7. Would it be all right with you . . .?

8. Is it okay with you . . .?

9. Would it bother you . . .?

Now present your own conversations.

I'd Rather You Didn't

(1) Actually, To be honest (with you), To tell (you) the truth, (2) I'd rather you didn't. I'd prefer it if you didn't/wouldn't. I'd prefer/rather that you not. I'd prefer you not to. (3) You see The reason is

A. Is it all right if I order steak for two?
B. **Actually,**(1) **I'd rather you didn't.**(2)
A. Oh, okay.
B. **You see**(3) . . . I'm a vegetarian.
A. Oh, I'm sorry. I didn't know that.

1. Would you mind . . .?

2. Do you mind . . .?

3. Would it be okay . . .?

4. Would you object . . .?

5. Is it okay . . .?

Now present your own
conversations.

I Can't Do That Without an Authorization

the landlord

A. Could I ask you to change the lock on our door?
B. I'm afraid I can't do that without **an authorization from**[1] the landlord.
A. Oh? How can I get his authorization?
B. Well, the best thing to do is to write a note asking him to **authorize me to**[2] change the lock on your door.
A. Okay. I'll do that.
B. I'm sorry. I don't mean to **make things difficult for you.**[3]
A. I understand.

[1] an authorization from
the permission of
the approval of
the consent of
the agreement of
a go ahead from

[2] authorize me to _____
permit me to _____
approve my _____ing
consent to my _____ing
agree to my _____ing
give the go ahead for me
to _____

[3] make things difficult/
complicated for you
complicate things
give you a hard time
give you "the runaround"

Mrs. Field in the Maintenance Department

1. fix the ceiling in my office

Mr. Thompson in the Payroll Department

2. give me an advance on my next paycheck

Mr. Blackwell in the Dean's office

3. switch my major to Accounting

the branch manager, Mrs. Watkins

4. hold our mail at the post office while we're away

the board of directors

5. change my title to "Senior Vice-President"

"I CAN'T DO THAT WITHOUT AN AUTHORIZATION"

Now present your own conversations.

You Mustn't Under Any Circumstances

A. Before you sign the lease, do you have any questions?
B. Yes. Are we allowed to sublet the apartment?
A. No. I'm afraid subletting the apartment isn't permitted.
B. I see. Well, is it all right to use the fireplace?
A. No. You mustn't use the fireplace under any circumstances.
B. Oh. Well, do you allow people to have pets?
A. No. That's out of the question. We don't permit anyone to have pets.
B. How about parking in front of the building?
A. I'm sorry. You're not supposed to park in front of the building.
B. Oh.
A. And before I forget, I should mention that you may not alter the apartment in any way without permission. Now, do you have any other questions?
B. No, I guess not. I think you've answered them all.

A. Before _____, do you have any questions?
B. Yes. Are we allowed to _____?
A. No. I'm afraid _____ing isn't permitted.
B. I see. Well, is it all right to _____?
A. No. You mustn't _____ under any circumstances.
B. Oh. Well, do you allow people to _____?
A. No. That's out of the question. We don't permit anyone to _____.
B. How about _____ing?
A. I'm sorry. You're not supposed to _____.
B. Oh.
A. And before I forget, I should mention that you may not _____ without permission. Now, do you have any other questions?
B. No, I guess not. I think you've answered them all.

1. Before you begin your freshman year here at Winchester College . . .

2. Before beginning your summer here at Camp Salamander . . .

3. Before you start your six weeks of basic training . . .

4. Before your tour of The Republic of Grenomia gets underway . . .

Create original conversations using the model dialog on p. 92 as a guide. Feel free to adapt and expand the model any way you wish.

Functions

Permission

Asking for . . .

Can/Could I (possibly) _____?
Can/Could I please _____?
May I (please) _____?
Is it all right/okay (with you) if I
_____?
Would it be possible for me to
_____?
I'd like to _____, if that's all
right/okay (with you).

Would you mind/object if I
_____ed?
Would it bother you if I
_____ed?
Do you mind if I _____?

Is it all right/okay (with you) if I
_____?
Would it be all right/okay (with you)
if I _____ed?
I'd like to _____, if that's all
right/okay (with you).

Granting . . .

Certainly.
Sure.
Of course.
By all means.
It's all right/okay with me.
Yes.

No, I wouldn't mind.
No, I don't mind.
No, of course not.
No, not at all.
No, it's all right/fine/okay with me.
No.

Go (right) ahead.
Be my guest.

I guess so.
I suppose so.
I don't see (any reason) why not.

If you want to _____,

it's { fine
      all right } with me.
      okay

Denying . . .

I'd rather you didn't.
I'd prefer it if you didn't/wouldn't.
I'd prefer/rather that you not.
I'd prefer you not to.

_____ing isn't allowed/permitted.
You mustn't _____ (under any
circumstances).
We don't permit anyone to _____.
You're not supposed to _____.
You may not _____ (without
permission).

That's out of the question.

I can't do that without

{ an authorization from
the permission of
the approval of   } _____
the consent of
the agreement of
a go ahead from

Inquiring about Permissibility

Is _____ing allowed/permitted?
Is it okay to _____?
Is it all right to _____?
Are you allowed/permitted to _____?
Are people allowed to _____?
Do they allow/permit _____ing?
Do they allow people to _____?

Indicating Permissibility

I don't think _____ing is
allowed/permitted.
I don't think you're allowed/
permitted to _____.
I don't think people are allowed/
permitted to _____.
I don't think they allow/permit
people to _____.
I don't think they allow/permit you
to _____.

Yes, _____ _____.
[less certain]
I think so.
I believe so.
Yes, as far as I know.

No, _____ _____.
[less certain]
I don't think so.
I don't believe so.
Not as far as I know.

Gratitude

Expressing . . .

Thanks (for telling me).

Apologizing

(Oh,) I'm sorry.

I don't mean to

{ make things difficult/
complicate for you.
complicate things.
give you a hard time.
give you "the runaround."

Attracting Attention

Excuse me, . . .
Pardon me, . . .

Surprise-Disbelief

Oh?

(Well,) how about that!
(Well,) what do you know!
(Well,) how do you like that!
Isn't that something!

Persuading-Insisting

Honestly.
Really.

Denying/Admitting

Admitting

You see . . .
The reason is . . .

Requests

Direct, Polite

Could I ask you to _____?

Could I ask you a favor?

Conversation Strategy

Hesitating

Hmm.

Let me think (for a minute).
Let me see.
Let's see now.

SCENES & IMPROVISATIONS
Chapters 7, 8, 9

Who do you think these people are?
What do you think they're talking about?
Create conversations based on these scenes and act them out.

1.

2.

3.

4.

5.

6.

7.

8.

How Would You Like to Go to the Zoo?
Would You By Any Chance Be Interested
in Seeing a Movie?
Can You Come?
We'd Like to Invite You and Your Wife Over
for Dinner
I Think I Should Be Going Now
I've Really Got to Go Now
I Don't Have Any Obligations or Commitments
on Friday

• Can • Gerunds • Have to/Have Got to • Must • Need to
• Present Continuous Tense to Express Future
• Present Perfect Tense • Supposed to • Would

How Would You Like to Go to the Zoo?

⁽¹⁾ How would you like to
_____?
Would you like to _____?
Do you want to _____?
Would you be interested in
_____ing?
How about _____ing?
Let's _____.

⁽²⁾ I'd love to.
I'd like to.
I'd like that.
That sounds like fun.
That sounds great/
terrific/wonderful.
That would be great/
terrific/wonderful.
I'd be happy to/glad to.

[stronger]
I'd be delighted to/
thrilled to.

⁽³⁾ a nice idea
a good idea
a nice thing to do
a nice/good way to spend
the day

A. **How would you like to**⁽¹⁾ go to the zoo this Sunday?
B. **I'd love to.**⁽²⁾ I haven't gone to the zoo in a long time.
A. Me neither. That's why I thought going to the zoo might be **a nice idea.**⁽³⁾

1. see a ballgame

2. play basketball

3. go sailing

4. take a ride in the country

5. pick strawberries

Now present your own conversations.

Would You By Any Chance Be Interested in Seeing a Movie?

see a movie?

(1) If you're not busy,
If you're free,
If you don't have any other plans,

(2) Would you (by any chance) be interested in _____ ing?
You wouldn't (by any chance) be interested in _____ ing, would you?

(3) can't
won't be able to

(4) I have to
I've got to
I'm supposed to

(5) asking
inviting me
the invitation

A. **If you're not busy,**(1) **would you by any chance be interested in**(2) seeing a movie with me this Saturday?
B. I'd love to, but I **can't.**(3) **I have to**(4) study for my college entrance exams.
A. That's too bad.
B. Thanks for **asking,**(5) though. Maybe we can see a movie some other time.

go out for dinner?

1. attend my cousin's wedding

have a picnic?

2. help my parents with the "spring cleaning"

see a play?

3. take care of my little sister

go out dancing?

4. participate in our annual school concert

play miniature golf?

5. work on my science project

"WOULD YOU BY ANY CHANCE BE INTERESTED IN SEEING A MOVIE?"

Now present your own conversations.

Can You Come?

I'm organizing a company picnic for this Saturday.

A. I'm organizing a company picnic for this Saturday. **Can you come?**(1)
B. I'd love to, but I'm not sure I can. I think I'm supposed to work overtime.
A. That's too bad. Is there any chance you could possibly get out of working overtime?
B. I'm not sure. **Let me check and get back to you.**(2)
A. Okay, but please try to come. It won't be much of a company picnic without you!
B. It's nice of you to say that. **I'll do my best.**(3)

I'm having a slumber party this Saturday night.

1. baby-sit

I'm planning a family reunion for next April 20th.

2. speak at my firm's annual meeting

I'm throwing a surprise party for my husband's birthday this Friday night.

3. be on duty

I'm putting together a softball game for this coming Saturday afternoon.

4. help my landlord paint the hallway

I'm scheduling a "pot luck supper" for the first Sunday in June.

5. collect for "The Heart Fund"

"CAN YOU COME?"

Now present your own conversations.

We'd Like to Invite You and Your Wife Over for Dinner

dinner
this Saturday evening
7:00

A. **We'd like to invite you and your wife over**[1] for dinner this Saturday evening. Would you be able to come?
B. This Saturday evening?
A. Yes, and we hope you'll be able to join us.
B. **Thank you for the invitation.**[2] We'd be **very happy**[3] to come.
A. Good.
B. What time should we **plan to arrive?**[4]
A. **How does 7:00 sound?**[5]
B. 7:00? Fine. We'll be looking forward to it.

[1] We'd like to invite you and your wife over
We'd like to have you and your wife over
We'd like you and your wife to be our guests
We'd like you and your wife to join us

[2] Thank you/Thanks for the invitation.
Thank you/Thanks for inviting us.
I appreciate the invitation.
It's (very) nice of you to invite us.

[3] very happy
very glad
pleased
delighted

[4] plan to arrive
plan to get there
plan on arriving
plan on being there

[5] How does 7:00 sound?
Is 7:00 convenient/all right?
Would 7:00 be convenient/all right?

brunch
this Sunday
noon

1. you and your husband

a barbecue
this Saturday afternoon
2:00

2. you and your family

cocktails
this Friday evening
6:00

3. you and your wife

a party celebrating our
15th wedding anniversary
this Saturday evening
7:30

4. you and your fiancé

a small get-together we're
having
this Saturday evening
8:00

5. you and your fiancée

"WE'D LIKE TO INVITE YOU AND YOUR WIFE OVER FOR DINNER"

Now present your own conversations.

I Think I Should Be Going Now

(1) bumped into
ran into

(2) be going
get going
be on my way
be getting on my way

(3) I need to
I have to
I've got to
I'm supposed to

(4) get together soon
keep in touch
stay in touch

(5) Take care.
Take it easy.

(6) So long.
Good-bye.
Bye.
Bye-bye.
See you.

A. Well, it's been really nice seeing you again.
B. Yes, it has. I'm glad we **bumped into**(1) each other.
A. Me, too. You know, I think I should **be going**(2) now. **I need to**(3) have this car back at the rental agency by 2:00.
B. Actually, I should get going, too.
A. Let's **get together soon.**(4)
B. Okay. I'll call you.
A. **Take care.**(5)
B. **So long.**(6)

1. get these packages to the post office before it closes

2. finish my lunch hour a little early today

3. pick up a few things at the supermarket on my way home

4. be at my piano lesson by 4:00

5. reach Denver by 7:00 tonight

Now present your own conversations.

I've Really Got to Go Now

A. **By the way,**[1] **what time is it?**[2]
B. It's about 1:30.
A. 1:30?! Already?! I didn't realize it was so late.
B. I didn't either.
A. **I've really got to go now.**[3] **I've got to**[4] get to my English class.
B. Oh! You'd better hurry! **See you soon.**[5]
A. So long.
B. Bye.

[1] By the way,
Incidentally,

[2] What time is it?
Do you have the time?

[3] I've (really) got to go now.
I've (really) got to be going now.
I (really) have to go now.
I'd (really) better go now.
I (really) need to go now.
I (really) should go now.
I have to/I've got to run.
I have to/I've got to get going.

[4] I've got to
I have to
I need to

[5] (I'll) see you soon/later/ tomorrow/next week/ . . .

1. get to the bank before it closes

2. pick up my daughter at school

3. catch a 3:00 plane

4. be home in time for dinner

5. put my makeup on before the show begins

Now present your own conversations.

INTERCHANGE
I Don't Have Any Obligations or Commitments on Friday

A. I'd love to continue this conversation, but I really need to go now. I have to get back to the office.

B. Well, let's get together soon.

A. Okay. Would you like to have lunch some day next week?

B. Sure. How about Monday?

A. Hmm. I'm afraid I can't make it on Monday. I've got to fly to Chicago on business.

B. Well unfortunately, I'm tied up on Tuesday. I'm supposed to have lunch with an important visitor from out of town, and I don't think there's any way I can get out of it. Are you free on Wednesday?

A. Wednesday? Let's see. Hmm. Somehow I think I've already got something scheduled for Wednesday. Oh, yes! I've got an appointment with my dentist to have my teeth cleaned, and it's essential that I keep it.

B. Well, I'm afraid Thursday is out for me. I'm expected to attend a meeting of our personnel committee, and it's very important for me to be there.

A. So that leaves Friday. I don't have any obligations or commitments on Friday. How about you?

B. Friday sounds good. Where should we meet?

A. You know, I really must be going now or I'll be very late. Can you give me a call tomorrow and we'll decide?

B. Fine. Speak to you then.

A. Sorry I have to rush off like this.

B. That's okay. I understand.

A. Good-bye.

B. So long.

A. I'd love to continue this conversation, but I really need to go now. I have to _____.
B. Well, let's get together soon.
A. Okay. Would you like to have lunch some day next week?
B. Sure. How about Monday?
A. Hmm. I'm afraid I can't make it on Monday. I've got to _____.
B. Well unfortunately, I'm tied up on Tuesday. I'm supposed to _____, and I don't think there's any way I can get out of it. Are you free on Wednesday?
A. Wednesday? Let's see. Hmm. Somehow I think I've already got something scheduled for Wednesday. Oh, yes! I've got an appointment with my _____ to _____, and it's essential that I keep it.
B. Well, I'm afraid Thursday is out for me. I'm expected to attend a _____, and it's very important for me to be there.
A. So that leaves Friday. I don't have any obligations or commitments on Friday. How about you?
B. Friday sounds good. Where should we meet?
A. You know, I really must be going now or I'll be very late. Can you give me a call tomorrow and we'll decide?
B. Fine. Speak to you then.
A. Sorry I have to rush off like this.
B. That's okay. I understand.
A. Good-bye
B. So long.

You're in the middle of talking with someone but you have to go now. Create an original conversation using the model dialog above as a guide. Feel free to adapt and expand the model any way you wish.

Functions

Ability/Inability

Inquiring about . . .

Can you _____?
Is there any chance you could
 (possibly) _____?
Would you be able to _____?

Expressing Inability

I can't.
I won't be able to.

I'm not sure I can.

I can't make it on _____.
I'm tied up on _____.

Invitations

Extending . . .

How would you like to _____?
Would you like to _____?
Do you want to _____?
Would you be interested in
 _____ing?
How about _____ing?
Let's _____.

Would you (by any chance) be
 interested in _____ing?
You wouldn't (by any chance) be
 interested in _____ing, would
 you?

We'd like to invite you (and
 _____) over for _____.
We'd like to have you (and
 _____) over for _____.
We'd like you (and _____) to be
 our guest(s) for _____.
We'd like you (and _____) to join
 us for _____.

Can you come?
Do you think you can come?
Do you think you'd be able to come?
Would you be able to come?
Can you make it?
Do you think you can make it?

Please try to come.

We hope you'll be able to join us.

If you're not busy, . . .
If you're free, . . .
If you don't have any other
 plans, . . .

Accepting . . .

I'd love to.
I'd like to.
I'd like that.
That sounds like fun.
That sounds great/terrific/
 wonderful.
That would be great/terrific/
 wonderful.
I'd be happy to/glad to.
[stronger]
I'd be delighted to/thrilled to.

We'd be { very happy / very glad / pleased / delighted } to come.

We'll be looking forward to it.

Thanks/Thank you for { asking. / inviting me. / the invitation. }
I appreciate the invitation.
It's (very) nice of you to invite me.

Declining . . .

I'd love to, but I can't.
I'd love to, but I won't be able to.

Obligation

Expressing . . .

I have to _____.
I've got to _____.
I'm supposed to _____.
I need to _____.

I'm expected to _____.

I don't think there's any way I can
 get out of it.

I'm tied up on _____.
I've got something scheduled for
 _____.

I don't have any obligations or
 commitments on _____.

Leave Taking

(You know,) I think I should
{ be going / get going / be on my way / be getting on / my way } (now).

(You know), I (really) must be going.
I've (really) got to go now.
I've (really) got to be going now.
I (really) have to go now.
I'd (really) better go now.
I (really) need to go now.
I (really) should go now.
I have to/I've got to run.
I have to/I've got to get going.

I should get going, too.

Well, it's been really nice seeing you
 again.

I'd love to continue this conversation,
 but . . .

Let's get together soon.
Let's keep in touch.
Let's stay in touch.

(I'll) see you soon/later/tomorrow/
 next week/ . . .

I'll call you.

Speak to you then.

Take care.
Take it easy.
So long.
Good-bye.
Bye.
Bye-bye.
See you.

Sorry I have to rush off like this.

Conversation Strategies

Checking and Indicating Understanding

*Checking One's Own
 Understanding*

This Saturday evening?
7:00?

Directing/Redirecting a Conversation

By the way, . . .
Incidentally, . . .

Obligation
Ability/Inability

11

I've Had a Lot of Experience Taking Shorthand
I Haven't Altered Men's Clothing Before
I'm Afraid I Wasn't Able to Do It
I Won't Be Able to Go Bowling With You
I Didn't Know That Was Required
Policies and Practices

• Able to • Adjectives • Can • Embedded Questions
• Gerunds • Have to/Have Got to • Impersonal
Expressions • Infinitives • Must • Need to • Passives
• Present Perfect Tense • Supposed to • Would

I've Had a Lot of Experience Taking Shorthand

(1) Can you
Are you able to
Do you know how to

(2) I've had a lot of experience
I'm very good at

(3) consider yourself
say you're

(4) experienced
capable

(5) I would say so.
Yes, I would.

A. **Can you**(1) take shorthand?
B. Yes, I can. **I've had a lot of experience**(2) taking shorthand.
A. Then **you'd consider yourself**(3) an **experienced**(4) stenographer?
B. **I would say so.**(5)

1. type technical reports
typist

2. repair foreign cars
mechanic

3. operate a computer
data processor

4. fix window frames and doors
carpenter

5. perform this operation
surgeon

Now present your own
conversations.

I Haven't Altered Men's Clothing Before

A. Can you alter men's clothing?
B. No, I can't. I've had **a lot of**(1) experience altering clothing, but I haven't altered MEN'S clothing before. However, **I'm sure**(2) **I'd be able to**(3) learn quickly.
A. That would be important. Altering men's clothing is a **key**(4) part of the job.

(1) a lot of
a good/great deal of
years of

(2) I'm sure
I'm confident
I'm certain
I know

(3) I'd be able to
I could

(4) key
essential
major
significant

1. edit scientific manuscripts

2. design solar buildings

3. operate a 70 millimeter projector

4. use a computerized cash register

5. drive a tractor-trailer truck

Now present your own conversations.

I'm Afraid I Wasn't Able to Do It

(1) disappointed
upset

(2) What makes you say that?
Why do you say that?
Why?
How come?

(3) I was supposed to
I said I would
I had promised to
I had promised you I would

(4) I wasn't able to
I couldn't

(5) The truth is (that)
The fact of the matter is that

(6) you were counting/
depending on me to
_____

you were counting/
depending on my
_____ing
you had expected me
to _____

A. You're going to be very **disappointed**[1] with me.
B. **What makes you say that?**[2]
A. Well, remember **I was supposed to**[3] save you a seat?
B. Yes . . .?
A. Well, uh . . . I'm afraid **I wasn't able to**[4] do it.
B. Oh? Why not?
A. **The truth is,**[5] I tried but the usher wouldn't let me.
B. Don't worry about it.
A. I feel bad. After all, **you were counting on me to**[6] save it.
B. Don't worry about it. These things happen.
A. You aren't upset?
B. No, that's okay.

1. fix your doorbell

2. pick up your dress at the cleaner's

3. buy some groceries on the way home

4. clean the apartment this week

5. get these copied for you

6. get at least a B on my Biology test

7. finish your sweater in time for your birthday

8. get you reservations at the Plaza Hotel

9. arrange a "blind date" for you for Saturday night

Now present your own conversations.

I Won't Be Able to Go Bowling With You

(1) I won't be able to
I'm not going to be able to
I can't

(2) insisting that I
requiring me to

[stronger]
making me
forcing me to

(3) there's nothing I can do
about it
there's no way I can get
out of it
I can't get out of it

(4) Let's plan on _____ing
Let's plan to _____
We can always _____
We'll _____

my foreman

A. Hi! It's me again!
B. Hi! What's up?
A. Well, since I talked to you about an hour ago, I've found out that **I won't be able to**(1) go bowling with you as we had planned. Something important has just come up.
B. Oh?
A. Yes. My foreman is **insisting that I**(2) work a double shift today, and **there's nothing I can do about it.**(3) I hope you understand.
B. Of course I do. **Let's plan on**(4) going bowling some other time.

my father

1. play tennis

my doctor

2. have lunch

the store manager

3. play racquetball

my producer

4. have drinks

my little sister

5. go out

Now present your own conversations.

I Didn't Know That Was Required

A. I'd like to **submit**[1] my request for maternity leave.
B. Have you had it approved by your supervisor?
A. Excuse me. Have I had it what?!
B. Approved by your supervisor. **You're supposed to**[2] have your request for maternity leave approved by your supervisor before it can be **processed.**[3]
A. Oh. I haven't done that. I didn't know that was **required.**[4]
B. Oh, yes. It's **essential.**[4]

[1] submit
hand in
turn in
give you

[2] You're supposed to
You're required to
You're expected to
You need to
You have to
You've got to
You must
It's necessary for you to
It's required that you

[3] processed
accepted
considered
reviewed
evaluated
acted upon
taken into consideration

[4] required
necessary
essential
mandatory

1. signed by your parents

2. notarized

3. checked by one of our secretaries

4. verified by your physician

5. signed by your spouse

Now present your own conversations.

INTERCHANGE
Policies and Practices

A. Let me **tell you about**[1] some of our policies and practices here at "Globe Insurance."

B. All right.

A. We require all our employees to arrive promptly for work, and we insist that they keep their lunch hours to a reasonable length.

B. I understand.

A. And employee character is very important to us. We expect everyone here at "Globe Insurance" to be industrious, cooperative, and honest.

B. I'm very glad to hear that.

A. We also try to do the best we can for our employees. We feel obligated to provide a safe working environment, and we make every effort to listen to our employees' concerns.

B. That's very admirable.

A. Now, perhaps you have some questions about working here. Is there any additional information I can provide?

B. Yes, as a matter of fact. I have a few questions.

A. Certainly.

B. Could you tell me whether I would be required to have a medical examination before I start work?

A. Yes, definitely.

B. And would I have to go through special training?

A. Yes, you would.

B. And would it be necessary for me to work weekends?

A. No, that wouldn't be necessary.

B. And one more question: do employees here have to go through a probation period?

A. No, they don't.

B. I see.

A. Do you have any other questions?

B. No, I don't.

A. [Silent pause]

B. Well, **I've probably taken up enough of your time.**[2] I'll look forward to hearing from you once my job application has been considered.

A. We'll be in touch with you shortly.

B. **I've enjoyed talking with you.**[3] Thank you very much.

A. You're very welcome.

(1) tell you about
fill you in on
outline for you
advise you of
make you aware of

(2) I've probably taken up
enough of your time.
I don't want to take up any
more of your time.

(3) I've enjoyed talking with
you.
It was nice meeting you.
It was a pleasure meeting
you.
I'm grateful for/I appreciate
this opportunity to talk/
meet with you.

A. Let me **tell you about**(1) some of our policies and practices here at
"_____."

B. All right.

A. We require all our employees to _____, and we insist that they
_____.

B. I understand.

A. And employee character is very important to us. We expect everyone here at
"_____" to be _____, _____, and _____.

B. I'm very glad to hear that.

A. We also try to do the best we can for our employees. We feel obligated to
_____, and we make every effort to _____.

B. That's very admirable.

A. Now, perhaps you have some questions about working here. Is there any additional
information I can provide?

B. Yes, as a matter of fact. I have a few questions.

A. Certainly.

B. Could you tell me whether I would be required to _____?

A. Yes, definitely.

B. And would I have to _____?

A. Yes, you would.

B. And would it be necessary for me to _____?

A. No, that wouldn't be necessary.

B. And one more question: do employees here have to _____?

A. No, they don't.

B. I see.

A. Do you have any other questions?

B. No, I don't.

A. [Silent pause]

B. Well, **I've probably taken up enough of your time.**(2) I'll look forward to hearing from
you once my job application has been considered.

A. We'll be in touch with you shortly.

B. **I've enjoyed talking with you.**(3) Thank you very much.

A. You're very welcome.

You're at a job interview. Create an original conversation using the model dialog above as a
guide. Feel free to adapt and expand the model any way you wish.

Functions

Obligation

Inquiring about . . .

Do I have to _____?
Would I have to _____?
Would I be required to_____?
Would it be necessary (for me) to
_____?

Expressing . . .

It's required/necessary/essential/
mandatory.

We require _____ to _____.
We insist (that) _____.
We expect _____ to _____.

You're supposed to _____.
You're required to _____.
You're expected to _____.
You need to _____.
You have to _____.
You've got to _____.
You must _____.
It's necessary for you to _____.
It's required that you _____.

_____ is insisting that I
_____.
_____ is requiring me to
_____.
[stronger]
_____ is making me _____.
_____ is forcing me to _____.

I was supposed to _____.
I said I would _____.
I had promised to _____.
I had promised you I would
_____.

I didn't know that was required/
necessary/essential/mandatory.

You were counting/depending on me
to _____.
You were counting/depending on my
_____ing.
You had expected me to _____.

We feel obligated to _____.

Ability/Inability

Inquiring about . . .

Can you _____?
Are you able to _____?
Do you know how to _____?

You'd consider yourself an
experienced/capable _____?
You'd say you're an experienced/
capable _____?

Expressing Ability

I can (_____).

I'm very good at _____ing.

I've had a lot of experience
_____ing.
I've had a good/great deal of
experience _____ing.
I've had years of experience
_____ing.

I'm sure/I'm confident/I'm certain/I
know I'd be able to learn quickly.
I'm sure/I'm confident/I'm certain/I
know I could learn quickly.

Expressing Inability

I wasn't able to _____.
I couldn't _____.

I won't be able to _____.
I'm not going to be able to _____.
I can't _____.

I haven't _____ed before.

There's nothing I can do about it.
There's no way I can get out of it.
I can't get out of it.

Denying/Admitting

Admitting

I'm afraid _____.

The truth is (that) _____.
The fact of the matter is (that) _____.

Leave Taking

(Well,) I've probably taken up
enough of your time.
(Well,) I don't want to take up any
more of your time.

I've enjoyed talking with you.
It was nice meeting you.
It was a pleasure meeting you.
I'm grateful for/I appreciate this
opportunity to talk/meet with you.

Remembering/Forgetting

Inquiring about . . .

Remember _____?

Indicating . . .

I forgot.
It (completely) slipped my mind.

Asking for and Reporting Information

What makes you say that?
Why do you say that?
Why?
How come?

What's up?

Perhaps you have some questions
about _____.

I have a few questions.

Could you tell me _____?

I was wondering _____.

I've found out that _____.

Asking for and Reporting Additional Information

Is there any (additional) information
I can provide?
Do you have any (other) questions?

Conversation Strategies

Initiating a Topic

Let me tell you about . . .
Let me fill you in on . . .
Let me outline for you . . .
Let me advise you of . . .
Let me make you aware of . . .

Hesitating

Well, . . .
Well, uh . . .

Initiating Conversations

Hi! It's me again!

Asking for Repetition

Excuse me.

Have I had it what?!

Please Clean Up Your Room Before Dinner
Please Retype the Letter to Mr. Casey
Could You Do Me a Favor?
I Was Wondering If You'd Be Willing
to Switch Seats With Me
I'd Like to, but I'm Afraid I Can't
Can I Take a Message?

• Can • Could • Gerunds • Have to/Have Got to
• Infinitives • Need to • Present Unreal Conditional
• Reported Speech • Should • Supposed to
• Verb + Object + Infinitive • Will • Wish-Clauses • Would

Please Clean Up Your Room Before Dinner

(1) Please _____.
Can you (please) _____?
Will you (please) _____?
Would you (please) _____?
I'd like you to _____.
I wish you would _____.

(2) What did you ask me to do?
What did you say?
What was that?

(3) Okay.
All right.
Sure.

A. Charlie. **Please**[1] clean up your room before dinner.
B. Sorry, I didn't hear you. **What did you ask me to do?**[2]
A. I asked you to clean up your room before dinner.
B. **Okay.**[3]

1. roll up the windows in the car

2. help me fold the laundry

3. change your clothes before our guests arrive

4. take the dog for a walk before you leave for work

5. give me a hand opening this jar of pickles

Now present your own conversations.

Please Retype the Letter to Mr. Casey

A. George. **Please**[1] retype *the letter to Mr. Casey*.
B. The letter to Mr. Casey?
A. Yes. And while you're at it, please get me the Jones file.
B. **Certainly.**[2] I'll do it right away.

[1] Please _____.
Can you (please) _____?
Will you (please) _____?
Would you (please) _____?
I'd like you to _____.
I wish you would _____.

[2] Certainly.
Of course.

1. put these glasses *through the dishwasher*
get some more spoons and forks

2. take *Mr. Anderson's blood pressure*
check his temperature

3. order me *a tuna fish sandwich*
call my dentist and reschedule my appointment

4. take these boxes *to the stockroom*
check our supply of glue

5. put these fan letters *in my dressing room*
call NBC and cancel my appearance on "The Today Show"

Now present your own conversations.

Could You Do Me a Favor?

give me a lift home?

lend me your vacuum cleaner?

A. **Could you do me a favor?**(1)
B. What is it?
A. **Could you possibly**(2) give me a lift home?
B. **All right.**(3)
A. Are you sure? I don't want to **inconvenience you.**(4)
B. **No problem.**(5) **I'd be happy to.**(6)
A. Thanks. I really appreciate it.

A. **Could you do me a favor?**(1)
B. What is it?
A. **Would you mind**(2) lending me your vacuum cleaner?
B. **No, I wouldn't mind.**(3)
A. Are you sure? I don't want to **inconvenience you.**(4)
B. **No problem.**(5) **I'd be happy to.**(6)
A. Thanks. I really appreciate it.

---

(1) Could you do me a favor?
Could I ask you a favor?
Could you do a favor for me?

- -

(2) Could you possibly _____?
Could you (please) _____?
Could I (possibly) ask you to _____?
Would you be willing to _____?
Do you think you'd be able to _____?
I wonder if you could (possibly) _____.

(3) All right.
→ Okay.
Sure.
Of course.

Would you mind _____ing?

→ No, I wouldn't mind.
No, of course not.
No, not at all.

- -

(4) inconvenience you
trouble you
bother you
put you to any trouble
put you out

(5) No problem.
No trouble at all.

(6) I'd be happy/glad to.
(It would be) my pleasure.

1. Could I ask you to . . .?

2. Would you mind . . .?

3. Would you be willing to . . .?

4. Would you mind . . .?

5. Would you mind . . .?

6. Do you think you'd be able to . . .?

7. I wonder if you could . . .

Now present your own conversations.

I Was Wondering If You'd Be Willing to Switch Seats With Me

A. Excuse me, but **I was wondering if you'd be willing to**[1] switch seats with me.
B. Switch seats?
A. Uh . . . yes. If you'd be willing to, I'd really appreciate it.
B. **All right.**[2]
A. Oh, thank you.
B. **My pleasure.**[3]

A. Excuse me, but **would you mind if I asked you to**[1] let me off in front of my house?
B. In front of your house?
A. Uh . . . yes. If you'd be willing to, I'd really appreciate it.
B. **No, I wouldn't mind.**[2]
A. Oh, thank you.
B. **My pleasure.**[3]

[1] [less direct, very polite]
I was wondering if you'd (be willing to) _____.
I was wondering if you could possibly _____.
Would you be kind enough to _____?
Could I possibly impose on you to _____?
[more direct, polite]
Could you possibly _____?
Could you (please) _____?
Could I (possibly) ask you to _____?
Would you be willing to _____?
Do you think you'd be able to _____?
I wonder if you could (possibly) _____.

[less direct, very polite]
Would you mind if I asked you to _____?
Would I be troubling you (too much) if I asked you to _____?
Would I be imposing on you if I asked you to _____?
[more direct, polite]
Would you mind _____ing?

[2] All right.
Okay.
→ Sure.
Of course.
I'd be happy/glad to.

→ No, I wouldn't mind.

- -
[3] My pleasure.   Don't mention it.   (I'm) glad to do it.   You're welcome.

1. I was wondering if you'd . . .

2. Would you mind . . .?

3. Would you be kind enough to . . .?

4. Would I be troubling you too much if I asked you to . . .?

5. Would you be willing to . . .?

6. Would I be imposing on you if I asked you to . . .?

7. I wonder if you could . . .

Now present your own conversations.

I'd Like to, but I'm Afraid I Can't

> (1) I'd like to
>   I'd love to
>
> (2) I have to
>   I've got to
>   I need to
>   I'm supposed to
>
> (3) I'm (really) sorry.
>   I'm awfully sorry.
>   I feel terrible.

A. Could I possibly ask you to help me get this refrigerator up the steps?
B. Gee, **I'd like to,**(1) but I'm afraid I can't. **I have to**(2) avoid lifting heavy things.
A. Oh, okay.
B. **I'm really sorry.**(3)
A. Don't worry about it. I understand.

1. Would you be willing to . . .?

2. I wonder if you could . . .

3. Would you mind . . .?

4. Would you mind if I asked you to . . .?

5. Do you think you'd be able to . . .?

Now present your own conversations.

INTERCHANGE
Can I Take a Message?

A. Hello. **May I please speak to**[1] Larry?
B. I'm afraid Larry isn't here right now. **Can I take a message?**[2]
A. Yes. This is his friend Bob **calling.**[3] Would you please **ask**[4] Larry to bring a few bottles of soda to the party tonight?
B. Okay. **Just a minute.**[5] **I'm writing this down.**[6] "Bob called. You should bring a few bottles of soda to the party tonight." Is that it?
A. Yes, I guess so. You might ask him to call me back if he has a chance.
B. All right. I'll give him the message.
A. Thanks very much.
B. Good-bye.
A. Good-bye.

A. Hello. **May I please speak to**[1] _____?
B. I'm afraid _____ isn't here right now. **Can I take a message?**[2]
A. Yes. This is _____ **calling.**[3] Would you please **ask**[4] _____ to _____
_____?
B. Okay. **Just a minute.**[5] **I'm writing this down.**[6] "_____ called. You should _____
_____." Is that it?
A. Yes, I guess so. You might ask him/her to call me back if he/she has a chance.
B. All right. I'll give him/her the message.
A. Thanks very much.
B. Good-bye.
A. Good-bye.

---

[1] May/Can I (please) speak to
_____?
I'd like to speak to _____
(please), (if he's/she's there).
Is _____ there?

[2] Can I take a message?
Can I give him/her a message?
Would you like to leave a message (for him/her)?

[3] calling
speaking

[4] ask
tell

[5] Just a minute.
Just a/one moment.

[6] I'm writing this down.
I'm taking this down.

Create an original telephone conversation using the model dialog above as a guide. Feel free to adapt and expand the model any way you wish.

CHAPTER 12 SUMMARY

Functions

Requests

Direct, Polite

Please _____.
Can you (please) _____?
Will you (please) _____?
Would you (please) _____?
I'd like you to _____.
I wish you would _____.

And while you're at it, please
_____.

Could you do me a favor?
Could I ask you a favor?
Could you do a favor for me?

Would you please ask/tell _____
   to _____?

Direct, More Polite

Could you possibly _____?
Could you (please) _____?
Could I (possibly) ask you to
   _____?
Would you mind _____ing?
Would you be willing to _____?
Do you think you'd be able to
   _____?
I wonder if you could (possibly)
   _____.

Less Direct, Very Polite

I was wondering if you'd (be willing
   to) _____.
I was wondering if you could
   possibly _____.
Would you be kind enough to
   _____?
Would you mind if I asked you to
   _____?
Would I be troubling you (too much)
   if I asked you to _____?
Could I possibly impose on you to
   _____?
Would I be imposing on you if I
   asked you to _____?

Responding to Requests

Okay.
All right.
Sure.
Certainly.
Of course.
I'd be happy/glad to.
(It would be) my pleasure.

No, I wouldn't mind.
No, of course not.
No, not at all.
No problem.
No trouble at all.

Attracting Attention

Charlie.

Excuse me, but . . .

Gratitude

Expressing . . .

Thanks (very much).

Responding to . . .

My pleasure.
Don't mention it.
(I'm) glad to do it.
You're welcome.

Appreciation

I really appreciate it.

Ability/Inability

Expressing Inability

I'd like to/love to, but I'm afraid I
   can't.

Obligation

Expressing . . .

I have to _____.
I've got to _____.
I need to _____.
I'm supposed to _____.

Apologizing

I'm (really) sorry.
I'm awfully sorry.
I feel terrible.

Offering to Do Something

Can I take a message?
Can I give him/her a message?
Would you like to leave a message
   (for him/her)?

Conversation Strategies

Asking for Repetition

Sorry, I didn't hear you.

What did you ask me to do?
What did you say?
What was that?

Initiating Conversations

(Hello.) May/Can I (please) speak to
   _____?
   I'd like to speak to _____
      (please), (if he's/she's there).
   Is _____ there?

Checking and Indicating Understanding

Checking One's Own Understanding

The letter to Mr. Casey?

SCENES & IMPROVISATIONS
Chapters 10, 11, 12

Who do you think these people are?
What do you think they're talking about?
Create conversations based on these scenes and act them out.

1.

2.

3.

4.

5.

6.

7.

8.

13

Do You Have Any Suggestions?
How About Going Window-Shopping?
I Strongly Advise You
Can I Offer You Some Advice?
I Need Your Advice on Something
Thanks for the Warning
Excellent Suggestions

• Adjectives • Could • Gerunds • Had Better
• Imperatives • Infinitives • Might • Must • Negative
Questions • Ought to • Past Perfect Tense • Past Tense
• Present Perfect Tense • Present Real Conditional
• Present Unreal Conditional • Should • Tag Questions
• Would

Do You Have Any Suggestions?

(1) suggestion(s)
    recommendation(s)

(2) How about _____?
    What about _____?
    I/I'd suggest _____.
    I/I'd recommend _____.

(3) Everybody says
    People say
    Everybody tells me
    Most people say
    I hear
    They say

a fresh tasting toothpaste   *Tooth-Brite*

A. I'm looking for a fresh-tasting toothpaste. Do you have any **suggestions?**(1)
B. A fresh-tasting toothpaste. Hmm. Well, **how about**(2) Tooth-Brite?
A. Tooth-Brite?
B. Yes. I think you'll like it. **Everybody says**(3) it's very fresh-tasting.
A. Okay. Thanks for the **suggestion.**(1)

a good adventure novel

Moby Dick

1.

a light snack

our fruit salad

2.

a firm mattress

the Posture-Perfect 400

3.

a fuel-efficient compact car

a Chevette

4.

an out-of-the-way vacation spot

VISIT GRENOMIA $2.50 ROUND TRIP

The Republic of Grenomia

5.

"DO YOU HAVE ANY SUGGESTIONS?"

Now present your own conversations.

How About Going Window-Shopping?

go window-shopping?

take a ride in the country?

A. What do you want to do today?
B. I don't know. Do you have any **ideas?**[1]
A. Well, **how about**[2] going window-shopping?
B. Oh, I don't know. **I don't think I'm in the mood to**[3] go window-shopping. Any other suggestions?
A. Well, let's see. **What if we**[2] took a ride in the country?
B. **Hmm.**[4] **Good idea.**[5] We haven't taken a ride in the country **in ages.**[6]

[1] ideas
     suggestions
     thoughts

[2] How about _____ing?
     What about _____ing?
     Let's _____.
     What if we _____ed?
     Why don't we _____?
     We could (always) _____.

[3] I don't think I'm in the mood to _____.
     I don't really feel like _____ing.

[4] Hmm.
     [more excited]
     Hey!
     Say!

[5] (That's a/What a) good idea.
     (That's a/What a) good suggestion.
     That sounds good/great.
     That sounds like a good idea.

[6] in ages
     in/for a long time

play squash?

go bowling?

1.

go fishing?

ride our bikes along the river?

2.

play bridge with the Carters?

see a play?

3.

cut firewood?

drive into town?

4.

bake cookies?

see a movie?

5.

"HOW ABOUT GOING WINDOW-SHOPPING?"

Now present your own conversations.

I Strongly Advise You

(1) I (strongly) advise you to _____.
I urge you to _____.
I recommend that you _____.
I recommend _____ing.

(2) important
necessary

(3) Definitely!
Absolutely!
Without question!

(4) you might _____
you could (possibly) _____
you could/would run the risk of _____ing
there's a chance you might/could _____

(5) warning
advice

guidance counselor

A. As your guidance counselor, **I strongly advise you to**[1] take Physics.
B. Do you really think that's **important?**[2]
A. **Definitely!**[3] If you don't, **you might**[4] have trouble getting into medical school.
B. Oh. Well, thank you for the **warning.**[5]

doctor

1. go on a low-fat diet
have a heart attack some day

lawyer

2. testify in your own defense
lose your case

dentist

3. brush after every meal
lose your teeth some day

loan officer

4. take out a smaller loan
have difficulty meeting the monthly payments

stockbroker

5. sell all your shares of Grenomia Mining, Limited
"lose your shirt"

"I STRONGLY ADVISE YOU"

Now present your own conversations.

Can I Offer You Some Advice?

I've been having this pain in my chest lately.

(1) You seem troubled/upset.
You don't seem to be yourself today.

(2) the matter
wrong
bothering you

(3) some advice
a piece of advice
a suggestion

(4) I think you should/ought to
_____.
I/I'd suggest that you _____.
I/I'd suggest _____ing.
If I were you, I'd _____.
It seems to me (that) you should _____.
Don't you think you should _____?
Don't you think it would/might be a good idea to _____?

A. **You seem troubled.**(1) Is anything **the matter?**(2)
B. Yes, as a matter of fact. I've been having this pain in my chest lately.
A. Well, can I offer you **some advice?**(3)
B. Sure. What?
A. **I think you should**(4) see a doctor.
B. You're probably right.

My old landlord refuses to return my security deposit.

1. take him to court

Bobby Jones has been teasing me all morning.

2. tell the teacher

My supervisor is forcing me to work this weekend.

3. file a complaint through the union

The pressure of this job is "burning me out."

4. take a few days off

I've fallen in love with somebody else and I don't know how to tell my boyfriend.

5. level with him

"CAN I OFFER YOU SOME ADVICE?"

Now present your own conversations.

I Need Your Advice on Something

> I've been offered a good full-time job.

A. I need your advice on something.
B. Sure. What is it?
A. I've been offered a good full-time job, and I don't know what to do about it.
B. Well, **have you considered**[1] putting the baby in a day-care center?
A. Hmm. **I hadn't thought of that.**[2]

> I'm tired of selling men's underwear.

1. switch to another department

> I'm fed up with taking the train to work.

2. form a car pool

3. join "Weight Watchers"

4. ask your landlord to call an exterminator

5. take a semester off

6. get a loan from the bank

7. see a therapist

8. enlist in the armed forces

9. separate for a little while

Now present your own conversations.

Thanks for the Warning

*Get out of the way!
That forklift is coming
toward you!*

A. **Careful!**(1)
B. **Huh?**(2)
A. You'd better get out of the way!
B. Oh?
A. Yes. That forklift is coming toward you! You might get run over!
B. **Thanks for the warning.**(3)

*Don't walk over there!
The floor is wet!*

A. **Careful!**(1)
B. **Huh?**(2)
A. You'd better not walk over there!
B. Oh?
A. Yes. The floor is wet! You might slip!
B. **Thanks for the warning.**(3)

*Stay away from the conveyer belt!
It sometimes catches people's
fingers!*

1. get hurt

*Don't cross the tracks!
There's a train coming!*

2. get hit

*Keep clear of the doorway!
It's the entrance to the
kitchen!*

3. get knocked down by a waiter

*Don't pet my dog!
He doesn't like children!*

4. get bitten

*"Choose your words carefully"
with the boss today!
He's in a rotten mood!*

5. get fired

"THANKS FOR THE WARNING"

Now present your own conversations.

INTERCHANGE
Excellent Suggestions

A. You've been to Paris, haven't you?
B. Yes. As a matter of fact, I used to live in Paris.
A. Well, I'm planning to visit there soon, and I was wondering if you could recommend some things to do.
B. Sure. You should definitely go to Notre Dame Cathedral. You also ought to see The Palace at Versailles. And you must visit The Louvre.
A. Those sound like excellent suggestions. Can you recommend any good places to eat?
B. Yes. Make it a point to eat at "Maxim's." And if you go there, I suggest that you order the duck. It's delicious.
A. That sounds good.
B. Oh, and one more thing. Be sure to have someone take your picture in front of The Eiffel Tower.
A. I'll do that.
B. Is there anything else I can tell you about?
A. I don't think so. You've been very helpful. Thanks a lot.
B. Send me a postcard, will you?
A. Okay.

A. You've been to _____, haven't you?
B. Yes. As a matter of fact, I used to live in _____.
A. Well, I'm planning to visit there soon, and I was wondering if you could recommend some things to do.
B. Sure. You should definitely go to _____. You also ought to see _____. And you must visit _____.
A. Those sound like excellent suggestions. Can you recommend any good places to eat?
B. Yes. Make it a point to eat at "_____." And if you go there, I suggest that you order the _____. It's delicious.
A. That sounds good.
B. Oh, and one more thing. Be sure to have someone take your picture in front of _____.
A. I'll do that.
B. Is there anything else I can tell you about?
A. I don't think so. You've been very helpful. Thanks a lot.
B. Send me a postcard, will you?
A. Okay.

You're planning a trip. Create an original conversation using the model dialog above as a guide and using functional expressions found throughout this chapter. Feel free to adapt and expand the model any way you wish.

Functions

Advice-Suggestions

Asking for . . .

I need your advice on something.

Do you have any suggestions/
   recommendations/ideas/thoughts?

Can you recommend _____?
I was wondering if you could
   recommend _____.

Any other suggestions?

Offering . . .

Can I offer you { some advice?
                  a piece of advice?
                  a suggestion?

I (strongly) advise you to _____.
I urge you to _____.
I recommend that you _____.
I recommend _____ing.

You should (definitely) _____.
You ought to _____.
You must _____.
Make it a point to _____.
Be sure to _____.

I think you should/ought to
   _____.
I/I'd suggest that you _____.
I/I'd suggest _____ing.
If I were you, I'd _____.
It seems to me (that) you should
   _____.
Don't you think you should
   _____?
Don't you think it would/might be a
   good idea to _____?

How about _____?
What about _____?
I/I'd suggest _____.
I/I'd recommend _____.

How about _____ing?
What about _____ing?
Let's _____.
What if we _____ed?
Why don't we _____?
We could (always) _____.

Have you considered _____ing?
Have you thought of/about
   _____ing?
Have you given any thought to
   _____ing?
You might consider _____ing.
Why don't you _____?
You could (always) _____.
How about _____ing?
What about _____ing?
It might be a good idea to _____.
What if you _____ed?
What if you were to _____?

Responding to . . .

(That's a/What a) good idea.
(That's a/What a) good suggestion.
That sounds good/great.
That sounds like a good idea.

I hadn't thought of that.
That hadn't occurred to me.

Warning

If you don't (_____),
   _____.

(Be) careful!
Look out!
Watch out!

(You'd better) *get out of the way!*
(You'd better) stay away from the
   _____!
(You'd better) keep clear of the
   _____!
You'd better not _____!
Don't _____!

You might _____.

Gratitude

Expressing . . .

Thanks/Thank you for _____.

Thanks a lot.

Want-Desire

Inquiring about . . .

What do you want to do today?

Expressing . . .

I don't think I'm in the mood to
   _____.
I don't really feel like _____ing.

Possibility/Impossiblity

Expressing . . .

You might _____.
You could (possibly) _____.
You could/would run the risk of
   _____ing.
There's a chance you might/could
   _____.

Asking for and Reporting
Information

Is anything { the matter?
             wrong?
             bothering you?

Everybody says . . .
People say . . .
Everybody tells me . . .
Most people say . . .
I hear . . .
They say . . .

Conversation Strategies

Hesitating

Hmm.
Well, . . .
(Well,) let's see . . .

Initiating a Topic

You seem troubled/upset.
You don't seem to be yourself today.

Asking for Repetition

Huh?
[more polite]
Excuse me?
Pardon (me)?

Checking and Indicating
Understanding

*Checking One's Own
   Understanding*

Tooth-Brite?

I Agree
That's Just What I Was Thinking
That Might Be True
I'm Afraid You're Right
That Isn't Exactly Right
That's Not True
I'm Not So Sure About That

• Adjectives • Emphatic Sentences • Might/May
• Negative Questions • Short Answers • Tag Questions

I Agree

A. We had a very good fourth quarter.
B. **I agree.**(1) We DID have a very good fourth quarter, didn't we.
A. **Absolutely!**(2)

1.

2.

3.

4.

5.

Now present your own conversations.

That's Just What I Was Thinking

That was a terrible movie!
The acting was awful . . .
and the storyline was impossible to follow.

A. That was a terrible movie!
B. It was.
A. I mean, the acting was awful . . .
B. **I agree.**(1)
A. . . . and the storyline was impossible to follow.
B. **That's just what I was thinking.**(2)

(1) I agree.
You're right.
I know.

[less formal]
I'll say!

(2) That's just/exactly what I
was thinking.
I couldn't agree with you
more.
I feel the same way.
That's exactly what I think.
My feelings exactly.

[less formal]
You can say that again!
You took the words right
out of my mouth!

She's an awful singer!
Her voice is so loud . . .
and she's singing off key.

1.

Mr. and Mrs. Wagner have such
wonderful children.
They're very well-mannered . . .
and they're so friendly to
everybody in the neighborhood.

2.

This bus driver drives like a
maniac!
He's constantly changing lanes . . .
and he's traveling much too fast.

3.

Walter made a fool of himself
at the party!
He drank too much . . . and he
told the same "corny" jokes
he's been telling for years.

4.

Dr. Frankenstein has been
acting very strangely recently.
He's very nasty to everybody
in the village . . .and I bet
he's up to something in his
laboratory.

5.

"THAT'S JUST WHAT I WAS THINKING"

Now present your own
conversations.

That Might Be True

A. This car is a very old model.
B. **That might be true.**(1) **But**(2) **wouldn't you agree that**(3) it's in excellent condition?
A. **I suppose you're right.**(4)

1.

2.

3.

4.

5.

Now present your own conversations.

I'm Afraid You're Right

You've been very quiet recently.

A. You know, I've noticed that you've been very quiet recently.
B. **I'm afraid you're right.**(1) I HAVE been very quiet recently, haven't I.
A. **It's true.**(2)

(1) I'm afraid you're right.
I'm afraid I have to agree.
I hate to admit/say it, but you're right.
I hate to admit/say it, but it's true.

(2) It's true.
I'll say!
No doubt about it!
Absolutely!
Definitely!

You've been gaining weight.

1.

You aren't as good-natured as you used to be.

2.

The grandchildren don't call as often as they used to.

3.

Your grades have been suffering since football practice started.

4.

Good old Rover isn't as young as he used to be.

5.

"I'M AFRAID YOU'RE RIGHT"

Now present your own conversations.

That Isn't Exactly Right

> The bread goes in Aisle Four.

> Aisle FIVE

(1) Mr./Ms./Mrs./Miss ——
    sir
    ma'am

(2) that isn't exactly/quite right
    that isn't exactly/quite
      correct
    that (really) isn't so
    I think you might be
      mistaken

(3) Thank you for calling that
    to my attention.
    Thank you for correcting
    me (on that).

A. The bread goes in Aisle Four.
B. Excuse me, **Mr.** Perkins,[1] but actually, **that isn't exactly right.**[2]
A. Oh?
B. Yes, Mr. Perkins. Actually, the bread goes in Aisle FIVE.
A. Oh. **Thank you for calling that to my attention.**[3]

> Our special tonight is baked chicken.

> BROILED FISH

1. Excuse me, Mrs. Alfredo . . .

> Our stock went up ten points today!

> DOWN ten points

2. Excuse me, sir . . .

> Children's Clothing is on the third floor.

> on the SECOND floor

3. Excuse me, Miss Whitehead . . .

> I see we're going to remove your appendix tomorrow.

> remove my TONSILS

4. Excuse me, Doctor . . .

> I've just had a very cordial and successful meeting with the Ambassador from Sweden.

> the Ambassador from SWITZERLAND

5. Excuse me, Mr. President . . .

"THAT ISN'T EXACTLY RIGHT"

Now present your own conversations.

That's Not True

A. You've been reading my boyfriend's letters, haven't you.
B. **That's not true.**(1)
A. **Come on!**(2) **Admit it!**(3) **I know**(4) you have.
B. That just isn't so. I HAVEN'T been reading his letters!
A. Well, **I'm not so sure.**(5)

1.

2.

3.

4.

5.

Now present your own
conversations.

I'm Not So Sure About That

A. **Don't you think that**[1] somebody should do something about all the violence on children's cartoon programs?
B. Well, **I'm not so sure about that.**[2]
A. Oh?
B. Yes. **I wish I could agree with you,**[3] but **if you ask me,**[4] kids aren't very affected by what they see on TV because they know it isn't real.
A. Well, **I disagree.**[5]

[1] Don't you think (that)
Wouldn't you say (that)
Wouldn't you agree that

[2] I'm not so sure (about that).
I don't know (about that).
I'm not sure (if) I agree (with you on that).
I wouldn't say that.
I wouldn't go as far as that.
I wouldn't go so far as to say that.

[3] I wish I could agree (with you)
I hate to disagree (with you)
I don't mean to disagree (with you)
I don't want to argue (with you) (about that)
I don't want to start/get into an argument (with you) (about it)

[4] if you ask me,
in my opinion,
as far as I'm concerned,
I personally think,
as I see it,
the way I see it,

[5] I disagree.
I don't agree.
I can't agree.
I don't think so.

You're having a disagreement with somebody. Create an original conversation using the model dialog on p. 146 as a guide. Feel free to adapt and expand the model any way you wish.

Functions

Agreement/Disagreement

Inquiring about . . .

Wouldn't you agree (that) _____?
Wouldn't you say (that)_____?
Don't you think (that)_____?

Expressing Agreement

I agree (with you).
You're/That's right.
That's/It's true.
I know.
[less formal]
I'll say!

Absolutely!
Definitely!
No doubt about it!

That's just/exactly what I was
  thinking.
I couldn't agree with you more.
I feel the same way.
That's exactly what I think.
My feelings exactly.
[less formal]
You can say that again!
You took the words right out of my
  mouth!

I suppose/guess you're right.
I suppose/guess that's true.
That might/may be true.
You might/may be right.
You have a point (there).
I see your point.
I know.
Yes.

Expressing Disagreement

I disagree.
I don't agree.
I can't agree.
I don't think so.

I'm not so sure (about that).
I don't know (about that).
I'm not sure (if) I agree (with you on
  that).
I wouldn't say that.
I wouldn't go as far as that.
I wouldn't go so far as to say that.

I wish I could agree (with you),
  but . . .
I hate to disagree (with you), but . . .
I don't mean to disagree (with you),
  but . . .
I don't want to argue (with you)
  (about that), but . . .
I don't want to start/get into an
  argument (with you) (about it),
  but . . .

(But/However,)
{ wouldn't you agree (that) _____?
{ wouldn't you say (that) _____?
{ don't you think (that) _____?

Correcting

Giving Correction

That isn't exactly/quite right.
That isn't exactly/quite correct.
That (really) isn't so.
I think you might be mistaken.

(Actually,) *the bread goes in Aisle
  FIVE.*
That just isn't so. *I do like your
  meatloaf.*

Responding to Correction

Thank you for calling that to my
  attention.
Thank you for correcting me on that.

Certainty/Uncertainty

Expressing . . .

I know _____.
I'm sure _____.
I'm positive _____.
I'm convinced _____.

I'm not so sure (about that).
I'm not so sure I believe that.

Denying/Admitting

Denying

That's not true.
That's/You're wrong.
You're mistaken.
That (just) isn't so.

Admitting

I'm afraid you're right.
I'm afraid I have to agree.
I hate to admit/say it, but you're
  right.
I hate to admit/say it, but it's true.

Persuading-Insisting

Come on!
Look!
Listen!

Admit it!
Face it!

Conversation Strategies

Initiating a Topic

You know, . . .

Don't you think (that) _____?
Wouldn't you say (that) _____?
Wouldn't you agree (that) _____?

Focusing Attention

If you ask me, . . .
In my opinion, . . .
As far as I'm concerned, .
I personally think . . .
As I see it, . . .
The way I see it . . .

I'm Positive
In All Likelihood
It Should Arrive Any Minute Now
She Must Have Gotten Stuck in Traffic
I Might Buy the Cheap One
It's a Possibility
There's Not Much Chance of That Happening
I Don't Know for Sure

• Future: Going to • Future: Will • Gerunds • Had
Better • Imperatives • Might/May • Might Have/May
Have • Must Have • Noun Clauses • Ought to • Present
Real Conditional • Present Unreal Conditional • Short
Answers • Should/Should Have

I'm Positive

(1) certain
sure
positive

(2) I'm positive/certain/sure.
Absolutely!
Positively!

(3) I definitely
There's no question (in my mind) I
I have no doubt (at all) (that) I

(4) There's no chance (that)
There's no possibility (that)

[less formal]
There's no way (that)

A. Do you want to go through with this?
B. Yes, I do.
A. Are you **certain?**(1)
B. **I'm positive.**(2) **I definitely**(3) want to go through with this.

A. Is it going to rain?
B. No, it isn't.
A. Are you **sure?**(1)
B. **Absolutely!**(2) **There's no chance**(4) it's going to rain.

1. Do we have a quiz tomorrow?
Yes . . .

2. Will this hurt?
No . . .

3. Are you going to raise taxes this year?
No . . .

4. Are you capable of running our overseas operations?
Yes . . .

5. Did the butler do it?
No . . .

Now present your own conversations.

In All Likelihood

A. What are you going to do next year?
B. **I'll probably**[1] go to *law school*.
A. Law school? Oh. Is that definite?
B. Well, I'm not **absolutely positive.**[2] But **in all likelihood**[3] that's what I'm going to do next year.

[1] I'll probably
    I'll most likely
    I'm pretty sure I'll
    Chances are I'll

[2] absolutely positive/sure/
    certain (about that)
    a hundred percent sure

[3] in all likelihood
    in all probability

1. go on *a tour of the English countryside*

2. *Seymour*

3. *at the next Board of Trustees meeting*

4. have *a "sweet sixteen" party*

5. buy *a yacht*

Now present your own conversations.

It Should Arrive Any Minute Now

(1)
It should
It ought to
It'll probably
It'll most likely
In all likelihood it'll
In all probability it'll
Chances are it'll

A. When will the next bus arrive from Boston?
B. **It should**(1) arrive any minute now.
A. · Any minute now?
B. Yes, according to the schedule.

1. in half an hour
according to the recipe
on the box

2. within thirty days
according to company
policy

3. in four days
according to my doctor

4. seven business days
according to usual bank
procedures

5. Minneapolis
according to the flight
plan

Now present your own
conversations.

152

She Must Have Gotten Stuck in Traffic

Our English teacher should have shown up for class by now.

She must have gotten stuck in traffic.

A. I'm getting a little **worried**(1) about our English teacher. She should have shown up for class by now.

B. Oh, **I wouldn't be concerned.**(2) **She must have**(3) gotten stuck in traffic.

A. I don't know. She **might have**(4) . . . but then again, I'm not so sure. I'm afraid something must have happened.

B. Now **don't jump to conclusions.**(5) I'm positive she'll show up for class soon.

My wife's plane should have landed by now.

It must have been late taking off.

1.

My husband should have been home by now.

He must have gotten tied up at the office.

2.

My daughter should have been home from her date by 11 p.m.

She must have lost track of the time.

3.

Our shipment of imported Christmas ornaments should have been delivered by now.

It must have been delayed at Customs.

4.

My request for a transfer should have been approved by now.

It must have gotten caught up in a lot of red tape.

5.

"SHE MUST HAVE GOTTEN STUCK IN TRAFFIC"

Now present your own conversations.

I Might Buy the Cheap One

(1) might
may

(2) On the other hand,
Then again,

(3) perhaps I'll
maybe I'll
I might
I may

(4) Take my advice!
Take it from me!
If you want my advice,

(5) be disappointed
be sorry
regret it

(6) I'll probably
I guess I'll
I suppose I'll

A. Which model washing machine are you interested in purchasing?
B. I'm not sure. I **might**(1) buy the cheap one. **On the other hand,**(2) **perhaps I'll**(3) buy the deluxe version.
A. **Take my advice!**(4) Don't buy the cheap one! You'll **be disappointed.**(5)
B. Oh. Well, in that case, **I'll probably**(6) buy the deluxe version.
A. You won't be sorry.

1. see "Moon Over Manhattan"
   see "Dancers in Love"

2. take a bus tour
   walk around on my own

3. request a sub-compact
   ask for a sedan

4. take Astronomy with Professor Bright
   take Zoology with Professor Hood

5. order the "Chicken Surprise"
   order the "Beef Delight"

Now present your own conversations.

It's a Possibility

A. What would you do if I told you I was **going to**[1] quit my job?
B. Quit your job?!
A. Yes, quit my job!
B. Well, I'd **probably**[2] say **you should**[3] think about it seriously before you make a decision. Why? You aren't really going to quit your job, are you?
A. Well, **it's a possibility.**[4]

[1] going to _____
planning to _____
intending to _____
thinking of _____ing
considering _____ing
playing/toying with the idea of _____ing

[2] probably
most likely

[3] you should
you ought to
you'd better

[4] It's a possibility.
There's a chance.
I might/may.
It could happen.
You never know!

1.

2.

3.

4.

5.

Now present your own conversations.

There's Not Much Chance of That Happening

(1) What do you think the
chances are of
What's the likelihood of
What's the possibility of

(2) Probably not very good.
It/That isn't very likely.
Pretty slim.

(3) There's not much chance of
that happening.
I doubt (if) that would/could/
will happen.
I don't think that will
happen.

(4) In fact,
To tell the truth,

A. **What do you think the chances are of**(1) my having twins?
B. **Probably not very good.**(2)   **There's not much chance of that happening.**(3)
A. Oh? Are you absolutely sure about that?
B. Yes, I'm pretty certain. **In fact,**(4) if you had twins, I'd be very surprised.

1.

2.

3.

4.

5.

Now present your own
conversations.

INTERCHANGE
I Don't Know For Sure

A. I've been meaning to ask you . . . What are you going to do when our English course is finished?
B. I don't know. I think I might enroll in a more advanced class.
A. Oh. Is there a good chance of your doing that?
B. Perhaps, but I don't know for sure. If I don't enroll in a more advanced class, maybe I'll get a private tutor. What do you think?
A. Excuse me?
B. What do you think I should do? Do you have any advice?
A. Hmm. Well, I don't know . . . uh . . . I suppose if I had to choose between enrolling in a more advanced class and getting a private tutor, I'd probably enroll in a more advanced class. But of course that's only my opinion.
B. That's interesting. Why would you do that?
A. Well . . . because there's an advantage to studying in a group and being able to practice speaking with lots of other students.
B. Hmm. That makes a lot of sense. I'll keep that in mind when I finally come to making my decision. And how about YOU?
A. Me?
B. Yes. What are YOU going to do when our English course is finished?
A. . . . .

A. I've been meaning to ask you . . . What are you going to do _____?
B. I don't know. I think I might _____.
A. Oh. Is there a good chance of your doing that?
B. Perhaps, but I don't know for sure. If I don't _____, maybe I'll _____ _____. What do you think?
A. Excuse me?
B. What do you think I should do? Do you have any advice?
A. Hmm . . . Well, I don't know . . . uh . . . I suppose if I had to choose between _____ing and _____ing, I'd probably _____ _____. But of course that's only my opinion.
B. That's interesting. Why would you do that?
A. Well . . . because _____.
B. Hmm. That makes a lot of sense. I'll keep that in mind when I finally come to making my decision. And how about YOU?
A. Me?
B. Yes. What are YOU going to do _____?
A. . . . .

You're discussing future plans (about work, school, personal matters, etc.) with a friend. Create an original conversation using the model dialog above as a guide, and using functional expressions found throughout this chapter. Feel free to adapt and expand the model any way you wish.

Functions

Probability/Improbability

Inquiring about . . .

What do you think the chances are
    of _____?
What's the likelihood of _____?
What's the possibility of _____?

Is there a good chance _____?

Expressing . . .

I'll probably _____.
I'll most likely _____.
I'm pretty sure I'll _____.
Chances are I'll _____.
I guess I'll _____.
I suppose I'll _____.

In all likelihood . . .
In all probability . . .

If I had to choose between _____
    and _____, I'd probably _____.

It should
It ought to
It'll probably
It'll most likely   } *arrive any minute*
In all likelihood it'll   *now.*
In all probability it'll
Chances are it'll

The chances are probably not very good.
The chances are pretty slim.
It/That isn't very likely.

There's not much chance of that
    happening.
I doubt (if) that would/could/will
    happen.
I don't think that will happen.

Fear-Worry-Anxiety

I'm (getting) (a little) { worried
                          concerned } about
                          anxious   } _____.
                          nervous

I'm afraid something must have
    happened (to him/her/them).

I wouldn't be concerned.
I wouldn't worry.
Don't worry.
Don't be concerned.

Possibility/Impossibility

Inquiring about . . .

What's the possibility of _____?

Expressing Possibility

I might _____.
I may _____.
Perhaps I'll _____.
Maybe I'll _____.

Perhaps.

It's a possibility.
There's a chance.
I might/may.
It could happen.
You never know!

_____ might have _____ed.
_____ may have _____ed.

Expressing Impossibility

There's no chance (that) _____.
There's no possibility (that) _____.
[less formal]
There's no way (that) _____.

Certainty/Uncertainty

Inquiring about . . .

Are you certain/sure/positive?

Are you (absolutely) sure about that?

Is that definite?

Expressing . . .

I'm (absolutely) positive/certain/sure
    (that _____).
Absolutely!
Positively!

I definitely _____.
There's no question (in my mind)
    _____.

I have no doubt (at all) (that)
    _____.

I'm pretty certain.

I'm not absolutely positive/sure/
    certain (about that).
I'm not a hundred percent sure.

I'm not (so) sure.
I don't know for sure.

Advice-Suggestions

Asking for . . .

What do you think (I should do)?
Do you have any advice?

Offering . . .

You should _____.
You ought to _____.
You'd better _____.

Take my advice!
Take it from me!
If you want my advice,

Don't jump to conclusions.
Don't get (yourself) "all worked up."
Don't get carried away.
Don't let your imagination run away
    with you.

There's an advantage to _____ing.

Deduction

_____ should have _____ed
    (by now).

_____ must have _____.
_____ probably _____.
_____ most likely _____.
Chances are _____.
I wouldn't be surprised if _____.
I/I'll bet _____.

Intention

Inquiring about . . .

What are you going to do (*next year*)?

You aren't really going to _____,
    are you?

Expressing . . .

      { going to _____.
        planning to _____.
I'm   { intending to _____.
      { thinking of _____ing.
        considering _____ing.
        playing/toying with the idea of
            _____ing.

Surprise-Disbelief

Quit your job?!

Conversation Strategies

Initiating a Topic

I've been meaning to ask you . . .

Focusing Attention

In fact, . . .
To tell the truth, . . .

Hesitating

Hmm.
Well, . . .
Well, I don't know . . .
Uh . . .

Checking and Indicating Understanding

*Checking One's Own
    Understanding*

Any minute now?

SCENES & IMPROVISATIONS
Chapters 13, 14, 15

Who do you think these people are?
What do you think they're talking about?
Create conversations based on these scenes and act them out.

1.

2.

3.

4.

5.

6.

7.

8.

Good Job!
Do You Approve of the Way I Clipped Fifi's Hair?
You Really Shouldn't Have Raised Your Voice
to the Boss
I Really Wish You Hadn't Removed
the Coffee Machine
I Apologize
I Hope You'll Forgive Me
Maybe You Ought to Apologize
I'm Afraid I Can't Keep My Promise

• Could Have • Gerunds • Passives • Past Tense • Past
Unreal Conditional • Present Perfect Tense • Sequence
of Tenses • Should Have • Wish-Clauses • Would

Good Job!

A. **Good job!**(1)
B. Do you really think so?
A. Yes. **Absolutely!**(2) You gave that presentation **very**(3) well.
B. I'm glad you approve.
A. As a matter of fact, I don't think I've ever seen a presentation given better than that.
B. **Thank you for saying so.**(4)

1. do that dance number

2. teach that lesson

3. run that race

4. handle that press conference

5. perform that triple-bypass operation

Now present your own conversations.

Do You Approve of the Way I Clipped Fifi's Hair?

A. **Do you approve of the way I**[1] clipped Fifi's hair?
B. Well . . . Can I **be frank**[2] with you?
A. **By all means.**[3] Please.
B. Well . . . **In all honesty,**[4] I think Fifi's hair could have been clipped a little better.
A. You know . . . come to think of it . . . you're probably right. **Please accept my apology.**[5] I promise I'll do better next time.

[1] Do you approve of the way I _____ed?
How do you like the way I _____ed?
What do you think of the way I _____ed?
What do you think of how I _____ed?
Did I _____ all right?

[2] be frank
be honest
be open
level

[3] By all means.
Sure.
Yes.

[4] In all honesty,
To be (perfectly) honest/frank,

[5] Please accept my apology.
Please forgive me.
I apologize.
I'm sorry.

1. type this report

2. assemble this radio

3. handle the union negotiations

4. prepare the spaghetti sauce

5. fly the plane

Now present your own conversations.

You Really Shouldn't Have Raised Your Voice to the Boss

A. You know . . . perhaps **it's none of my business**(1) . . . but you really shouldn't have raised your voice to the boss.
B. Oh?
A. Yes. I don't know **whatever prompted you to do it,**(2) but raising your voice to the boss was not a very good idea.
B. Hmm. **You're probably right.**(3)

1. take yesterday off
   without permission

2. invite your entire sixth-
   grade class to your
   birthday party

3. contradict the principal
   at today's faculty
   meeting

4. disregard the warning
   light on the dashboard

5. tell the bank teller your
   real name

Now present your own
conversations.

I Really Wish You Hadn't Removed the Coffee Machine

(1)	guess suppose
(2)	as a result of because of
(3)	I hadn't thought of that. That hadn't occurred to me. That never entered my mind.
(4)	known realized
(5)	I apologize. Please forgive me. I'm sorry. Please accept my apology.

A. You know . . . I hate to say it . . . but I really wish you hadn't removed the coffee machine.
B. Oh? I'm sorry, but I **guess**(1) I didn't see anything wrong with that.
A. But don't you realize that **as a result of**(2) your removing the coffee machine, employee morale is at an all-time low?!
B. Hmm. **I hadn't thought of that.**(3) If I had **known**(4) that employee morale was going to be at an all-time low, I wouldn't have removed it. **I apologize.**(5)

1. let Peter have the car tonight

2. ask for garlic and pepperoni on this pizza

3. promise the kids new bicycles for Christmas

4. make me get such a short haircut

5. tell the foreman how fast we can produce these teddy bears

Now present your own conversations.

I Apologize

A. **I apologize for**[1] being late.
B. **That's okay.**[2]
A. You know, this is the first time I've ever been late. **I'm really sorry.**[3]
B. **Don't worry about it.**[4]

1. forget our anniversary

2. fall asleep in class

3. shout at you

4. come back late from lunch

5. "mess up" my lines

Now present your own conversations.

I Hope You'll Forgive Me

A. **I'd like to**[1] apologize for behaving rudely at your party last night.
B. It's all right.
A. **I'm really sorry about it.**[2] **I hope you'll forgive me.**[3]
B. Don't worry about it. **These things happen.**

[1] I'd like to
I want to
I've got to

[2] I'm really sorry about it.
I really regret it.

[3] I hope you'll forgive me.
Please forgive me.

[4] These things happen.
We all make mistakes.
You're only human.

I added up your bill wrong.

1.

I forgot to deliver yesterday's paper.

2.

I gave you the wrong answers to the math homework.

3.

I accused you of taking money from the petty cash box.

4.

I failed to get your input before I decided who to hire as your assistant.

5.

"I HOPE YOU'LL FORGIVE ME"

Now present your own conversations.

Maybe You Ought to Apologize

(1) upset
annoyed
taken aback

(2) Maybe you ought to/
should _____.
Maybe you should
consider _____ing.
It might be a good idea to
_____.
Why don't you _____?

(3) patch things up
clear the air
smooth things over
iron things out
set things straight

Your hamburgers
are overcooked.

A. You know . . . I think you hurt Dad's feelings when you told him his hamburgers were overcooked.
B. Hmm. I didn't realize that. Do you think he's angry with me?
A. I don't know if "angry" is the right word, but it seems to me he's a little **upset**.(1)
B. I feel terrible.
A. **Maybe you ought to**(2) apologize to him. That might help **patch things up**(3) between you two.
B. Good idea! Thanks.

You're a little
overweight.

1. Michael

You're spoiling
your grandchildren.

2. your mother

Your new jingle for
"Sudsy Soap" isn't
creative enough.

3. Barry

I think we're spending too
much time on grammar, and
not enough on conversation.

4. our English teacher

Your new boyfriend
is a "nerd."

5. your sister

"MAYBE YOU
OUGHT TO
APOLOGIZE"

Now present your own
conversations.

INTERCHANGE
I'm Afraid I Can't Keep My Promise

A. You're going to have to forgive me.
B. Oh? Why?
A. Well, remember I had promised you I'd help you study for the TOEFL* exam?
B. Yes, I remember.
A. Well, **I hate to have to tell you this,**[1] but I'm afraid I can't keep my promise.
B. Oh? Why not?
A. Well . . . you see . . . I have to go to the Immigration Office to renew my visa. Otherwise, I'd be able to help you study for the TOEFL exam.
B. I understand.
A. You know, **I don't make a habit of breaking promises to people.**[2] I hope you're not upset with me.
B. No, not at all. **These things happen.**[3]

[1] I hate to have to tell you this I don't feel very good about telling you this I wish I didn't have to tell you this	[2] I don't make a habit of breaking promises to people. I don't like to/usually break promises (I make) to people. I'm not one to go back on my word.	[3] These things happen. It's not your fault.

A. You're going to have to forgive me.
B. Oh? Why?
A. Well, remember I had promised you I'd _____?
B. Yes, I remember.
A. Well, **I hate to have to tell you this,**[1] but I'm afraid I can't keep my promise.
B. Oh? Why not?
A. Well . . . you see . . . _____.
   Otherwise, I'd be able to _____.
B. I understand.
A. You know, **I don't make a habit of breaking promises to people.**[2] I hope you're not upset with me.
B. No, not at all. **These things happen.**[3]

You can't keep a promise you've made to somebody. Create an original conversation using the model dialog above as a guide and using functional expressions found throughout the chapter. Feel free to adapt and expand the model any way you wish.

*TOEFL: Test of English as a Foreign Language

Functions

Approval/Disapproval

Inquiring about . . .

Do you approve of the way I
_____ed?
How do you like the way I
_____ed?
What do you think of the way I
_____ed?
What do you think of how I
_____ed?
Did I _____ all right?

Expressing Approval

Good job!
Fine job!
Well done!
Excellent!
Very good!

Good idea!

You _____ed {
very well.
extremely well.
exceptionally well.
unbelievably well.
}

Expressing Disapproval

In all honesty, _____.
To be (perfectly) honest/frank,
_____.

I think _____ could have been
_____ed better.

You (really) shouldn't have
_____ed.
_____ing was not a very good
idea.

I (really) wish you hadn't
_____ed.

As a result of your _____ing,
_____.

Complimenting

Expressing Compliments

I don't think I've ever seen a
_____ better than _____.

Apologizing

I apologize.
I'm sorry.
Please forgive me.
Please accept my apology.

I apologize
Forgive me
[less formal]
Sorry
} for _____ing.

I'd like to
I want to
I've got to
} apologize for _____ing.

I'm really/very sorry (about it).
I feel terrible (about it).
I (really) regret it.

I hope you'll forgive me.
Please forgive me.

You're going to have to forgive me.

Granting Forgiveness

That's/It's okay.
That's/It's all right.
Don't worry about it.
No problem.
These things happen.
We all make mistakes.
You're only human.
It's not your fault.
I understand.

Promising

Offering a Promise

I promise I'll _____.

I had promised (_____) I'd
_____.

Breaking a Promise

I can't keep my promise.

I don't make a habit of breaking
promises to people.
I don't like to/usually break promises
(I make) to people.
I'm not one to go back on my word.

Wish-Hope

I hope _____.

Remembering/Forgetting

Inquiring about . . .

Remember I had promised you I'd
_____?

Indicating . . .

I remember.

Denying/Admitting

Admitting

I hate to have to tell you this, but . . .
I don't feel very good about telling
you this, but . . .
I wish I didn't have to tell you this,
but . . .

Gratitude

Expressing . . .

Thank you for *saying so.*
Thank you for *the compliment.*
It's nice of you to *say that/so.*

Agreement/Disagreement

Expressing Agreement

You're probably right.
I suppose/guess you're right.

Advice-Suggestions

Offering . . .

Maybe you ought to/should _____.
Maybe you should consider
_____ing.
It might be a good idea to _____.
Why don't you _____?

Responding to . . .

I hadn't thought of that.
That hadn't occurred to me.
That never entered my mind.

Conversation Strategies

Initiating a Topic

Perhaps it's none of my business,
but . . .
Perhaps I'm out of place saying so,
but . . .
Perhaps it isn't my place to say so,
but . . .
Perhaps I'm speaking out of turn,
but . . .
[less formal]
Perhaps I'm sticking my nose where
it doesn't belong, but . . .

You know, . . .

I hate to say it . . . but . . .

Hesitating

Well . . .
You know . . .
Come to think of it . . .
You see . . .

It's a Shame
You Know What I Wish?
If Only I Could Communicate With My Boss
I Could Kick Myself!
I Regret Having to Fire Mr. Smith
I've Been Thinking

• Adjectives • Comparatives • Could • Gerunds • Hope-
Clauses • Past Unreal Conditional • Present Unreal
Conditional • Short Answers • Wish-Clauses

It's a Shame

*This restaurant is so **expensive** . . . we can't eat here tonight.*

A. **It's a shame**[1] this restaurant is so expensive.
B. **I agree.**[2] I wish it were cheaper.
A. **Me, too.**[3] I was hoping we could eat here tonight, but it **looks like**[4] that's out of the question.
B. I'm afraid so.

*The weather is so **bad** . . . we can't go to the beach.*

1.

*This machine is so **slow** . . . we won't be able to finish copying this report today.*

2.

*The boss is in such a **bad** mood . . . I can't ask him to give me tomorrow off.*

3.

*The union's wage demands are so **high** . . . we won't be able to negotiate an agreement by midnight.*

4.

*These instructions are so **complicated** . . . we won't be able to put this bicycle together for Patty's birthday.*

5.

"IT'S A SHAME"

Now present your own conversations.

You Know What I Wish?

> It's a shame we don't have a newer car.

> We spend so much money on repairs.

A. You know what I wish?
B. What?
A. I wish we had a newer car.
B. I know. **It's too bad**(1) we don't. If we had a newer car, we wouldn't spend so much money on repairs.
A. **That's exactly what I was thinking.**(2)

(1) It's too bad (that)
It's a shame (that)
It's a pity (that)

(2) That's exactly/just what I was thinking.
That's exactly what I think.

[less formal]
You can say that again!
You took the words right out of my mouth!

> It's a pity the baby-sitter isn't available tonight.

> We have to skip our exercise class at the health club.

1.

> I'm disappointed we can't afford a washer and dryer.

> We need to walk eight blocks to the laundromat every week.

2.

> It's too bad it didn't snow a lot last night.

> School is open today.

3.

> It's a shame they don't allow children to visit the patients.

> You have to wave to the kids through the window.

4.

> It's disappointing we didn't get the contract for the new "XYZ Missile."

> We were forced to lay off thirty percent of our workers.

5.

"YOU KNOW WHAT I WISH?"

Now present your own conversations.

If Only I Could Communicate With My Boss

(1) I've been meaning
I keep forgetting
I keep meaning

(2) Do you really want to know?
Do you want to know the truth?

(3) the truth is
the fact of the matter is

(4) That's too bad.
That's a shame/a pity.
What a shame/a pity.

(5) If only I could
I wish I could

(6) It's not that easy/simple.
It's easier said than done.

A. **I've been meaning**(1) to ask you . . . How are you enjoying your new job?
B. **Do you really want to know?**(2)
A. Yes.
B. Well, **the truth is,**(3) I'm not enjoying my new job at all.
A. **That's too bad.**(4) I'm sorry to hear that.
B. **If only I could**(5) communicate with my boss.
A. Why can't you?
B. **It's not that easy.**(6) Communicating with my boss is very difficult.
A. I'm sure it is. But don't give up trying.
B. Oh, don't worry. I won't.

1.

2.

3.

4.

5.

6.

7.

8.

9.

Now present your own conversations.

I Could Kick Myself!

(1) I could kick myself!

[stronger]
I could kill myself!
I could shoot myself!
I could (just) die!

(2) I made a terrible mistake.

[less formal]
I (really) goofed!

[much less formal]
I (really) blew it!

(3) Do you mean (to say)
Are you saying
Does that mean

(4) It's all my fault.
I'm (entirely) to blame.
It's all my doing.

(5) That's too bad!
That's terrible!
That's awful!

A. **I could kick myself!**(1)
B. Why?
A. **I made a terrible mistake.**(2) I forgot to fill up the tank before we left . . . and now I wish I hadn't.
B. Oh! **Do you mean to say**(3) we're out of gas?!
A. Yes, we are . . . and **it's all my fault.**(4) If I hadn't forgotten to fill up the tank before we left, we wouldn't be out of gas.
B. **That's too bad!**(5)

1.

2.

3.

4.

5.

6.

7.

8.

9.

Now present your own conversations.

I Regret Having to Fire Mr. Smith

(1) I regret _____ing.
I regret (that) I _____.
I'm sorry about _____ing.
I'm sorry (that) I _____.

(2) a/any choice
any alternative
any other option
any other recourse

(3) Perhaps
Apparently
Evidently

(4) I wasn't aware of that.
I didn't know that.

(5) under the circumstances
given the circumstances
given the situation

I have to fire Mr. Smith. He was caught embezzling funds from the bank.

A. You know, **I regret**[1] having to fire Mr. Smith.
B. Well, then why are you going to do it?
A. I don't have **a choice.**[2] **Perhaps**[3] you're not aware that he was caught embezzling funds from the bank.
B. Oh! No, **I wasn't aware of that.**[4] That's too bad!
A. Yes, it really is. If he hadn't been caught embezzling funds from the bank, I wouldn't have to fire him.
B. Well, **under the circumstances,**[5] I can see why it's necessary.

I'm forced to go out of business. The new shopping mall has taken all my customers away.

1.

I have to take the car keys away from you. I saw you speeding down Main Street yesterday.

2.

I'm required to evict you. The building is going to be converted into a condominium.

3.

I'm breaking up with my boyfriend. He has a drinking problem.

4.

I'm requiring Johnny to repeat third grade. He doesn't know his multiplication tables.

5.

"I REGRET HAVING TO FIRE MR. SMITH"

Now present your own conversations.

INTERCHANGE
I've Been Thinking

A. You know, I've been thinking.
B. What?
A. I regret I didn't start studying English when I was young.
B. Really?
A. Yes. I wish I had begun when I was about five or so.
B. Hmm. What makes you say that?
A. Well, if I had begun studying English earlier, I wouldn't be having so much trouble with pronunciation.
B. Oh. I can understand why you feel that way.

A. You know, I've been thinking.
B. What?
A. I'm sorry I'm so shy.
B. Really?
A. Yes. I wish I felt more comfortable around large groups of people.
B. Hmm. What makes you say that?
A. Well, if I weren't so shy, I wouldn't feel so uneasy at parties like these.
B. Oh. I can understand why you feel that way.

A. You know, I've been thinking.
B. What?
A. I regret/I'm sorry _____.
B. Really?
A. Yes. I wish _____.
B. Hmm. What makes you say that?
A. Well, if _____.
B. Oh. I can understand why you feel that way.

You've been thinking about something you regret. Create an original conversation using the model dialog above as a guide and using functional expressions found throughout this chapter. Feel free to adapt and expand the model any way you wish.

CHAPTER 17 SUMMARY

Functions

Regret

It's a shame (that) _____.
It's a pity (that) _____.
(It's) too bad (that) _____.
I'm disappointed (that) _____.
It's disappointing (that) _____.

I regret _____ing.
I regret (that) I _____.
I'm sorry about _____ing.
I'm sorry (that) I _____.

I wish I hadn't _____ed.

I could kick myself!
[stronger]
I could kill myself!
I could shoot myself!
I could (just) die!

Agreement/Disagreement

Expressing Agreement

I agree (with you).
You're/That's right.
That's true.
I know.

That's exactly/just what I was
  thinking.
That's exactly what I think.
[less formal]
You can say that again!
You took the words right out of my
  mouth!

Me, too.
I think so, too.
I feel the same way.

Under the circumstances, I can see
  _____.
Given the circumstances, I can see
  _____.
Given the situation, I can see
  _____.

Wish-Hope

I wish *it were cheaper*.

I wish I could _____.
If only I could _____.

I was hoping _____.

Denying/Admitting

Admitting

The truth is . . .
The fact of the matter is . . .

I made a terrible mistake.
[less formal]
I (really) goofed!
[much less formal]
I (really) blew it!

It's all my fault.
I'm (entirely) to blame.
It's all my doing.

Deduction

It looks like _____.
It appears (as if/as though) _____.
It seems (as if/as though) _____.

Satisfaction/Dissatisfaction

Inquiring about . . .

How are you enjoying _____?

Expressing Dissatisfaction

I'm not enjoying_____ (at all).

Sympathizing

That's too bad.
That's a shame/a pity.
What a shame/a pity.
That's terrible.
That's awful.
I'm sorry to hear that.

Remembering/Forgetting

Indicating . . .

I forgot to _____.

Asking for and Reporting Information

What makes you say that?

Perhaps ⎫
Apparently ⎬ you're not aware that
Evidently ⎭ _____.

Conversation Strategies

Initiating a Topic

You know *what I wish?*

I've been meaning to ask you . . .
I keep forgetting to ask you . . .
I keep meaning to ask you . . .

(You know,) I've been thinking . . .

Clarification

Asking for Clarification

Do you mean (to say) _____?
Are you saying _____?
Does that mean _____?

Nice Day Today, Isn't It
Don't You Just Hate People Who Cut in Line?
Let Me Put It This Way
What You're Really Saying
Excuse Me for Interrupting
By the Way . . .
In My Opinion

• Gerunds • Negative Questions • Relative Clauses with
Who • Sequence of Tenses • Short Answers

Nice Day Today, Isn't It

(1) Pardon (me)?
Excuse me?
What did you say?
What was that?
Come again?

(2) saying (that)
commenting (that)

A. Nice day today, isn't it.
B. **Pardon me?**(1)
A. I was just **saying**(2) it's a nice day today.
B. Oh, yes. It is.

1.

2.

3.

4.

5.

Now present your own conversations.

Don't You Just Hate People Who Cut in Line?

Look at that man! He's cutting in line!

annoying!

A. **Don't you just hate people who**[1] cut in line?
B. Yes. **To me,**[2] cutting in line is very annoying.
A. It sure is.

Look at those people! They're throwing litter all over the park!

inconsiderate!

A. **I can't stand it when people**[3] throw litter all over the park.
B. I can't either. **To me,**[2] throwing litter all over the park is very inconsiderate.
A. It sure is.

[1] Don't you just hate people who _____?
Doesn't it bother you when people _____?
Aren't you annoyed when people _____?
[less formal]
Doesn't it get to you when people _____?
Wouldn't you like to clobber people who _____?

[2] To me,
As far as I'm concerned,
[less formal]
In my book,

[3] I can't stand it when people _____.
I can't stand people _____ing.
It really bothers me when people _____.
[more informal]
I can't take it when people _____.

Look at that man! He's smoking in the elevator!

rude!

1.

Look at that customer! He's complaining about every little thing!

obnoxious!

2.

Look at that young man! He's refusing to give up a seat to a senior citizen!

selfish!

3.

Look at that woman! She's parking in an area reserved for the handicapped!

thoughtless!

4.

Look at those people! They're kissing in public!

tacky!

5.

"DON'T YOU JUST HATE PEOPLE WHO CUT IN LINE?"

Now present your own conversations.

Let Me Put It This Way

The X-rays suggest that an extraction is indicated.

A. The X-rays suggest that an extraction is indicated.
B. **I'm afraid I'm not following you.**(1)
A. Okay. **Let me put it this way**:(2) I'm going to have to pull your tooth.
B. Oh, now **I understand.**(3)

And then the opposing sides disengaged.

1. "The war ended."

Your position doesn't fit into our plans for reorganization.

2. "You're fired."

I'm sensing a degree of strain in our relationship.

3. "I think we should break up."

The bookkeeper tells me she's "moving on to greener pastures."

4. "The bookkeeper is going to quit."

The stork is going to visit our house very soon.

5. "I'm going to have a baby."

"LET ME PUT IT THIS WAY"

Now present your own conversations.

What You're Really Saying

A. Your new sport jacket is a very unusual color.
B. **What you're really saying is**[1] you don't like it.
A. Now **don't jump to conclusions!**[2] I didn't say I didn't like it. I just said it was a very unusual color.
B. Oh.

[1] What you're (really) saying is
What you're trying to say is
What you mean is
In other words

[2] Don't jump to conclusions!
Don't read too much into what I'm saying!

1.

2.

3.

4.

5.

Now present your own conversations.

Excuse Me for Interrupting

(1) Excuse me for interrupting,
Forgive me for interrupting,
(I'm) sorry for interrupting,
(I'm) sorry to interrupt,

(2) Wait a minute!
Hold on (a minute)!

(3) Did you say
Was that

A. **Excuse me for interrupting,**(1) but you have an important call on line 5.
B. Thank you. Oh, **wait a minute!**(2) **Did you say**(3) line 9?
A. No. Line 5.
B. Oh, okay.

1.

2.

3.

4.

5.

Now present your own conversations.

*I.R.S.: Internal Revenue Service
C.I.A.: Central Intelligence Agency

By the Way . . .

the merger with the State Street Bank

The new Xerox machine arrived this morning.

A. Now, **regarding**[1] the merger with the State Street Bank, . . .
B. **Oh, by the way,**[2] the new Xerox machine arrived this morning.
A. Oh, I didn't know that. Now **as I was saying,**[3] regarding the merger with the State Street Bank, **in my opinion,**[4] . . .
B. Excuse me for interrupting, but I'm afraid it's getting late. **I've really got to go now.**[5]
A. Oh. That's too bad. We haven't really had a chance to talk about the merger with the State Street Bank.
B. I know. I'm sorry. Let's continue the conversation soon.

[1] regarding _____,
regarding the issue of _____,
as far as _____ is concerned,

[2] (Oh,) by the way,
(Oh,) incidentally,
(Oh,) before I forget,
I don't mean to change the subject, but

[3] as I was saying,
to get back to what I was saying,
to get back to what we were talking about,

[4] in my opinion,
as I see it,
the way I see it,
if you ask me,
the thing to keep in mind is

[5] I've (really) got to go now.
I've (really) got to be going now.
I (really) have to go now.
I'd (really) better go now.
I (really) need to go now.
I (really) should go now.
I have to/I've got to run.
I have to/I've got to get going.

my request for maternity leave

We've ordered new uniforms for all the employees.

1.

my broken stove

I'm thinking of painting the front hallway.

2.

our plans to get married

My roommate, Sarah, just got a new job.

3.

my suggestion for increasing productivity

The supervisor on the night shift quit yesterday.

4.

Einstein's theory of relativity

Did you know that there's going to be a big dance this Saturday night?

5.

"BY THE WAY..."

Now present your own conversations.

INTERCHANGE
In My Opinion

A. What's your opinion about nuclear energy?
B. Nuclear energy. Now, that's quite an issue! I actually have some pretty strong viewpoints regarding nuclear energy. Are you interested in hearing them?
A. Yes.
B. Well, in my opinion, nuclear energy is our best hope for the future.
A. But don't you think it poses a threat to the safety of the population?
B. Not really. As I see it, nuclear reactors are a clean and safe source of electricity.
A. Well, if you ask me, people don't realize how dangerous radiation can be.
B. The thing to keep in mind is our oil and gas resources are limited. And furthermore, . . .
A. Let me say one more thing.
B. Okay.
A. I'd just like to point out that I think too many accidents are happening at nuclear power plants all over the country.
B. You know, we could probably go on talking about this forever and never come to an agreement.
A. You're probably right. I guess we just don't see "eye to eye" when it comes to nuclear energy.
B. I guess not.

A. What's your opinion about _____?

B. _____. Now, that's quite an issue! I actually have some pretty strong viewpoints regarding _____. Are you interested in hearing them?

A. Yes.

B. Well, in my opinion, _____
_____.

A. But don't you think _____
_____?

B. Not really. As I see it, _____
_____.

A. Well, if you ask me, _____
_____.

B. The thing to keep in mind is _____
_____.

And furthermore, . . .

A. Let me say one more thing.

B. Okay.

A. I'd just like to point out that I think _____
_____.

B. You know, we could probably go on talking about this forever and never come to an agreement.

A. You're probably right. I guess we just don't see "eye to eye" when it comes to
_____.

B. I guess not.

You're exchanging opinions with somebody you disagree with. You each have three very good reasons for thinking the way you do. List the reasons in the following chart, and then create an original conversation using the model dialog above as a guide. Feel free to adapt and expand the model any way you wish.

OPINIONS ABOUT _____

1. _____   1. _____
   _____   _____

2. _____   2. _____
   _____   _____

3. _____   3. _____
   _____   _____

CHAPTER 18 SUMMARY

Functions

Complaining

Don't you just hate people who
_____?
Doesn't it bother you when people
_____?
Aren't you annoyed when people
_____?
[less formal]
Doesn't it get to you when people
_____?
Wouldn't you like to clobber people
who _____?

_____(ing) is (very) annoying/
inconsiderate/rude/obnoxious/
selfish/thoughtless/tacky.

I can't stand it when people _____.
I can't stand people _____ing.
It really bothers me when people

_____.
[less formal]
I can't take it when people

_____.

Agreement/Disagreement

Expressing Agreement

Yes.

It sure is.

I _____ either.

You're (probably) right.

Expressing Disagreement

But don't you think _____?

Not really.

We don't see "eye to eye" when it
comes to _____.

Correcting

No. *Line 5.*

Leave Taking

(I'm afraid) it's getting late.

I've (really) got to go (now).
I've (really) got to be going (now).
I (really) have to go (now).
I'd (really) better go (now).
I (really) need to go (now).
I (really) should go (now).
I have to run.
I have to get going.
I've got to run.
I've got to get going.

Advice-Suggestions

Offering . . .

Don't jump to conclusions!
Don't read too much into what I'm
saying!

Conversation Strategies

Clarification

Asking for Clarification

[less direct]
I'm afraid I'm not following you.
I'm not really sure what you're
getting at.
I'm not quite clear as to what you
mean (by that).
[more direct]
What do you mean (by that)?
What does that mean?
Could you clarify that (for me)?

Giving Clarification

Let me put it this way: . . .
Let me put it another way: . . .
What I'm (really) saying is . . .
What I'm trying to say is . . .
What I mean is . . .
What I'm getting at is . . .
In other words . . .
[less formal]
Let me try that again.
Let me try that one more time.

What you're (really) saying is . . .
What you're trying to say is . . .
What you mean is . . .
In other words . . .

I didn't say _____.

I just said _____.

Focusing Attention

To me, . . .
As far as I'm concerned, . . .
In my opinion, . . .
As I see it, . . .
The way I see it, . . .
If you ask me, . . .
The thing to keep in mind is . . .
[less formal]
In my book, . . .

(And) furthermore, . . .

Let me say one more thing.

I'd (just) like to point out that . . .

Directing/Redirecting
a Conversation

(Oh,) by the way, . . .
(Oh,) incidentally, . . .
(Oh,) before I forget, . . .
I don't mean to change the subject,
but . . .

(Now) as I was saying, . . .
(Now) to get back to what I was
saying, . . .
(Now) to get back to what we were
talking about, . . .

Initiating Conversations

Nice day today, isn't it.

Checking and Indicating
Understanding

*Checking One's Own
Understanding*

Did you say _____?
Was that _____?

Indicating Understanding

(Now) { I understand.
         I follow you.
         I see.

Interrupting

Excuse me for interrupting, (but) . . .
Forgive me for interrupting, (but) . . .
(I'm) sorry for interrupting, (but) . . .
(I'm) sorry to interrupt, (but) . . .

Initiating a Topic

(Now,) regarding _____, . . .
(Now,) regarding the issue of
_____, . . .
(Now,) as far as _____ is
concerned, . . .

Asking for Repetition

Pardon (me)?
Excuse me?
What did you say?
What was that?
Come again?

SCENES & IMPROVISATIONS
Chapters 16, 17, 18

Who do you think these people are?
What do you think they're talking about?
Create conversations based on these scenes and act them out.

1.

2.

3.

4.

5.

6.

7.

8.

Functions

Ability/Inability

Inquiring about . . .

Can you _____?
Are you able to _____?
Do you know how to _____?   11

Can you _____?
Is there any chance you could (possibly)_____?
Would you be able to _____?   10

You'd consider yourself an experienced/capable _____?
You'd say you're an experienced/capable _____?   11

Expressing Ability

I can (_____).   11

I'm (very) good at _____ing.   11

I've had a lot of experience _____ing.
I've had a good/great deal of experience _____ing.
I've had years of experience _____ing.   11

I'm sure/I'm confident/I'm certain/I know I'd be able to learn quickly.
I'm sure/I'm confident/I'm certain/I know I could learn quickly.   11

Expressing Inability

I can't _____.
I won't be able to _____.
I'm not going to be able to _____.   10,11

I wasn't able to _____.
I couldn't _____.   11

I'm not sure I can.   10

I can't make it on _____.
I'm tied up on _____.   10

I'd like to/love to, but I'm afraid I can't.   12

There's nothing I can do about it.
There's no way I can get out of it.
I can't get out of it.   11

Advice-Suggestions

Asking for . . .

What do you think (I should do)?
Do you have any advice?   15

Any suggestions?   5

Any other suggestions?   13

Do you have any suggestions/recommendations/ideas/thoughts?   13

Can you recommend _____?
I was wondering if you could recommend _____.   13

I need your advice on something.   13

Offering . . .

Can I offer you some advice?
Can I offer you a piece of advice?
Can I offer you a suggestion?   13

I (strongly) advise you to _____.
I urge you to _____.
I recommend that you _____.
I recommend _____ing.   13

You should (definitely) _____.
You ought to _____.
You must _____.
You'd better _____.
Make it a point to _____.
Be sure to _____.   13,15

You should _____.
Why don't you _____?
How about _____ing?   3

I think you should/ought to _____.
I/I'd suggest that you _____.
I/I'd suggest _____ing.
If I were you, I'd _____.
It seems to me (that) you should _____.
Don't you think you should _____?
Don't you think it would/might be a good idea to _____?   13

Maybe you ought to/should _____.
Maybe you should consider _____ing.
It might be a good idea to _____.
Why don't you _____?   5,16

Have you considered _____ing?
Have you thought of _____ing?
Have you thought about _____ing?
Have you given any thought to _____ing?
You might consider _____ing.
Why don't you _____?
You could (always) _____.
How about _____ing?
What about _____ing?
It might be a good idea to _____.
What if you _____ed?
What if you were to _____?   13

How about _____ing?
What about _____ing?
I/I'd suggest _____.
I/I'd recommend _____.   13

How about _____ing?
What about _____ing?
Let's _____.
What if we _____ed?
Why don't we _____?
We could (always)_____.
Would you be interested in _____(ing)?   5,13

Maybe we should _____.
Maybe we shouldn't _____.   5

They say that _____ is very good.
One of my favorite _____s is _____.   5

Is _____ okay?   5

There's an advantage to _____ing.   15

Take my advice!
Take it from me!
If you want my advice, _____.   15

Don't jump to conclusions!
Don't get (yourself) "all worked up."
Don't get carried away.
Don't let your imagination run away with you.   15

Don't jump to conclusions!
Don't read too much into what I'm saying!   18

Responding to . . .

(That's a/What a) good idea.
(That's a/What a) good suggestion.
That sounds good/great.
That sounds like a good idea.   13

I hadn't thought of that.
That hadn't occurred to me.   13

That never entered my mind.   16

Agreement/Disagreement

Inquiring about . . .

Wouldn't you agree (that) _____?
Wouldn't you say (that) _____?
Don't you think (that) _____?   14

Expressing Agreement

I agree (with you).
You're/That's right.
That's/It's true.
I know.
[less formal]
I'll say!
You can say that again!   7,14,17

Absolutely!
Definitely!
No doubt about it!   14

Me, too.
I think so, too.
I feel the same way.   17

Yes.   18

It sure is.   18

I _____ either.   18

That's just/exactly what I was
thinking.
I couldn't agree with you more.
I feel the same way.
That's exactly what I think.
My feelings exactly.
[less formal]
You can say that again!
You took the words right out of my
mouth!   14,17

You're probably right.
I suppose/guess you're right.   16

I suppose/guess you're right.
I suppose/guess that's true.
That might/may be true.
You might/may be right.
You have a point (there).
I see your point.
I know.
Yes.   14

Under the circumstances, I can see
_____.

Given the circumstances, I can see
_____.

Given the situation, I can see
_____.   17

Expressing Disagreement

I disagree.
I don't agree.
I can't agree.
I don't think so.   14

I wish I could agree (with you),
but . . .
I hate to disagree (with you), but . . .
I don't mean to disagree (with you),
but . . .
I don't want to argue (with you)
(about that), but . . .
I don't want to start/get into an
argument (with you) (about it),
but . . .   14

I'm not so sure (about that).
I don't know (about that).
I'm not sure (if) I agree (with you on
that).
I wouldn't say that.
I wouldn't go as far as that.
I wouldn't go so far as to say that. 14

(But/However,)
{ wouldn't you agree (that) ___?
  wouldn't you say (that) ___?
  don't you think (that) ___?   14,18

We don't see "eye to eye" when it
comes to _____.   18

Apologizing

I'm sorry.
Excuse me.   1

(Oh,) I'm sorry.   9

I apologize.
I'm sorry.
Please forgive me.
Please accept my apology.   16

I apologize
Forgive me
[less formal]   } for _____ing.
Sorry   16

I'd like to
I want to   } apologize for _____ing.
I've got to   16

I'm really/very/awfully sorry (about it).
I feel terrible (about it).
I (really) regret it.   12,16

I hope you'll forgive me.
Please forgive me.   16

You're going to have to forgive me. 16

I don't mean to { make things difficult/
                  complicated for you.
                  complicate things.
                  give you a hard time.
                  give you "the
                  runaround."   9

Appreciation

I appreciate it/that.
I'd appreciate it/that.
It's nice/kind of you to offer.
Thanks for offering.
I appreciate your offering.
That's (very) nice/kind of you.
That would be nice.   8

I really appreciate it.
I appreciate it very much.   8,12

It was very nice of you (to _____). 8

I want to express my appreciation to
_____.   8

I can't begin to tell you how much I
appreciate _____.   8

You're very kind/nice.   8

Approval/Disapproval

Inquiring about . . .

Do you approve of the way I
_____ed?
How do you like the way I _____ed?
What do you think of the way I
_____ed?
What do you think of how I
_____ed?
Did I _____ all right?   16

Expressing Approval

Good Job!
Fine job!
Well done!
Excellent!
Very good!   16

Good idea!   16

You _____ed { very well.
              extremely well.
              exceptionally well.
              unbelievably well.   16

Expressing Disapproval

In all honesty, _____.
To be (perfectly) honest/frank,
_____.   16

I think _____ could have been
_____ed better.   16

You (really) shouldn't have _____ed.
_____ing was not a very good
idea.   16

I (really) wish you hadn't _____ed. 16

As a result of your _____ing,
_____.   16

Asking for and Reporting Information

Where are you from?
   Japan.
What do you do?
   I'm an English teacher.
Which *apartment do you live in?*
How long *have you been studying here?*
Who *is your doctor?*
Whose *family are you in?*
What kind of *music do you play?*
When *are you due?*   1

How about you?
What about you?
And you?   1

Have you { heard from
           run into
           talked to
           seen   } _____ lately?
           spoken to
           been in touch
           with   2

How's _____ doing?
How is _____?
How has _____ been?
   Fine.
   Great.
   Wonderful.
   Not too well.
   Not so well.
   Not very well.   2

Did _____ have anything to say?   1

Have you heard anything about
_____?
Do you know anything about _____?   2

Tell me a little about yourself.   2

What do you want to know?
What would you like to know?
What can I tell you?   2

Is anything { the matter?
              wrong?
              bothering you?   13

Do you/Would you (by any chance)
know _____?
Do you/Would you (by any chance)
happen to know _____?   3

Could you (please/possibly) tell me
_____?
Do you/Would you (by any chance)
know _____?
Can you (please) tell me _____?
Would you (possibly/by any chance)
be able to tell me _____?   4

Did you hear (that) _____?   3

Where did you hear that?
How do you know (that)?
Who told you (that)? 3

*School isn't really going to be closed
  tomorrow, is it?* 3

What happened? 3

What's up? 11

What makes you say that?
Why do you say that?
Why?
How come? 11,17

Have you by any chance ever
  _____ed? 3

Can you tell me what it's like? 3

Which one is that? 3

Perhaps you have some questions
  about _____. 11

I have a few questions. 11

I was wondering _____. 11

I've found out that _____. 11

People say . . .
They say . . .
People/They tell me . . .
Most people say . . .
Everybody says . . .
Everybody tells me . . .
I hear . . .
I've heard . . .
Word has it (that) . . . 2,13

I heard it on the radio/on TV/on the
  news.
I saw/read it in the paper. 3

Perhaps
Apparently } you're not aware that
Evidently   _____.
                                    17

Asking for and Reporting Additional Information

What else have you heard?
Have you heard anything else?
Do you know anything else? 2

Can you tell me anything else?
Can you tell me anything more?
What else can you tell me? 3

What did you do next?
What did you do after that?
And then what did you do?
What was the next thing you did? 3

What else would you like to know? 3

Is there any (additional) information I
  can provide?
Do you have any (other) questions? 11

As a matter of fact, . . .
In fact, . . . 3

Attracting Attention

Excuse me, . . .
Pardon me, . . . 8,9

Excuse me, but . . . 12

Charlie. 12

Certainty/Uncertainty

Inquiring about . . .

Are you positive/certain/sure (about
  that)? 3,15

Are you (absolutely) sure about that?
                                    15

Is that definite? 15

Expressing Certainty

I'm (absolutely) positive/certain/sure
  (that _____).
Absolutely!
Positively! 15

I'm positive/certain/sure.
I'm absolutely positive/certain/sure.
I'm a hundred percent sure.
There's no doubt about it.
I'm absolutely positive. 3

I know _____.
I'm sure _____.
I'm positive _____.
I'm convinced _____. 14

I definitely _____.
There's no question (in my mind)
  _____.
I have no doubt (at all) (that) _____.
                                    15

I'm pretty certain. 15

Expressing Uncertainty

I don't know for sure.
I'm not (so) sure.
I'm not (completely/absolutely)
  positive.
I'm not absolutely positive/certain/sure
  (about that).
I'm not a hundred percent
  positive/sure. 3,15

I'm not sure.
I'm not certain.
I don't know yet. 9

I don't think so.
Not as far as I know. 3

I'm not so sure (about that).
I'm not so sure I believe that. 14

I doubt it. 3

Complaining

It's too _____. 5

I was (a little) disappointed.
I wasn't very pleased with it.
It was (a little) disappointing. 5

I'm { annoyed with
      upset with
      [stronger]
      mad at
      angry at
      furious with } _____.
                                    5

He's always
He's constantly } _____ing.
He keeps on
                                    5

His _____ing { bothers
                annoys } me.
                upsets
                                    5

I'm tired of _____(ing).
I'm sick of _____(ing).
I'm sick and tired of _____(ing). 5

Don't you just hate people who
  _____?
Doesn't it bother you when people
  _____?
Aren't you annoyed when people
  _____?
[less formal]
Doesn't it get to you when people
  _____?
Wouldn't you like to clobber people
  who _____? 18

_____(ing) is (very) annoying/
  inconsiderate/rude/obnoxious/selfish/
  thoughtless/tacky. 18

I can't stand it when people _____.
I can't stand people _____ing.
It really bothers me when people
  _____.
[less formal]
I can't take it when people _____. 18

Complimenting

Expressing Compliments

That was { a very good
           quite a
           [less formal] } _____!
           some
                                    5

I thought it was { excellent.
                   wonderful.
                   terrific.
                   magnificent.
                   fabulous.
                   superb.
                                    5

I (really) like _____.
I love _____. 5

It's very _____.
It's so _____. 5

It's one of the _____est _____s I've
  ever _____ed. 5

I don't think I've ever seen a _____
  better than _____. 16

Responding to Compliments

Thanks/Thank you (for saying so).
It's nice of you to say so/that.
I'm glad you like it. 5

Oh/Aw, go on!
Oh/Aw, come on!
Oh! 5

You're just saying that. 5

195

Congratulating

That's fantastic!
That's great/wonderful/
  exciting/marvelous!   2

Congratulations!   2

I'm very happy to hear that.
I'm very happy for you.   2

Correcting

Giving Correction

That isn't exactly/quite right.
That isn't exactly/quite correct.
That (really) isn't so.
I think you might be mistaken.   14

(Actually,) *the bread goes in aisle FIVE.*
  14

That just isn't so. *I do like your meat
loaf.*   14

Responding to Correction

Thank you for calling that to my
  attention.
Thank you for correcting me
  (on that).   14

Deduction

You must be _____.   2

_____ must have _____.
_____ probably _____.
_____ most likely _____.
Chances are _____.
I wouldn't be surprised if _____.
I/I'll bet _____.   15

_____ should have _____ed (by
  now).   15

It looks like _____.
It appears (as if/as though) _____.
It seems (as if/as though) _____.   17

Denying/Admitting

Denying

That's not true.
That's/You're wrong.
You're mistaken.
That (just) isn't so.   14

Admitting

The truth is (that) _____.
The fact of the matter is (that)
  _____.   11,17

You see . . .
The reason is . . .   9

I'm afraid _____.   11

I'm afraid you're right.
I'm afraid I have to agree.
I hate to admit it/say it, but you're
  right.
I hate to admit it/say it, but it's
  true.   14

I hate to have to tell you this, but . . .
I don't feel very good about telling
  you this, but . . .
I wish I didn't have to tell you this,
  but . . .   16

I made a terrible mistake.
[less formal]
I (really) goofed!
[much less formal]
I (really) blew it!   17

It's all my fault.
I'm (entirely) to blame.
It's all my doing.   17

Describing

He's/She's about your height, sort of
  heavy, with *dark curly* hair.   2

He's/She's very _____.   2

It's the _____one with the _____.   3

It's a (very) _____ _____.   3

It's one of the _____est _____s I
  know.   3

Directions-Location

Asking for Directions

Could you please tell me how to get to
  _____?   4

Giving Directions

Go to _____.
Turn _____.
Walk _____ blocks.   4

Disappointment

I was (a little) disappointed.
I wasn't very pleased with it.
It was (a little) disappointing.   5

I'm (very) disappointed with/in
  _____.   7

Fear-Worry-Anxiety

I'm (getting) (a little)
  { worried
  concerned
  anxious } about ___.
  nervous
  15

I'm afraid something must have
  happened (to him/her/them).   15

I wouldn't be concerned.
I wouldn't worry.
Don't worry.
Don't be concerned.   15

Granting Forgiveness

That's/It's okay.
That's/It's all right.
Don't worry about it.
No problem.
These things happen.
We all make mistakes.
You're only human.
It's not your fault.
I understand.   16

Gratitude

Expressing . . .

Thanks (very much).
Thank you (very much).   8,12

Thanks/Thank you for _____.   13

Thanks a lot.   13

Thanks (for telling me).   9

Thank you for *saying so.*
Thank you for *the compliment.*
It's nice of you to *say that/so.*   5,16

I'm very grateful (to _____).   8

I want to thank _____.
I want to express my gratitude to
  _____.   8

I keep forgetting to thank you for
  _____.   8

Responding to . . .

You're welcome.
Don't mention it.
No problem.
Glad to be of help.
I'm glad to do it.
It was nothing (at all).   8,12

I'm glad I could do it/help/be of help.
(It was) my pleasure.
Any time.   8,12

Greeting People

Hello.
[less formal]
Hi.
[more formal]
How do you do?   1

(It's) nice to meet you.
(It's) nice meeting you.
(I'm) happy to meet you.
(I'm) glad to meet you.
(I'm) pleased to meet you.   1

How are you?
How have you been?
[less formal]
How are you doing?
How are things?
How's it going?
  Fine (thank you/thanks).
  Good.
  All right.
  Okay.
  Not bad.   1

Identifying

My friend *Paul*, my brother *Tom*, . . .   1

She's the one who _____.   1

The one *the children gave you.*   3

Indifference

Whenever _____ is fine with me.
(Whoever . . . Whatever . . . However
  . . . Whichever . . . Wherever . . .)
  6

It doesn't make any difference (to me).
It doesn't matter (to me).
It's all the same to me.
I don't care.
I don't feel strongly about it one way
   or the other. 6

It doesn't matter to me whether you
   _____ or not. 6

It's (entirely) up to you.
It's (entirely) your decision.
It's for you to decide. 6

Instructing

(Please) _____. 4

First, . . .
Then, . . .
After that, . . .
Next, . . .
And finally, . . . 4

Intention

Inquiring about . . .

What are you going to do (next
   year)? 15

What are you doing this afternoon? 7

Have you decided _____? 7

You aren't (really) going to _____,
   are you? 15

Expressing . . .

I'm going to _____.
I'm planning to _____.
I plan to _____.
I intend to _____.
I've decided to _____. 7

I'm going to _____.
I'm planning to _____.
I'm intending to _____.
I'm thinking of _____ing.
I'm considering _____ing.
I'm playing/toying with the idea of
   _____ing. 15

I've been thinking of _____ing.
I'm thinking of _____ing.
I've been thinking about _____ing.
I'm thinking about _____ing. 7

I've been meaning to _____ (for a
   long time). 7

I've thought about it for a long time.
I've given it a lot of thought.
I've given it a lot of serious
   consideration. 7

I've decided it's time to do it. 7

I haven't made up my mind yet. 7

I was planning to _____.
I was going to _____.
I intended to _____.
I thought I would _____. 7

I was intent on _____ing.
I was determined to _____. 7

I'll _____ { right away.
right now.
as soon as I can.
the first chance I get. 7

Introductions

Introducing Oneself

My name is _____.
I'm _____. 1

Introducing Others

Let me introduce (you to) _____.
I'd like to introduce (you to) _____.
I'd like you to meet _____.
[less formal]
Meet _____.
This is _____. 1

Invitations

Extending . . .

Would you like to join me?
Do you want to join me?
Would you be interested in joining
   me? 7

How would you like to _____?
Would you like to _____?
Do you want to _____?
Would you be interested in
   _____ing?
How about _____ing?
Let's _____. 10

Would you (by any chance) be
   interested in _____ing?
You wouldn't (by any chance) be
   interested in _____ing, would
   you? 10

We'd like to invite you (and _____)
   over for _____.
We'd like to have you (and _____)
   over for _____.
We'd like you (and _____) to be our
   guest(s) for _____.
We'd like you (and _____) to join us
   for _____. 10

Can you come?
Do you think you can come?
Do you think you'd be able to come?
Would you be able to come?
Can you make it?
Do you think you can make it? 10

Please try to come. 10

We hope you'll be able to join us. 10

If you're not busy, . . .
If you're free, . . .
If you don't have any other
   plans, . . . 10

Accepting . . .

I'd love to.
I'd like to.
I'd like that.
That sounds like fun.
That sounds great/terrific/
   wonderful.
That would be great/terrific/wonderful.

I'd be happy to/glad to.
[stronger]
I'd be delighted to/thrilled to. 7,10

We'd be { very happy
very glad
pleased
delighted } to come. 10

We'll be looking forward to it. 10

Thanks/Thank you for { asking.
inviting me.
the invitation.
I appreciate the invitation.
It's (very) nice of you to invite me. 10

Declining . . .

I'd love to, but I can't.
I'd love to, but I won't be able to. 10

Leave Taking

(You know,) I think I should
{ be going
get going
be on my way
be getting on
   my way } (now).
(You know,) I (really) must be going.
I've (really) got to go now.
I've (really) got to be going now.
I (really) have to go now.
I'd (really) better go now.
I (really) need to go now.
I (really) should go now.
I have to/I've got to run.
I have to/I've got to get going. 10,18

I should get going, too. 10

Well, it's been really nice seeing you
   again. 10

I'd love to continue this conversation,
   but . . . 10

(I'm afraid) it's getting late. 18

Let's get together soon.
Let's keep in touch.
Let's stay in touch. 10

('I'll) see you soon/later/tomorrow/next
   week/ . . . 10

I'll call you. 10

Speak to you then. 10

Take care.
Take it easy.
So long.
Good-bye.
Bye.
Bye-bye.
See you. 10

Sorry I have to rush off like this. 10

(Well,) I've probably taken up enough
   of your time.
(Well,) I don't want to take up any
   more of your time. 11

I've enjoyed talking with you.
It was nice meeting you.
It was a pleasure meeting you.
I appreciate/I'm grateful for this
   opportunity to talk/meet with you. 11

Likes/Dislikes

Inquiring about . . .

How do you like _____?
What do you think of _____? 5

How did you like _____? 5

Did you like _____? 5

Don't you like _____? 5

Expressing Likes

I like _____.
I love _____. 5

Expressing Dislikes

I don't (really) like/enjoy _____ very
  much.
I don't (particularly) care for _____.
I'm not (really) crazy about _____.
[stronger]
I hate _____. 5

Obligation

Inquiring about . . .

Do I have to _____?
Would I have to _____?
Would I be required to _____?
Would it be necessary (for me) to
  _____? 11

Expressing . . .

I have to _____.
I've got to _____.
I'm supposed to _____.
I need to _____. 10,12

I'm expected to _____. 10

You're supposed to _____.
You're required to _____.
You're expected to _____.
You need to _____.
You have to _____.
You've got to _____.
You must _____.
It's necessary for you to _____.
It's required that you _____. 11

We require _____ to _____.
We insist (that) _____.
We expect _____ to _____. 11

It's required/necessary/essential/
  mandatory. 11

_____ is insisting that I _____.
_____ is requiring me to _____.
[stronger]
_____ is making me _____.
_____ is forcing me to _____. 11

I was supposed to _____.
I said I would _____.
I had promised to _____.
I had promised you I would _____. 11

I don't think there's any way I can get
  out of it. 10

I'm tied up on _____.
I've got something scheduled for
  _____. 10

I didn't know that was required/
  necessary/essential/mandatory. 11

You were counting/depending on me
  to _____.
You were counting/depending on my
  _____ing.
You had expected me to _____. 11

I don't have any obligations or
  commitments on _____. 10

We feel obligated to _____. 11

Offering to Do Something

Do you want me to _____?
Would you like me to _____?
I'll _____, if you'd like.
I'll/I'd be happy/glad to _____, (if
  you'd like). 8

Let me (_____). 8

Can I take a message?
Can I give him/her a message?
Would you like to leave a message
  (for him/her)? 12

Offering to Help

Making an Offer

(Do you) want any help?
(Do you) need any help?
(Do you) want a hand?
(Do you) need a hand?
Can I help?
Can I give you a hand? 8

Would you like me to help you
  _____?
Do you want me to help you _____?
I'd be glad/happy to help you _____,
  (if you'd like).
Let me help you _____.
Would you like any help _____ing?
Would you like me to give you a hand
  _____ing? 8

Can I do anything to help?
Is there anything I can do to help?
Can I help? 8

I'd be happy/glad to give you a hand.
I'd be happy/glad to lend a hand.
I'd be happy/glad to help. 8

Let me give you a hand.
I'm happy to lend a hand. 8

Let me _____.
Allow me to _____.
I'll _____. 8

May/Can I help you?
May/Can I assist you? 8

Is there anything/something in
  particular I can help you find?
Is there anything/something you're
  looking for in particular? 8

Is there anything else I can help you
  with? 8

Please let me know if I can be of any
  further assistance.
Please feel free to call on me if I can be
  of any further assistance.
If I can be of any further assistance,
  please don't hesitate to ask/let me
  know. 8

Responding to an Offer

If you don't mind.
If you wouldn't mind.
If it's no trouble. 8

I don't want to {
  trouble you.
  bother you.
  inconvenience you.
  put you to any
    trouble.
  put you out. 8

Don't worry about it.
That's okay/all right. 8

Permission

Asking for . . .

Can/Could I (possibly) _____?
Can/Could I please _____?
May I (please) _____?
Is it all right/okay (with you) if I
  _____?
Would it be possible for me to
  _____?
I'd like to _____, if that's all right/
  okay (with you).
Would it be all right/okay (with you) if
  I _____ed? 9

Would you mind/object if I _____ed?
Would it bother you if I _____ed?
Do you mind if I _____? 9

Granting . . .

Certainly.
Sure.
Of course.
By all means.
It's all right/okay with me.
Yes. 9

No, I wouldn't mind.
No, I don't mind.
No, of course not.
No, not at all.
No, it's all right/fine/okay with me.
No. 9

Go (right) ahead.
Be my guest. 9

I guess so.
I suppose so.
I don't see (any reason) why not. 9

If you want to ___, it's
{
  fine
  all right } with me.
  okay 9

Denying . . .

I'd rather you didn't.
I'd prefer it if you didn't/wouldn't.
I'd prefer/rather that you not.
I'd prefer you not to. 9

198

_____ing isn't allowed/permitted.
You mustn't _____ (under any circumstances).
We don't permit anyone to _____.
You're not supposed to _____.
You may not _____ (without permission). 9

That's out of the question. 9

I can't do that without
{ an authorization from
the permission of
the approval of
the consent of
the agreement of
a go ahead from } _____. 9

Inquiring about Permissibility

Is _____ing allowed/permitted?
Is it okay to _____?
Is it all right to _____?
Are you allowed/permitted to _____?
Are people allowed to _____?
Do they allow/permit _____ing?
Do they allow people to _____? 9

Indicating Permissibility

I don't think _____ing is allowed/permitted.
I don't think you're allowed/permitted to _____.
I don't think people are allowed/permitted to _____.
I don't think they allow/permit people to _____.
I don't think they allow/permit you to _____. 9

Yes, _____ _____.
[less certain]
I think so.
I believe so.
Yes, as far as I know. 9

No, _____ _____.
[less certain]
I don't think so.
I don't believe so.
Not as far as I know. 9

Persuading-Insisting

I mean it!
I'm (really) serious.
I'm being honest with you. 5

Listen!
Look!
(No,) really!
(No,) I mean it!
(No,) honestly!
(Oh,) come on! 8,9,14

I insist. 8

Let me, for a change.
Let me, for once. 8

There's no sense in your _____ing.
There's no reason (for you) to _____.
You don't have to _____.
You shouldn't have to _____. 8

Admit it!
Face it! 14

Possibility/Impossibility

Inquiring about . . .

What's the possibility of _____? 15

Expressing Possibility

I might _____.
I may _____.
I thought I might _____.
I thought I'd _____.
Perhaps I'll _____.
Maybe I'll _____. 7,15

Perhaps. 15

You might _____.
You could (possibly) _____.
You could/would run the risk of _____ing.
There's a chance you might/could _____. 13

It's a possibility.
There's a chance.
I might/may.
It could happen.
You never know! 15

_____ might have _____ed.
_____ may have _____ed. 15

Expressing Impossibility

There's no chance that _____.
There's no possibility (that) _____.
[less formal]
There's no way (that) _____. 15

Preference

Inquiring about . . .

Would you { prefer _____?
rather have _____?
like _____? } 6

Would you like to
Would you prefer to
Would you rather
Do you want to
Would you care to } _____ (or _____)? 6

How would you like it? 6

Do you have any strong feelings about it? 6
Do you have any feelings about it one way or another?
Do you care one way or the other?
Do you have a preference/any preferences? 6

Expressing . . .

I'd prefer _____.
I'd rather have _____.
I'd like _____. 6

I'd prefer to _____.
I'd rather _____.
I'd like to _____.
I'd much rather _____. 6

Probability/Improbability

Inquiring about . . .

What do you think the chances are of _____?
What's the likelihood of _____?
What's the possibility of _____? 15

Is there a good chance _____? 15

Expressing Probability

I'll probably _____.
I'll most likely _____.
I'm pretty sure I'll _____.
Chances are I'll _____.
I guess I'll _____.
I suppose I'll _____. 7,15

In all likelihood . . .
In all probability . . . 15

If I had to choose between _____ and _____, I'd probably _____. 15

It should
It ought to
It'll probably
It'll most likely } arrive any
In all likelihood it'll } minute now.
In all probability it'll
Chances are it'll } 15

Expressing Improbability

The chances are probably not very good.
The chances are pretty slim.
It/That isn't very likely. 15

There's not much chance of that happening.
I doubt (if) that would/could/will happen.
I don't think that will happen. 15

Promising

Asking for a Promise

Can I { rely on
depend on
count on } you to _____? 7

Can I { depend on
count on
rely on
be sure of } that? 7

Promise? 7

Offering a Promise

Promise.
I promise I'll _____.
I promise to _____. 7,16

I promise (you) _____.
I guarantee (you) _____.
I assure you _____.
I give you my word _____.
You can be sure _____. 7

Absolutely.
Definitely.
Positively. 7

199

You can $\left\{\begin{array}{l}\text{rely on}\\ \text{depend on}\\ \text{count on}\end{array}\right\}$ me. 7

I won't let you down.
I won't disappoint you. 7

I had promised (_____)
I'd _____. 16

Breaking a Promise

I can't keep my promise. 16

I don't make a habit of breaking
    promises to people.
I don't like to/usually break promises
    (I make) to people.
I'm not one to go back on my
    word. 16

Regret

It's a shame (that) _____.
It's a pity (that) _____.
(It's) too bad (that) _____.
I'm disappointed (that) _____.
It's disappointing (that) _____. 17

I regret _____ing.
I regret (that) I _____.
I'm sorry about _____ing.
I'm sorry (that) I _____. 17

I wish I hadn't _____ed. 17

I could kick myself!
[stronger]
I could kill myself!
I could shoot myself!
I could (just) die! 17

Remembering/Forgetting

Inquiring about . . .

Did you (happen to) remember to
    _____?
You didn't (by any chance) remember
    to _____, did you? 3

Remember _____? 11

Remember I had promised you I'd
    _____? 16

Indicating . . .

I remember. 16

You remember. 3

Oh, that one. 3

I forgot (all about it).
I completely forgot.
It (completely) slipped my mind. 3,11

I forgot to _____. 17

Requests

Direct, Polite

Please _____.
Can you (please) _____?
Will you (please) _____? 12

Would you (please) _____?
I'd like you to _____.
I wish you would _____. 12

And while you're at it, please
    _____. 12

Could you do me a favor?
Could I ask you a favor?
Could you do a favor for me?
Could I ask you to _____? 9,12

Would you please ask/tell _____ to
    _____? 12

Direct, More Polite

Could you possibly _____?
Could you (please) _____?
Could I (possibly) ask you to _____?
Would you mind _____ing?
Would you be willing to _____?
Do you think you'd be able to _____?
I wonder if you could (possibly)
    _____. 2,12

$\left.\begin{array}{l}\text{Would you mind}\\ \text{Would it bother you}\\ \text{Would it disturb you}\end{array}\right\}$ if I _____ed? 6

Less Direct, Very Polite

I was wondering if you'd (be willing
    to) _____.
I was wondering if you could possibly
    _____.
Would you be kind enough to _____?
Would you mind if I asked you to
    _____?
Would I be troubling you (too much) if
    I asked you to _____?
Could I possibly impose on you to
    _____?
Would I be imposing on you if I asked
    you to _____? 12

Responding to Requests

Okay.
All right.
Sure.
Certainly.
Of course.
I'd be happy/glad to.
(It would be) my pleasure. 12

No, I wouldn't mind.
No, of course not.
No, not at all.
No problem.
No trouble at all. 12

Satisfaction/Dissatisfaction

Inquiring about . . .

How do you like _____?
What do you think of _____? 5

How are you enjoying _____? 17

How did you like _____? 5

Did you (really) like it? 5

Are you $\left\{\begin{array}{l}\text{satisfied}\\ \text{happy}\\ \text{pleased}\end{array}\right\}$ with it? 5

Is it _____ enough? 5

What seems to be the problem (with
    it)?
What seems to be the matter (with it)?
What's the problem/matter/wrong
    (with it)? 5

Expressing Satisfaction

It's $\left\{\begin{array}{l}\text{fine.}\\ \text{very nice.}\\ \text{perfect.}\end{array}\right.$ 5

It's just what I $\left\{\begin{array}{l}\text{had in mind.}\\ \text{wanted.}\\ \text{was looking for.}\end{array}\right.$ 5

I wouldn't want it any _____er. 5

Expressing Dissatisfaction

It's too _____. 5

I'm not enjoying _____ (at all). 17

I really $\left\{\begin{array}{l}\text{expected it to be}\\ \text{thought it would be}\\ \text{hoped it would be}\end{array}\right\}$ _____er. 5

It wasn't as _____ as I thought it
    would be. 5

Surprise-Disbelief

Assistant manager?!
1:30?! Already?!
Quit your job?!
They're going to make the park across the
    street into a parking lot?! 2,3,10,15

School isn't really going to be closed
    tomorrow, is it? 3

I didn't realize _____. 10

Oh? 9

You're kidding!
No kidding!
You're joking!
I don't/can't believe it.
Oh, come on!
No!
That can't be!
You've got to be kidding! 3

Gee!
Boy!
Wow! 7

(Well,) how about that!
(Well,) what do you know!
(Well,) how do you like that!
Isn't that something! 9

Sympathizing

That's too bad!
That's a shame/a pity!
What a shame/a pity! 2,7,17

That's terrible!
That's awful! 17

I'm (very) sorry to hear (about) that.
I'm (very/so) sorry. 2,17

Want-Desire

Inquiring about . . .

When do you want to _____?
Who would you like to _____?
What would you like to do?
How would you like me to _____?
Which _____ would you rather _____?
Where do you want _____ to _____?
6
What do you want to do today? 13

Expressing . . .

I'd like _____.
I'll have _____.
I want _____. 6

I (really) don't feel like _____ing.
I'm not (really) in the mood to _____.
I don't think I'm in the mood to _____.
I'd (really) prefer not to _____. 6
_____ wants me to _____. 6

Warning

Don't _____! 15

(You'd better) *get out of the way!*
(You'd better) *stay away from the _____!*
(You'd better) keep clear of the _____!
You'd better not _____!
Don't _____! 13
If you don't (_____), _____. 13

(Be) careful!
Look out!
Watch out! 13
You might _____. 13
You'll be disappointed.
You'll be sorry.
You'll regret it. 15

Wish-Hope

I wish *it were cheaper.* 17
I (really) wish you hadn't _____ed. 16
I wish I could _____.
If only I could _____. 17
I hope _____. 16
I was hoping _____. 17

Conversation Strategies

Asking for Repetition

Excuse me. 11,13,18

Pardon (me)?
What did you say?
What was that?
Come again? 13,18

(Sorry.) I didn't hear you. 4,12

I didn't (quite) catch that.
I didn't get that.
I missed that.
I'm lost.
I'm not following you. 4

What did you say?
Could/Would you (please) repeat that?
Could/Would you say that again?
Would you mind saying that again?
Would you mind repeating that? 4

What did you ask me to do?
What did you say?
What was that? 12

WHEN do you want me to _____?
WHEN should I _____?
WHEN did you tell me to _____? 4

Could you repeat the last two
{ instructions?
  directions?
  steps?
  things you
    said? 4

I forgot the last part. 4

Have I had it what?! 11

Huh? 13

Checking and Indicating Understanding

Checking Another Person's Understanding

(Have you) got it?
Do you follow me?
Okay? 4

Are you with me (so far)?
Okay (so far)?
Are you following me (so far)? 4

Do you think you've got it now?
Have you got all that? 4

Checking One's Own Understanding

Let me see.
Let me see if I understand.
Let me see if I've got that (right).
Let me repeat that back. 4

Did you say _____?
Was that _____? 18

This Saturday evening?
7:00?
The letter to Mr. Casey?
"Tooth-Brite"?
Any minute now? 10,12,13,15

Indicating Understanding

Now I've got it.
I understand.
I see.
I'm with you.
I follow you. 4,18

Uh-húh.
Um-hḿm.
Yes.
(That's) right. 4

Clarification

Asking for Clarification

Do you mean (to say) _____?
Are you saying _____?
Does that mean _____? 17

[less direct]
I'm afraid I'm not following you.
I'm not really sure what you're getting at.
I'm not quite clear as to what you mean (by that).
[more direct]
What do you mean (by that)?
What does that mean?
Could you clarify that for me? 18

Giving Clarification

Let me put it this way: . . .
Let me put it another way: . . .
What I'm (really) saying is . . .
What I'm trying to say is . . .
What I mean is . . .
What I'm getting at is . . .
In other words . . .
[less formal]
Let me try that again.
Let me try that one more time. 18

What you're (really) saying is . . .
What you're trying to say is . . .
What you mean is . . .
In other words . . . 18

CHAPTER 1

Pages 2–3: "I Don't Think We've Met"

Model

- In the United States it is common to initiate a conversation by introducing oneself.
- "Hello." is both formal and informal. "Hi." is informal, and therefore a more common form of greeting. "How do you do?" is a formal greeting.
- The subject and verb are often omitted in conversation as in "(It's) nice to meet you." and "(I'm) happy to meet you."
- Appropriate questions to ask when people meet for the first time often involve what the two speakers have in common. For example, in an English class: "Where are you from?"; at a clinic: "Who is your doctor?"
- "What do you do?" is a very common question asked when two people meet. In the United States, profession and personal identity are very strongly linked.
- It is NOT appropriate for people meeting for the first time to ask about salary, age, marital status, or religion.
- Short answers to information questions are more common in conversation than full-sentence answers. For example, "Where are you from?" "Japan.", as opposed to "I'm from Japan." ("What do you do?" requires a full answer: "I'm a dancer.")

Exercises

6: "Major"—the field or major course of study (such as History, Chemistry, Philosophy) chosen by college students.

Page 4: "Let Me Introduce . . ."

Model

- The greetings "How are you doing?", "How are things?", and "How's it going?" are informal. "How are you?" and "How have you been?" are used in both formal and informal situations.
- "Meet_____." and "This is _____." are lines of introduction that are used in very informal situations.
- Short answers such as "Fine." and "All right." are very common in both formal and informal situations.
- The exchange: "How are you?" "Fine." has become almost a ritual in American society. The speaker asking the question "How are you?" is not necessarily asking how the other person is feeling, but rather is extending a greeting. In response to this "greeting," the other speaker automatically answers "Fine.", "Good." even if he or she isn't!

Page 5: "Don't I Know You From Somewhere?"

Model

- "Excuse me, but . . ." is a common way to initiate a conversation. In this case, it is said with hesitation because Speaker A is not absolutely sure who Speaker B is.
- When a speaker uses a negative question to get information, the speaker expects a positive answer.
- The question "Don't I know you from somewhere?" is so common that it has become a type of cliché. It is sometimes used to indicate that the speaker has an ulterior motive (usually in striking up a conversation with a member of the opposite sex).
- In line 3, Speaker A is positive that he is correct and persists by saying "Sure." or "Of course."
- In line 4, Speaker B realizes that Speaker A has made a mistake. "No, I'm afraid not." and "You must have me confused with somebody else." are very polite ways of telling Speaker A that he is wrong.

Exercises

2: In the United States, boys and girls often play on the same team in certain sports such as baseball and tennis.
5: The FBI (Federal Bureau of Investigation) is the U.S. government agency that investigates federal crimes.
5: The "10 Most Wanted" list is a constantly updated list of the most dangerous and sought-after criminals in the country.

Pages 6–7: "Guess Who I Saw Yesterday!"

Models

- To say "Guess . . ." and "You won't believe . . ." are powerful ways to initiate a new topic of conversation and to capture the interest of the listener. These phrases signal to the listener that the topic and related information will be interesting and relevant.
- In line 6, the phrase "Oh, sure you do!" emphasizes that Speaker A is VERY sure that Speaker B knows the person being talked about.
- In line 10, by saying "How IS she?", Speaker B is enthusiastically asking for information about the person mentioned.

Exercises

5: "Board of Education." Each city in the United States has a board or committee which makes major decisions concerning schools in the area.
6: "Have a crush on"—be infatuated with a member of the opposite sex.
7: "Retirement." When many older Americans stop working, usually around the age of 65, they often move to a warmer climate to spend their retirement years.

CHAPTER 2

Page 10: "Good News!"

Model

- "I have some good news." is a common way to get someone's attention and set the scene for a happy announcement.
- In line 2, Speaker B is expressing interest in Speaker A's good news by saying "Really?"
- In lines 4, 5, and 7, Speaker B appropriately reacts to Speaker A's good news by congratulating her friend.

Exercises

1: "A raise"—a raise in pay or salary.
2: Oxford University is an extremely prestigious British university. For an American to be accepted by Oxford is a great honor.
3: Nobel Prizes are awarded annually to people who work for the interests of humanity. Examples are the Nobel Peace Prize, the Nobel Prize for Medicine, and the Nobel Prize for Literature.
4: Many companies in the United States give awards and recognition to hardworking employees as an incentive.

Page 11: "Bad News!"

Model

- "I have some bad news." prepares the listener for an unpleasant announcement. The listener hears this and is prepared to sympathize.

Exercises

1: In the United States, dogs and cats are usually considered "members of the family." For most Americans, losing a pet is a very serious matter.

Pages 12–13: "Have You Heard from . . . ?"

Models

- To "hear from" and "be in touch with" can mean by letter or by telephone. To "talk to" and "speak to" can mean by telephone or face to face. To "run into" and "see" mean to meet someone face to face.
- In line 3, Speaker B says "As a matter of fact, I have." because it is a coincidence that Speaker A has mentioned that person.
- Even though the subject of the conversation is not present, it is appropriate to express congratulations or sympathy about what has been reported.

Exercises

6: The PTA (Parent Teacher Association) is a group of parents whose children attend the same school and who often meet with the school's teachers and other parents to discuss school issues.

Page 14: "What Do They Look Like?"

Model

- In line 3, Speaker B says, "I'm afraid I don't remember what he looks like." as a polite way of asking Speaker A to describe the person.
- In line 5, Speaker A uses the expression, "You can't miss him." meaning that Charlie Jones is VERY recognizable.
- When describing someone, the adjectives "heavy" and "thin" are more appropriate and polite than the adjectives "fat" and "skinny," which can be insulting.

Exercises

3: "Ms." is a title for women which is commonly used in the United States in place of both Miss and Mrs.

Page 15: "What Are They Like?"

Model

- In the expressions "They say . . ." and "They tell me . . . ," the pronoun "they" is used to mean "everybody" or "many people."
- In line 4, by saying "Hmm.", Speaker A is acknowledging the new information he has heard.
- In line 6, the phrase "Really? That's interesting." has very little meaning. It is most often used simply to acknowledge that the new information has been heard and understood.

Exercises

4: A senator is a U.S. political representative. Two senators from each of the fifty states are elected to represent their state in the United States Senate in Washington, D.C.

Pages 16–17: "Tell Me a Little About Yourself"

Model

- In the first line, "So" signals a change in the topic of conversation.
- "Gee—uh . . ." and "Well, let's see . . ." are common ways to hesitate and give oneself time to think before speaking.

- "Tell me a little about yourself." is a very open-ended request. It is a common way of asking for information about a person being met for the first time.
- "What do you do?" (line 4) is probably the most common question asked when meeting someone for the first time. Americans generally define themselves and others by profession.

Exercises

2: The majority of American politicians pay writers to write their speeches for them.

2: A congressman is a political representative who serves in the United States House of Representatives in Washington, D.C.

4: Exercise classes, along with health food and jogging, have become more and more popular for both men and women in the United States.

CHAPTER 3

Page 20: "Which One?"

Model

- "You should _____.", "Why don't you_____?", and "How about _____ing?" are common expressions for offering advice or suggestions.
- In line 4, "Hmm." indicates that the speaker is thinking and trying to remember.
- In line 5, Speaker A says "You remember." Speaker A is positive that Speaker B knows the object being talked about.

Page 21: "What's It Like There?"

Model

- With the expressions, "In my opinion . . . ," "If you ask me . . . ," and "As far as I'm concerned . . . ," a speaker focuses attention on the information to follow. These introductory phrases tell the listener that what follows is the speaker's opinion.
- When Americans plan a vacation, they are often primarily interested in knowing what the weather and the people are like.

Page 22: "As Far As I Know . . ."

Model

- "Do you/Would you by any chance know_____?" are polite ways of asking for information when approaching strangers.
- In line 3, Speaker B begins her answer to Speaker A's question by saying "As far as I know." This phrase is a common way to answer a question without appearing "too knowledgeable" and is therefore polite. Again in line 6, Speaker B is being polite when she says with uncertainty, "I don't think so." It isn't until Speaker A questions her certainty that Speaker B finally says "Yes, I'm positive."
- In line 4, "Hmm." indicates that Speaker A is thinking about or "digesting" this new information.
- This lesson illustrates the importance of the notion of time and schedule to Americans. In the model conversation, Speaker A is extremely concerned about the arrival time of the President. In the exercises, similar concern about time is expressed.

Page 23: "Did You Remember?"

Model

- "Uh-oh!" is a common expression used when someone suspects that something bad has happened.
- A family dog is considered important enough in the United States that if it is not fed on schedule, there is concern.
- In line 4, "Well," signals that the speaker has accepted the situation and is ready to decide on what action is to be taken.
- In line 4, "I guess one of us should go and do it." is similar to a suggestion. Speaker B is really suggesting that Speaker A do what was forgotten but does not directly say so.

Exercises

2: It is becoming more common in the United States for husbands and wives to share household chores such as cleaning, cooking, and setting the table.

Page 24: "Did You Hear?"

Model

- The announcement on the radio that schools are closed is probably due to a snowstorm. This is common during winter storms when traveling to school could be dangerous.

Exercises

4: City Hall is the location of the offices of city government.

Page 25: "Have You Heard the News?"

Model

- Declarative sentences spoken with question intonation are common ways of expressing surprise and disbelief. ("They're going to make the park across the street into a parking lot?!")

Pages 26–27: "What Happened?"

Model

- It is common and often considered polite to encourage a person telling a story by asking questions as the events unfold: "And then what did you do?", "What did you do after that?" This shows interest on the part of the listener.

CHAPTER 4

Page 32: "What Did You Say?"

Model

- In line 2, Speaker B says "I'm sorry." It is polite to apologize when asking for repetition. It is less polite simply to say "What?" or "Huh?"
- Playing "portable stereos" in public places is popular in the United States.

Page 33: "I'm Sorry. I Didn't Hear You"

Model

- By emphasizing the question word "WHEN . . . ?" or "WHAT . . . ?" Speaker B is indicating which piece of information he failed to hear or is not sure he heard correctly.

Pages 34–35: "Have You Got It?"

Model

- When asking strangers, the polite forms "Could you please tell me _____?, Could you possibly tell me_____?", and the like are more appropriate than direct questions such as "How do you get to the post office?"
- The expressions "(Have you) got it?, Do you follow me?, Okay?, Do you think you've got it now?" are used to check whether the person you are talking to has understood what you have said.
- The expressions "Let me see., Let me see if I understand., Let me see if I've got that (right)." are used to check your own understanding of what someone else has said. They would normally be followed by a repetition of the information that you are checking.
- The expressions "Uh-húh., Um-hḿm., Yes., (That's) right." are used to show that what the other speaker has said is correct. They give encouragement and tell the speaker to continue talking.
- In line 10, "Hmm . . ." indicates that the speaker has momentarily forgotten and is thinking.
- In line 13, by saying "Okay." the speaker indicates that she has understood.

Exercises

2: Self-service gas stations are popular in the United States. If gas customers pump their own gas, they usually pay less money for it.

Pages 36–37: "Are You With Me So Far?"

Model

- The expressions "Are you with me (so far)?, Okay (so far)?, Are you following me (so far)? Have you got all that?" are used to check another person's understanding of what you have said.
- The expressions "Yes, I'm with you., Now I've got it., I understand., I see., I'm with you." indicate that you have understood what the other person has said.

CHAPTER 5

Page 40: "Thanks For Saying So"

Model

- In line 2, Speaker B asks "Did you really like it?". This is a polite and gracious way to respond to a compliment. It indicates that the speaker is pleased, yet humble.
- Expressing gratitude is expected when responding to a compliment: "Thanks/Thank you (for saying so)., It's nice of you to say so/that."

Page 41: "You're Just Saying That!"

Model

- A typical way to make a compliment is by saying you like something and then telling why with a descriptive adjective. The superlative adjective is used to make a strong compliment.

- Instead of responding to a compliment with a simple "Thank you.", the following exchange is very common. The speaker responds to a compliment with an expression of disbelief: "Oh, go on! You're just saying that!" The speaker is not questioning the other person's sincerity, but instead is responding to the compliment with humility. The other person then normally insists that the compliment was sincere: "No, I mean it!, I'm (really) serious., I'm being honest with you."

Exercises

3: "Interesting" is an adjective with little meaning. The speaker is either not sure how she feels about the painting, or, out of politeness, does not wish to say what she *really* thinks about it!

Page 42: "Just What I Had in Mind!"

Model

- A declarative sentence with question intonation is often used to check whether the other speaker is satisfied. For example, line 3: "It isn't too heavy?", line 7: "So you're satisfied with it?"

Page 43: "I'd Like a Refund, Please"

Model

- These expressions are used to find out the cause of a person's dissatisfaction: "What seems to be the problem (with it)?, What seems to be the matter (with it)?, What's the problem/the matter/wrong (with it)?"
- In the United States it is not unusual to return something you have purchased or you have received as a gift. Most department stores have a "Return Counter." A store will usually give a refund (return your money) and/or allow you to exchange the item for another and pay any difference in cost. Some stores won't give refunds or exchanges. If they don't, there are usually signs in the store telling a customer the store policy.
- In line 5, the customer uses the polite expression "I don't think so." or any of the alternatives rather than simply saying "No."
- In lines 9 and 11, the customer expresses surprise and disappointment when she exclaims "No refunds??" and "Oh."

Exercises

2: "Flashy"—very brightly colored, often with a wild pattern.

Page 44: "I Was a Little Disappointed"

Model

- By beginning a response with "To tell (you) the truth,/Honestly,/To be honest (with you)," the speaker is "setting the scene" for expressing a reaction of disappointment about something.
- "I was (a little) disappointed., I wasn't very pleased with it., It was a little disappointing." are expressions of disappointment and are also used as a way of complaining.

Page 45: "I'm Really Annoyed"

Model

- To be "mad at", "angry at", and "furious with" are very strong emotional states.
- Voicing a complaint to a friend is different from and much easier than complaining directly to the person responsible for the annoyance.
- In line 6, Speaker B says "I don't understand." Speaker B sees a direct and logical solution to the problem and cannot understand why Speaker A has not taken this step.
- The present continuous tense is often used to express a habitual action when emphasizing the frequency of the action.

Pages 46–47: "Would You Like to Get Together This Weekend?"

Model

- The questions "Would you like to_____?" and "Do you want to_____?" are very similar.
- By saying "Well," before answers and questions, the speakers are being polite by avoiding being too direct.
- In line 27, Speaker A says "But if you don't like seafood, we can go someplace else." He assumes that Speaker B will reject this suggestion since she has rejected every other one!
- After this long discussion, Speaker B says "Then it's settled." or any of the alternative lines. This indicates that a good decision for both speakers has been made.

CHAPTER 6

Page 50: "I'd Prefer a Baked Potato"

Model

- Restaurants in the United States almost always offer a choice of side dishes with the main course.
- When ordering items on a menu, the indefinite article "a/an" is normally used. For example, "I'll have a hamburger, a salad . . ." When the particular food being ordered is a specialty of the restaurant, the definite article is used. For example, "I'll have the chicken, the fish . . ." In this case, the particular dish is listed as a specialty on the menu and the definite article refers to that specific dish.

- The amount of cooking time for beef (steak, hamburger, roast beef) varies from "rare" (the shortest cooking time), "medium rare", "medium", "medium well" to "well done" (the longest cooking time).

Page 51: "I'd Much Rather See a Movie"

Model

- Accompanying a preference with expressions such as "To be honest" or "I think" and asking "Is that okay?" is a polite way of showing that the speaker is being considerate of the other person's feelings.

Pages 52–53: "A Serious Disagreement"

Model

- Line 1: "You've seemed troubled for the past few days." makes it clear that Speakers A and B are close enough friends so that A has noticed a change in B's behavior. Since they are good friends, Speaker A feels that it is appropriate to ask questions about B's problem.
- In line 3, "Well, to tell the truth" indicates that Speaker B is about to admit that there is a problem.
- In line 6, Speaker B says "To make a long story short, ..." This expression is used when people want to leave out details and get right to the main point.

Exercises

6: In the United States, older relatives are sometimes sent to special homes for senior citizens where they are taken care of by professionals.

7: A parish is a local church community.

9: In the United States, workers sometimes "go on strike" (stop working) if they have a serious disagreement with their employers.

Page 54: "It Doesn't Make Any Difference"

Model

- In line 2, "Oh." indicates that Speaker B is a little surprised; she probably hadn't been thinking about when the two were going to leave the party. The "I don't know." which follows further indicates that she doesn't have strong feelings about the matter.
- In line 4, Speaker A asks "You don't have any strong feelings about it?" Declarative sentences are often used as questions to check understanding.
- At large parties in the United States, guests do not necessarily arrive at the party or leave at specific times. Rather, they may arrive and leave as they wish.

Page 55: "It's Entirely Up to You"

Model

- In line 3, Speaker A is being very considerate and respectful of Speaker B by double-checking "Are you sure?" and by using the expression "I mean . . ." along with the polite statement which follows.
- In line 4, Speaker B is being equally as polite and considerate by saying "Honestly" along with his statements of indifference.

Exercises

5: "Security Blanket." Young children often choose a special blanket which they like to have with them at all times "for security." The child in Exercise 5 is about twelve years old and the mother feels that it is certainly time for her daughter to give up her "security blanket."

Pages 56–57: "The International Gourmet"

Model

- The expressions: "Well, . . . Let me see, . . . Let's see, . . . Hmm, . . . Okay, . . . Uh, . . . I think, . . . I guess . . ." are common ways of hesitating or "buying·time" until you can think of what you want to say.

CHAPTER 7

Page 62: "I Promise"

Model

- To say the words "I promise" is to make a strong commitment to do something.
- In line 3, Speaker A emphasizes the importance of his request by double-checking with Speaker B: "You won't forget? It's really important."
- In line 4, recognizing how important this request is to Speaker A, Speaker B reassures him by saying "Don't worry. You can rely on me."

Exercises

5: In the United States, restaurant kitchens must maintain a standard of cleanliness determined by the local government in order to operate. A health inspector makes periodic visits to check that these standards are kept.

Page 63: "I Won't Let You Down"

Model

- In lines 3 and 5, Speaker A checks with Speaker B: "Can I depend on that?", "Now remember, I'm counting on you." The request is clearly important enough for the speaker to ask for reassurance twice.
- The single word expressions "Absolutely!, Definitely!, Positively!" indicate a strong statement of commitment.
- In line 5, Speaker A says "Okay." after Speaker B repeats his promise. This is a common way of responding to a promise and means "We both understand."
- A businessperson's workday normally begins at 9 a.m. and ends at 5 p.m. This businessman clearly needs his car by the end of the workday so that he can drive home.

Exercises

1: For a portion of the summer, children are often sent to overnight camp for fun and exercise (and as a vacation for their parents!).

Pages 64–65: "He Gave Me His Word"

Models

- "How come?" is equivalent to "Why?"
- In line 7, the expression "After all," implies "It's logical."

Exercises

4: "Overtime" means working more than the usual 40 hours per week.

Page 66: "I've Made a Decision"

Model

- The expression "You know" has a variety of meanings in English. In this instance, "You know" specifically introduces a new topic of conversation.
- "Gee!, Boy!, Wow!" are informal expressions for indicating surprise.
- In line 4, Speaker B expresses surprise and also comments on the importance of what Speaker A has announced: "That's a big decision!"

Page 67: "I'll Probably Stay Home and Read a Book"

Model

- The greeting "Hi! It's me!" is a very casual way to begin a telephone conversation. The speakers clearly know each other well enough to recognize one another's voice.
- In line 2, Speaker B answers "Oh, hi!" In this case, "Oh," indicates that Speaker B understands who "me" is in line 1.
- In line 3, Speaker A begins his question with "Tell me, . . ." This expression indicates that Speaker A wants to get directly to the point, the reason that he is calling.
- In line 3, when Speaker A asks "What are you doing this afternoon?", an invitation will probably follow. By responding "I'm not sure. I'll probably . . ." and asking "How about you?", Speaker B is communicating the fact that he is open to suggestions.
- In line 6, Speaker A says "Well," before announcing his plans. "Well," is used because the speaker wishes to avoid being too direct.

Page 68: "I Haven't Made Up My Mind Yet"

Model

- In line 1, "to ask" means "to invite."
- The subject "it" is sometimes dropped in casual conversation. In line 5, Speaker A says "Sounds like a difficult decision." ("[It] sounds like a difficult decision.")
- Similarly, short questions such as "Promise?" ("[Do you] promise?") and short answers such as "Promise." ("[I] promise.") are common in conversation.
- A prom is a formal dance, usually for high school students (ages 14–18). The "senior prom," a tradition in many U.S. high schools, is a dance attended by members of the senior class during the season of their graduation from high school.

Exercises

4: "Break up with"—end a romantic relationship with someone.

Page 69: "I Was Planning to Do Room 407 a Little Later"

Model

- In line 1, to "do" a room means to clean it.
- In line 2, Speaker B makes an excuse to a superior by stating a past intention ("I was planning to do it a little later.")

Pages 70–71: "I Changed My Mind"

Model

- In the United States, to say "Let's have lunch together sometime soon." is not necessarily an invitation. It is a common and polite way of saying good-bye.

CHAPTER 8

Page 74: "Do You Want Me to Wash the Dishes?"

Model

- "No. Don't worry about it." and "That's okay/all right." are polite ways of declining an offer.
- When making an offer and then being refused, Americans consider persuading or insisting to be polite and very appropriate.
- When responding to an offer, appreciation, in addition to gratitude, is the expected response.

Page 75: "Want Any Help?"

Model

- Making an observation ("I see you're changing the oil.") is a common way to initiate a conversation.
- Dropping the auxiliary and subject from the beginning of questions is common in casual conversation. For example, "(Do you) want any help?"
- "If you don't mind.", "If you wouldn't mind.", and "If it's no trouble." are common and polite ways of accepting an offer.

Pages 76–77: "Let Me Give You a Hand"

Model

- In line 6, Speaker A interrupts Speaker B as he is trying to refuse the offer. By doing this, along with strongly insisting and even ordering ("You're not moving that desk by yourself!"), Speaker A is not being rude. Rather, Speaker A is showing care and concern for Speaker B.

Page 78: "May I Help You?"

Model

- "May/Can I help you?" and "May/Can I assist you?" are common expressions used by salespeople when approaching customers.
- In line 2, Speaker B responds to Speaker A's offer of help by saying "I'm just looking." This expression is commonly used when you don't want a salesperson's assistance.
- In line 5, Speaker A begins to tell Speaker B that the store doesn't have any digital watches by saying "I'm afraid . . ." This expression is a polite way of giving bad news.
- In line 8, "I guess not." is a polite way of saying "No" to the salesperson.

Exercises

5: More and more "sugar free" food products are being produced in the United States, due to Americans' concern about their weight, the care of their teeth, and their general health.

Page 79: "Can I Do Anything to Help?"

Model

- In line 2, Speaker B hesitates when responding to Speaker A ("Well, uh . . .") because he has just been hurt and is not sure how to answer.
- Rollerskating on city streets is a popular activity in many parts of the United States.
- In line 5, Speaker A reacts to Speaker B's accident by saying "Oh, no!". By saying this he is indicating that he thinks the accident was a terrible thing and that he sympathizes with Speaker B.
- In most situations, asking for repetition by simply saying "Huh?" or "What?" is not polite. In this situation, however, Speaker B is somewhat confused and disoriented because of the accident.
- In line 9, Speaker A is offering his hand to help Speaker B up when he says "Well, here."
- When offering help, "Allow me . . ." is formal and very polite.

Exercises

1: To be "mugged" means to be attacked by a thief on the street.

Page 80: "I'm Very Grateful to You"

Model

- In this conversation, Speaker A strongly insists on thanking Speaker B because the favor (lending the calculator) was an important one.

Exercises

5: "Fix someone up"—arrange for two people to meet each other with the hope that they will become romantically involved.

Page 81: "Words Can't Express . . ."

Model

- At a formal award ceremony such as this, very formal and flowery language is appropriate and expected.

CHAPTER 9

Pages 84–85: "Is Smoking Allowed Here?"

Models

- The passive construction and the pronouns "they" and "you" are often used when referring to some authority. The identity or source of this authority is not known or not important.
- In models 2 and 4, Speaker A says "Oh, okay." as a way of accepting the negative response he has just been given by Speaker B.

Page 86: "Please Don't Pick the Flowers"

Model

- In line 1, Speaker A is trying to be polite and not seem critical of Speaker B's actions by using the less direct "Excuse me, but I don't think . . ."
- In line 5, "Hmm." indicates that Speaker B is considering this new information while reading the sign.

Page 87: "Can I Possibly Have the Car Tonight?"

Model

- In line 1, before Speaker A directly asks for permission, he says "Could I ask you a favor?" He does this to signal to Speaker B that he wishes to make a request.
- Saying "Yes" tentatively can be done by using the expressions "I guess so.", "I suppose so.", and "I don't see (any reason) why not."
- In lines 6–7, ". . . it wouldn't hurt to ask." is a non-direct way of telling Speaker A that he should ask his mother.

Exercises

5: A hot tub (pronounced "HOT tub") is a large tub filled with very warm water in which one or more people sit to relax. Hot tubs are very popular in the United States, especially on the West Coast.

Pages 88–89: "Would You Mind If I Served Leftovers for Dinner?"

Models

- "Leftovers" consist of food not eaten at a previous meal that is for use in a later meal.
- In line 3 of the first model, "No," indicates a positive response to Speaker A's request for permission.

Exercises

2: To "skip" dessert means to go without it.
8: A "teddy bear" is a stuffed toy in the shape of a bear that is named after Theodore "Teddy" Roosevelt, the twenty-sixth president of the United States.

Page 90: "I'd Rather You Didn't"

Model

- The expressions "You see, . . ." "The reason is . . ." are used to preface an admission.
- In line 3, "Oh," indicates that Speaker A was expecting a positive response to his request. He acknowledges the negative response when he says "okay."
- In line 5, "Oh," indicates that Speaker A understands Speaker B's reason for denying permission. Speaker A also politely apologizes for not knowing the reason beforehand.

Page 91: "I Can't Do That Without an Authorization"

Model

- In line 2, Speaker B politely begins his negative response by saying "I'm afraid I can't. . . ."
- In line 4, "Oh?" indicates that Speaker A is surprised and a little disappointed at the negative response.
- In line 5, Speaker B begins his explanation by saying "Well,". Here "Well," signals the beginning of a long, yet definitive explanation.
- In this conversation, Speaker B apologizes for not having the authority himself to do what Speaker A wants. Speaker A's "I understand." indicates that she recognizes that another authority is responsible and not Speaker B.

CHAPTER 10

Page 98: "How Would You Like to Go to the Zoo?"

Model

- In line 3, Speaker A says "Me neither." This is a short conversational response meaning "I haven't either." or "Neither have I."

Exercises

4: Going for a drive in the country is a popular form of recreation in the United States.
5: In the United States, fruit farmers often allow the public to pick fruit. As a form a recreation, people pay a small fee to pick the fruit and take it home.

Page 99: "Would You By Any Chance Be Interested in Seeing a Movie?"

Model

- The expressions "Would you (by any chance) be interested in _____ing?" and "You wouldn't (by any chance) be interested in _____ing, would you?" are very indirect and allow the person being invited to comfortably decline.
- "College entrance exams." To be accepted into an American college or university, students usually need to take college entrance (or "college board") examinations.
- In line 5, Speaker A expresses disappointment when he says "That's too bad."
- In line 6, Speaker B thanks Speaker A for the invitation. Saying "Thank you" when declining an invitation is always appropriate and expected.
- Speaker B suggests that they see a movie "some other time." This is a typical expression used when declining an invitation.

Exercises

2: "Spring cleaning." After a long winter, people often set aside some time to clean the inside and outside of their homes very well.
5: "Miniature golf." This is a popular form of recreation, which is similar to the game of golf but is played in a very small area.

Page 100: "Can You Come?"

Model

- "Company picnic." Large and small businesses in the United States often have a yearly picnic for employees.
- Speaker A really wants Speaker B to come to the company picnic. In line 5, she urges him to come by asking "Is there any chance you could possibly get out of working overtime?"
- Speaker A is complimenting Speaker B in line 8 when she says "It won't be much of a company picnic without you." She is saying that Speaker B will be very missed if he doesn't come.
- "Get out of"—avoid the responsibility of doing something.
- "Do one's best"—try very hard.
- "Not be much of a"—not be very successful.
- "Get back to"—give an answer at a later time.

Exercises

1: "Slumber party." Young girls often have parties where friends come to sleep overnight.
3: "Throw a party"—have a party.
4: "Put together a game"—organize a game.
5: "Pot luck supper." This is a common type of party where each guest brings something that he or she has cooked at home. "Pot luck" means that any combination of food is possible.

Page 101: "We'd Like to Invite You and Your Wife Over for Dinner"

Model

- In line 9, Speaker A says "How does 7:00 sound?" Asking if a certain time is all right is an indirect and polite way of naming a time.

Exercises

1: "Brunch"—a combination of breakfast and lunch, usually eaten on Sundays.
2: "Barbecue"—a meal cooked outdoors on a fire.
5: "Get-together"—a small, informal party.

Page 102: "I Think I Should Be Going Now"

Model

- These speakers have been talking for some time. In line 1, Speaker A marks the end of this conversation by saying "Well," and initiates the leave-taking "ritual":
  1. Both speakers express pleasure at having seen one another.
     "It's been really nice seeing you again."
     "I'm glad we bumped into each other."
  2. Both speakers say they need to leave.
     "I think I should be going now."
     "I should get going, too."
  3. Reasons for leaving are given.
     "I need to have this car back at the rental agency by 2:00."
  4. Promises to see one another again are made.
     "Let's get together soon."
     "Okay. I'll call you."
  5. The speakers finally say their actual "good-byes."

  In the United States, the leave-taking process almost always includes the above steps.
- In line 3, Speaker A begins the announcement that he is going to leave by saying "You know,". This serves to make the announcement less direct and, therefore, more polite.
- By saying "Actually," in line 5, Speaker B is really saying "Now that you've brought up the subject of leaving, I should leave, too."

Page 103: "I've Really Got to Go Now"

Model

- The speakers have been talking for some time. When Speaker A says "By the way," she redirects the conversation to the topic of time and taking leave.
- In line 7, Speaker B begins by saying "Oh!" This is a way of acknowledging the importance of Speaker Λ's obligation to get to English class.
- In "You'd better hurry!", "had better" is a strong suggestion or recommendation.
- The expression "(I'll) see you soon/later/tomorrow/next week/. . ." is not a promise or commitment of any kind. It is simply part of the leave-taking process.

Pages 104–105: "I Don't Have Any Obligations or Commitments on Friday"

Model

- The speakers have been talking for some time. When Speaker A says "I'd love to continue this conversation, but . . ." she is setting the scene for the beginning of the leave-taking process.
- In line 3, "Well," indicates that Speaker B understands the situation and is also ready to begin the leave-taking process.
- Both speakers are checking their schedules by looking in their appointment books. Business people usually carry such a book in order to keep track of their obligations and commitments.
- In line 18, when Speaker A says "You know," she is politely reminding Speaker B of her need to leave.

CHAPTER 11

Page 108: "I've Had a Lot of Experience Taking Shorthand"

Model

- In line 3, "Then" is equivalent to "Therefore" or "In that case."
- In line 3, Speaker A asks a question using a declarative sentence with question intonation. This form is commonly used when an affirmative answer is expected.
- In line 5, the job candidate does not want to be too direct. She wants to show confidence, but at the same time humility. This is why she responds "I would say so."

Page 109: "I Haven't Altered Men's Clothing Before"

Model

- Because it is so important to show ability and confidence at a job interview, Speaker B tells what she IS able to do, rather than simply saying "No" to the interviewer's question.

Pages 110–111: "I'm Afraid I Wasn't Able to Do It"

Model

- In lines 1 and 3, Speaker A is preparing Speaker B for the bad news: first by warning him that he will be disappointed, and then by reminding Speaker B of what he had asked him to do.
- In line 3, "Well," is used to hesitate briefly and call attention to the information that will follow.
- In line 4, Speaker B has clearly been prepared for bad news as he tentatively asks "Yes . . . ?"
- In line 6, Speaker B's "Oh?" is a way of asking for an explanation that is expected.
- Speaker B is very understanding in this situation. He tells Speaker A not to worry about what happened. In line 11, he says "These things happen." This indicates that he completely excuses Speaker A and has no bad feelings toward him.
- Speaker A is very apologetic and checks to be sure that Speaker B understands the situation when he asks "You aren't upset?"

Exercises

8: "Booked"—full.
9: "Blind date." When a man and a woman arrange to go on a date without having met each other, it is a "blind date."
"Slip one's mind"—forget.

Page 112: "I Won't Be Able to Go Bowling With You"

Model

- "What's up?" is a very informal expression used to ask for information.
- Lines 1 and 2 indicate that the speakers are good friends and had been talking on the phone earlier that day.
- "Come up"—happen unexpectedly.
- In line 10, by saying "Let's plan on going bowling some other time." Speaker B is telling Speaker A not to worry about the change in plans, and that he understands the situation.

Exercises

2: Fever "breaks" when the body temperature begins to return to normal.

Page 113: "I Didn't Know That Was Required"

Model

- In line 3, Speaker A expresses surprise at what Speaker B has said. She is questioning the new information she has heard when she asks "Have I had it what?!"
- Throughout this conversation the passive voice is used. This is typical when a source of authority (the agent) is either not known or not important.
- In line 7, Speaker A again expresses surprise when she says "Oh."

Exercises

2: A Notary Public is a person qualified by law to certify officially the authenticity of certain documents. He or she signs and stamps (notarizes) these papers.

5: When two people share a bank account, it is called a "joint bank account."

Pages 114–115: "Policies and Practices"

Model

- In lines 2 and 5, Speaker B says "All right." and "I understand." to show that he is listening to and understands what Speaker A is saying.
- When Speaker A says "Now," in line 13, he is changing the focus of attention from himself to the interviewee.
- Line 29 [silent pause] means that both speakers are taking the time to review in their own minds whether they have exchanged all the necessary information.
- It is the responsibility of Speaker B to break the silence and initiate the process of formal leave taking. In line 30, Speaker B breaks the silence by using the indirect "Well,".
- In line 32, "be in touch with"—contact by phone or by letter.

CHAPTER 12

Page 118: "Please Clean Up Your Room Before Dinner"

Model

- Saying a person's name is a common way to attract his or her attention.
- The requests "Please_____., Can you (please)_____?, Will you (please)_____?, Would you (please)_____?, I'd like you to_____., I wish you would_____." are polite and informal, and are used between people who know each other well.

Exercises

1: "Roll up" the windows means to close the car windows.

Page 119: "Please Retype the Letter to Mr. Casey"

Model

- Repeating back information with question intonation is a common way of checking understanding ("The letter to Mr. Casey?")
- In line 3, "While you're at it . . ." means "at the same time."
- The responses "Certainly." and "Of course." are appropriate when speaking to a person of authority.

Exercises

5: "The Today Show" is a popular TV morning news program in the United States. Famous people are interviewed on this type of program.

Pages 120–121: "Could You Do Me a Favor?"

Models

- Asking for a favor ("Could you do me a favor?") is a polite and indirect way of preparing the other person for a request.
- The expressions for requests in these model dialogs are polite and are used when asking someone to do something you consider important.
- In line 5 (Model 2), Speaker B responds to Speaker A's request by saying "No, I wouldn't mind." She is actually saying "yes" to the request. She is responding negatively to the question "Would you mind_____?"

Exercises

5: "Keep an eye on"—watch for problems.

Pages 122–123: "I Was Wondering If You'd Be Willing to Switch Seats With Me"

Models

- "Excuse me, but . . ." is a very polite way of attracting someone's attention.
- In line 5, Speaker A hesitates, "Uh . . . yes," while thinking of what to say next.
- In line 8, when Speaker A says "Oh, thank you.", he or she is relieved and very grateful to Speaker B.

Exercises

5: In the United States, it is a common practice for restaurant employees to sing "Happy Birthday" to customers who are celebrating birthdays.

Page 124: "I'd Like to, But I'm Afraid I Can't"

Model

- Lines 1 and 3 are an example of a common exchange involving requests. In line 3, Speaker B is expressing regret when he says "Gee." When saying no to a request, Americans usually say "I'd like to, but I can't."
- In line 5, Speaker A acknowledges and accepts Speaker B's response to his request when he says "Oh, okay."
- People generally feel badly when they have to refuse a request. In line 6, Speaker B clearly feels badly and apologizes ("I'm really sorry.")

Exercises

4: A "Little League" team is a baseball team made up of children.
5: In the United States, 55 miles per hour is the maximum speed limit on most highways. (The policeman in Exercise 5 doesn't like to give speeding tickets and is being extremely polite about it.)

Page 125: "Can I Take a Message?"

Model

- The form of this telephone conversation is very common.
    1. The caller initiates the conversation by saying "Hello."
    2. The caller asks to speak to someone.
    3. The person answering the phone tells the caller the person is not at home.
    4. The person answering the phone asks if he can take a message.
    5. The caller says yes and identifies himself.
    6. The caller gives the message to the person answering the phone.
    7. The person answering the phone says that he or she will convey the message.
    8. The caller expresses gratitude.
    9. The speakers say good-bye.
- In line 6, Speaker A asks "Is that it?" This expression means "Is that everything?"
- In line 7, Speaker B says "I guess so." This is a less direct way of saying "Yes."
- In the United States, a friend is often asked to bring food or beverages to a party given by a close friend.

CHAPTER 13

Page 130: "Do You Have Any Suggestions?"

Model

- In line 3, the salesclerk repeats "A fresh-tasting toothpaste." as a way of hesitating while he thinks of a brand to recommend.
- The expressions: "Everybody says . . ., People say . . ., Everybody tells me . . ., Most people say . . ., I hear . . ., They say . . ." are used when reporting generally known information.

Page 131: "How About Going Window-Shopping?"

Model

- In line 3, Speaker A begins to make a suggestion by saying "Well,". This makes the suggestion which follows less direct and more open to discussion.
- In line 4, Speaker B prefaces her negative response by saying "Oh, I don't know." By being less direct, the speaker is softening the negative answer to come.
- In line 5, Speaker B says "Any other suggestions?" This is a shorthand form of the question "Do you have any other suggestions?"

Page 132: "I Strongly Advise You"

Model

- Speaker A is an authority figure in this situation and makes her advice very strong when she says in line 1, "As your guidance counselor, . . ."
- The expressions: "I (strongly) advise you to_____., I urge you to_____., I recommend that you_____., I recommend_____ing." are strong, authoritative ways of giving advice.
- In line 3, Speaker B questions Speaker A's advice because, in this case, she really does not want to take Physics!
- In line 6, Speaker B finally accepts this new information when she says "Oh."

Exercises

5: "Lose your shirt"—lose all of your money or investments.

Page 133: "Can I Offer You Some Advice?"

Model

- "You seem troubled/upset., You don't seem to be yourself today.": A person who knows another person well will feel it is appropriate to make this comment in order to express concern and ask what the matter is.
- The two speakers in the model clearly know each other well. Speaker A not only recognizes that Speaker B has a problem, but is familiar enough with him that he asks about the problem.
- The expressions: "Is anything the matter/wrong/bothering you?" are common ways of asking a friend to be truthful about how he or she feels.

- Because it is important to be very tactful when giving advice, Speaker A uses the indirect "Well," and ASKS if he can offer some advice in line 4.

Exercises

1: "Security deposit." In the United States, when a tenant agrees to rent an apartment, the landlord often requires a security deposit. This money is to be returned when the tenant moves out.
4: "Burning me out." To be burnt out means that an activity or responsibility is causing too much pressure or stress. "Take time off"—take time away from work.
5: "Level with"—tell someone the truth.

Pages 134–135: "I Need Your Advice on Something"

Model

- The two speakers are friends. It is usually a friend, or someone known well, who is asked for this kind of advice.
- The expressions in this model dialog are less direct ways of offering suggestions when someone asks for advice.
- In the last line of the conversation, Speaker A says "Hmm. I hadn't thought of that." This means that she thinks Speaker B's advice is good and she will think seriously about doing what Speaker B suggests.
- It is becoming increasingly common in the United States for mothers of young children to work outside the home. While a mother works, the child often stays at a day-care center where he or she is taken care of by professional childcare workers.

Exercises

2: "Be fed up with"—be very tired of something and ready to stop.
3: "Weight Watchers" is a club for overweight people who wish to lose weight.
5: "Have it up to here"—be very tired of something and ready to stop.
7: In the United States, many people see a psychiatrist or therapist when feeling depressed.
8: The U.S. military helps pay for the college education of those who enlist.
9: "Be at each other's throats" means that two people are very annoyed with each other.

Page 136: "Thanks for the Warning"

Models

- The expressions "(Be) careful!, Look out!, Watch out!" are used when warning someone of an immediate danger.
- The situations in Model 1 and Model 2 are both situations that could result in injury. In such situations, it is common and acceptable to use the imperative form, "Careful!"
- In both models, Speaker B quickly answers "Huh?" in line 2. This is an informal response, but appropriate because in each case the person responding is surprised and caught off guard.
- In line 5, Speaker B is asking Speaker A why something is dangerous when he or she says "Oh?"

Page 137: "Excellent Suggestions"

Model

- In line 10, Speaker B says "Make it a point to eat at Maxim's." This expression means "Really try to . . ."
- In line 13, Speaker B says "Oh," to signal that she has just remembered something important.

CHAPTER 14

Page 140: "I Agree"

Model

- A tag question, such as the one in line 2, "didn't we," is often used to emphasize agreement.

Page 141: "That's Just What I Was Thinking"

Model

- In line 3, "I mean," indicates that Speaker A wants to support his previous statement with further information.
- In line 4, Speaker B is not being impolite when she interrupts Speaker A. She interrupts to show Speaker A that she strongly agrees.

Exercises

1: "Off key"—not in tune with the music.
4: "Corny jokes" are jokes which are very simple and not very funny.
5: "Up to something"—to be doing something secretively.

Page 142: "That Might Be True"

Model

- In line 2, Speaker B is tentatively agreeing with Speaker A ("That might be true."), but at the same time is expressing his own opinion, "But wouldn't you say that . . .?"
- In line 2, Speaker B uses a negative question because he wants and expects Speaker A to agree with his opinion.

Exercises

5: "Leaves a lot to be desired" is a polite way of saying that something is not very good.

Page 143: "I'm Afraid You're Right"

Model

- In this conversation, Speaker A makes a personal observation about Speaker B. The two speakers are clearly good friends.
- In line 3, Speaker B reluctantly agrees with Speaker A's observation ("I'm afraid you're right.") This is because she is not very happy about the reality of the situation.
- In the United States, being quiet and withdrawn is often considered unusual behavior and may indicate that something is wrong.

Exercises

1 & 2: The first speaker's observations in these two exercises are only acceptable when made by a very close friend or relative. It would be extremely rude to make such observations about people you do not know well.

Page 144: "That Isn't Exactly Right"

Model

- In this conversation, Speaker A is Speaker B's superior (his boss). Speaker B therefore corrects Speaker A using very indirect expressions ("Excuse me, Mr. Perkins, but actually . . ."), which makes the correction polite and acceptable.
- In line 6, Speaker A says "Oh." He is indicating that he understands his mistake.

Page 145: "That's Not True"

Model

- In this conversation, Speaker A is confronting Speaker B in a very direct way. The speakers are sisters, so Speaker A feels quite free to be very direct.
- The expressions: "Come on!, Look!, Listen!, Admit it!, Face it!" are informal ways of persuading someone.
- In line 5, Speaker A says "Well," as a way of hesitating and showing doubt.

Pages 146–147: "I'm Not So Sure About That"

Model

- Speaker A initiates this conversation with a negative question. She is assuming that Speaker B will agree with her opinion.
- In line 3, Speaker B indirectly (politely) disagrees with Speaker A's opinion by saying "I'm not so sure about that."
- In line 4, Speaker A shows surprise and asks for clarification when she says "Oh?"
- In line 5, Speaker B politely says he disagrees and expresses his own opinion on the topic.
- In the last line, Speaker A expresses disagreement and doubtfulness when she says "Well, . . ."

CHAPTER 15

Page 150: "I'm Positive"

Models

- In the first model, the father of the bride is asking his daughter if she wants to "go through with this." Her decision to get married is a big step and her father wants her to be absolutely sure at this important moment.

Exercises

5: Sherlock Holmes is a fictitious British detective made famous in the mystery novels of Sir Arthur Conan Doyle. Holmes' good friend Doctor Watson frequently aids him in solving mysterious crimes.

Page 151: "In All Likelihood"

Model

- In line 3, Speaker A repeats Speaker B's response to his question as a way of showing interest in her decision.
- In line 3, Speaker A says "Oh." as he contemplates this new information.

Exercises

4: In the United States, when young girls turn sixteen years old, they frequently have a special "sweet sixteen" birthday party to which they invite both boys and girls.

5: A popular kind of American TV show is the "game show." On these programs, contestants can win large prizes if they answer questions correctly or make the right decisions.

Page 152: "It Should Arrive Any Minute Now"

Model

- In line 2, Speaker B uses an expression of probability rather than certainty because although his response is probably correct, he can't be absolutely sure.
- In line 3, Speaker A is looking for reassurance when she checks, "Any minute now?"

4: In the United States, when a customer deposits a check in a bank, the check normally takes a period of time to "clear" (for funds to be transferred). Until the check clears, the customer usually does not have access to those funds.

Page 153: "She Must Have Gotten Stuck in Traffic"

Model

- In line 2, "show up"—arrive.
- In line 3, Speaker B says "Oh," as a way of lessening the seriousness of the situation and making Speaker A feel better.
- Speaker B keeps on trying to put Speaker A's mind at ease by forming intelligent hypotheses about why the teacher is late for class.
- In line 3, "get stuck"—be unable to move.
- In line 5, Speaker A says "I don't know" meaning he is not sure he agrees with Speaker B's idea.
- In line 7, Speaker B continues to try to stop Speaker A from worrying when she says "Now. . . ." In English, the word "now" is often used to calm or to soothe.

Exercises

2: "Be tied up"—be busy.
3: "Lose track of time"—not be conscious of the time of day.
5: "Be caught up"—be entangled.

Page 154: "I Might Buy the Cheap One"

Model

- In line 2, Speaker A uses the verb "purchase" when he approaches Speaker B. Salespeople use this word; in normal conversation, people usually use the verb "buy."
- In line 3, Speaker B is very indirectly asking for advice when he expresses uncertainty.
- Normally it is impolite to use the imperative "Don't . . . !" with strangers. When it is prefaced with an expression such as "Take my advice, . . ." it is appropriate.
- In line 5, Speaker A advises and warns Speaker B when he says "Don't buy the cheap one! You'll be disappointed." In English, advice is frequently accompanied by a warning.

Exercises

3: A "subcompact" is a very small car by U.S. standards.

Page 155: "It's a Possibility"

Model

- In line 5, Speaker B is trying not to be too direct when reacting to Speaker A's news (though she clearly thinks what Speaker A plans to do is a bad idea). She begins to give her opinion tactfully by saying "Well,".
- Speaker B is being tactful and forceful at the same time. In line 6, she asks the question "Why?", does not wait for Speaker A to answer, and then asks a negative question, indicating how strongly she feels about Speaker A's plans.

Exercises

1: "Drop out." In the United States, if a young person does not complete the four years needed for a college degree, he or she "drops out."
5: "Run away from home and join the circus." Young children sometimes consider leaving home, or actually do so when their home or family situation becomes very stressful. In earlier days, joining the circus was a common childhood fantasy.

Page 156: "There's Not Much Chance of That Happening"

Model

- In line 4, Speaker A responds by saying "Oh?" and asking whether Speaker B is sure, in order to check how certain Speaker B is about the prediction.

Exercises

5: The speakers are talking about characters in an episode of a daily "soap opera." This type of TV drama depicts the ongoing problems of its characters.

Page 157: "I Don't Know For Sure"

Model

- In line 9, Speaker A doesn't understand that Speaker B is asking for advice, so he asks "Excuse me?"
- Speaker A does not want to be too direct with his advice, so he hesitates and makes sure that Speaker B understands that he is only expressing his personal opinion.

CHAPTER 16

Page 162: "Good Job!"

Model

- In line 2, Speaker B says "Do you really think so?" When receiving compliments, it is common and very polite to question the complimenter's sincerity.
- In line 7, Speaker B thanks Speaker A for the compliment. Gratitude is always expected when a compliment is given.

Page 163: "Do You Approve of the Way I Clipped Fifi's Hair?"

Model

- In the United States, people do not generally like to criticize others. When expressing disapproval, it is important to be indirect and tactful. In this conversation, in line 2, Speaker B hesitates and prepares Speaker A for her disapproving words when she says, "Can I be frank with you?" In line 4, Speaker B uses the passive voice to "soften" the criticism by making it a little less direct.
- In line 6, Speaker A politely accepts Speaker B's expression of disapproval and apologizes.

Exercises

5: In this situation, the pilot is being "playful" with the young passenger.

Page 164: "You Really Shouldn't Have Raised Your Voice to the Boss"

Model

- In line 1, Speaker A makes it very clear that he does not want to insult or directly reprimand Speaker B. He wants to point out Speaker B's mistake as a favor to a friend.
- In line 3, by responding "Oh?" Speaker B is in fact asking "Do you really think so?"
- In line 5, to say that something is "not a very good idea" is a very tactful way of expressing disapproval.
- In line 6, Speaker B says "Hmm." while thinking about the criticism that Speaker A has offered.

Page 165: "I Really Wish You Hadn't Removed the Coffee Machine"

Model

- Speaker A delicately initiates the topic of the coffee machine because she does not wish to criticize her manager too directly. She does this by saying "I hate to say it . . . but."
- Speaker A expresses disapproval of Speaker B's action by pointing out the negative results of his action (employee morale is down).

Exercises

1: "Not sleep a wink"—not sleep at all.
4: "Laughing stock"—the object of ridicule.

Page 166: "I Apologize"

Model

- In line 3, Speaker A draws attention to new information by introducing it with "You know,".

Exercises

5: "Mess up"—make mistakes.

Page 167: "I Hope You'll Forgive Me"

Exercises

2: In the United States, it is common for private residents to have their daily newspapers delivered to their door by a young person in the neighborhood.
4: "Petty cash"—cash kept on hand by small businesses for minor expenses.

Page 168: "Maybe You Ought to Apologize"

Model

- Speaker A (a mother) knows Speaker B (her son) well enough to notice that Speaker B has hurt his father's feelings. While Speaker A doesn't actually suggest that Speaker B should apologize until the end of the conversation, this is the reason that Speaker A has brought up the entire subject.
- In the summertime in the United States, it is a tradition to have outdoor barbecues. The cooking at these barbecues is generally done by the man in the family.

Exercises

3: "Jingle"—a little song used in radio and TV commercials to advertise a product.
5: "Nerd"—a derogatory term used to describe someone who is considered unusual in some way. Children, who tend to identify very strongly with the behavior, manner of dress, and opinions of their friends, frequently use this term to refer to someone who doesn't conform to the group.

Page 169: "I'm Afraid I Can't Keep My Promise"

Model

- This conversation is an example of a common pattern or formula used when apologizing for a broken promise or commitment:
  1. Speaker A sets the scene by announcing that bad news is coming.
  2. Speaker A reminds Speaker B of a promise that was made earlier.
  3. Speaker A admits that the promise was not fulfilled.
  4. Speaker A gives a reason or excuse for not fulfilling the promise.
  5. Speaker A asks for forgiveness.
- The TOEFL, Test of English as a Foreign Language, is a standardized test that must be taken by most foreign students wishing to study at U.S. colleges and universities.

CHAPTER 17

Page 172: "It's a Shame"

Model

- Both speakers are very disappointed and throughout this conversation are expressing regret.
- In line 5, Speaker B says "I'm afraid so." This phrase is used to express unhappy, reluctant agreement.
- "Out of the question"—impossible.

Page 173: "You Know What I Wish?"

Model

- The phrase "You know what I wish?" is commonly used to initiate a topic and at the same time express a wish.
- In line 4, "I know." means "I know what you mean."

Pages 174–175: "If Only I Could Communicate With My Boss"

Model

- In line 3, Speaker B is preparing Speaker A for an unexpected, negative response to her question when he says "Do you really want to know?"
- The expressions for admitting "The truth is . . ., The fact of the matter is . . ." are used when negative information is to follow.
- In the last line of the conversation, Speaker B makes it clear to Speaker A that he has already made up his mind to continue trying very hard when he says "Oh, don't worry."

Exercises

5: "Keep up with"—learn as quickly as.

Pages 176–177: "I Could Kick Myself!"

Model

- In line 1, Speaker A expresses his frustration with himself. In line 3, he admits making a mistake and describes the error to Speaker B.
- The expressions: "I could kill myself!, I could shoot myself!, I could (just) die!" are strong, colorful ways of expressing regret and are not meant literally.
- In line 5, Speaker B responds with "Oh!" This indicates that she has realized the seriousness of the problem.

Exercises

4: The Boy Scouts of America is a national organization that encourages young boys ("cub scouts" who later become "boy scouts") to be good citizens. Groups led by a scout leader, often one of the scout's fathers, take hikes in the woods, go camping, and do other activities. A Girl Scout's organization offers similar activities for young girls.
7: "Put off"—postpone.
8: "On the spot"—immediately.

Page 178: "I Regret Having to Fire Mr. Smith"

Model

- In line 2, Speaker B begins to speak by saying "Well," making what she has to say less direct. It is not appropriate to be too direct in this situation. Someone has made a decision and it is not Speaker B's place to oppose that decision.
- In line 5, Speaker B expresses surprise at the new information when she says "Oh!"
- In the last line of the conversation, Speaker B again says "Well," this time meaning "Now I understand."

Exercises

1: In the United States, shopping malls (large enclosed shopping centers, often situated away from the center of cities) have come to replace smaller downtown shopping areas because of the convenience they offer: large parking lots and a variety of stores in one location.
3: Many apartment buildings in the United States are being converted into condominiums. This is forcing many tenants, who had previously paid rent for their apartments, to either buy the apartments or move out.

Page 179: "I've Been Thinking"

Model

- In line 2, Speaker B responds to Speaker A's initiating a topic by responding "What?" meaning "What have you been thinking?"
- In line 5, Speaker B responds by asking "Really?". This is expressing surprise and showing interest in what Speaker A is saying.
- In line 8, Speaker B is thinking over the new information when responding "Hmm."
- In the last line of the conversation, Speaker B says "Oh." meaning "I understand."

CHAPTER 18

Page 182: "Nice Day Today, Isn't It"

Model

- It is common to shorten a phrase such as "(It's a) nice day today." It is also very common to initiate a conversation with a stranger by introducing the topic of the weather.
- Speaker B was not expecting to be spoken to and did not hear Speaker A's comment. In line 2, he responds by asking for repetition, "Pardon me?"
- In line 4, Speaker B indicates that he now understands Speaker A's comment when he says "Oh, yes."

Exercises

In all of the exercises, two strangers are talking. The exercises are all examples of common and appropriate ways of initiating conversations with strangers.

Page 183: "Don't You Just Hate People Who Cut in Line?

Models

- Cutting in line and throwing litter in parks are annoying to most people. When Speaker A in Model 1 uses a negative question, he is expecting agreement. Similarly in Model 2, Speaker A expects agreement with her comment about littering.
- In both conversations, the speakers are complaining about people who are not conforming to known standards of appropriate public behavior.

Exercises

4: In the United States, handicapped people by law have the right of access to public places. This includes ramps at building entrances, elevators, and reserved parking areas.
5: "Tacky"—a slang expression meaning inappropriate or not in style.

Page 184: "Let Me Put It This Way"

Model

- In line 1, Speaker A is using "technical jargon," special vocabulary that is understood by members of the profession (in this case, dentistry), but may not be understood by the general public.
- In line 3, Speaker A agrees to "translate" what he is trying to say into simpler language so Speaker B will understand.

Page 185: "What You're Really Saying

Model

- In line 3, Speaker A does not want Speaker B to feel insulted. She calms him by saying "Now" and advises him not to misinterpret her comment. She is insisting that nothing more was implied by her comment about his jacket.
- In line 5, Speaker B concedes that he was perhaps mistaken when he says "Oh."

Page 186: "Excuse Me for Interrupting"

Model

- It is polite and appropriate to apologize when interrupting.

Exercises

4: There are three major TV networks in the United States: ABC, NBC, and CBS. Each one has a large news department with many reporters.
5: The Internal Revenue Service (IRS) is the federal agency in charge of collecting taxes. The Central Intelligence Agency (CIA) is responsible for national security.

Page 187: "By the Way . . ."

Model

- In line 3, Speaker B interrupts Speaker A and redirects the conversation.
- Xerox is the name of a large U.S. corporation and is also the brand name of the copying machines produced by that company. Occasionally the brand name of a very well-known product will, over time, become a general label. For instance, many people refer to all copying machines as "Xerox" machines, even though they are not produced

by the Xerox Company. Similarly, many refer to all cola drinks as "Coke" and all tissues as "Kleenex," both of which are brand names.

Pages 188–189: "In My Opinion"

Model

- By repeating the topic of Speaker A's question, "Nuclear energy." in line 2, Speaker B is indicating that he has a lot to say about the issue.
- In line 6, Speaker A says "But don't you think" as a way of counteracting Speaker B's comment.
- In line 11, Speaker A interrupts Speaker B because she feels strongly about her opinion and wishes to express it.
- In line 15, "You know," is an indirect and therefore polite way of creating a pause in the discussion.
- "See eye to eye"—agree.
- "I guess not." is a polite, indirect way of expressing agreement.

INDEX OF FUNCTIONS AND CONVERSATION STRATEGIES

INDEX OF GRAMMATICAL STRUCTURES

224

BULLET
PARK

BULLET
PARK

a novel by

JOHN CHEEVER

ALFRED A. KNOPF, New York 1969

To

Robert and Susan Cowley

PART
ONE

PART
ONE

I

Paint me a small railroad station then, ten minutes before dark. Beyond the platform are the waters of the Wekonsett River, reflecting a somber afterglow. The architecture of the station is oddly informal, gloomy but unserious, and mostly resembles a pergola, cottage or summer house although this is a climate of harsh winters. The lamps along the platform burn with a nearly palpable plaintiveness. The setting seems in some way to be at the heart of the matter. We travel by plane, oftener than not, and yet the spirit of our country seems to have remained a country of railroads. You wake in a pullman bedroom at three a.m. in a city the name of which you do not know and may never discover. A man stands on the platform with a child on his shoulders. They are waving goodbye to some traveler, but what is the child doing up so late and why is the man crying? On a siding beyond the platform there is a lighted dining car where a waiter sits alone at a table, adding up his accounts. Beyond this is a water tower and beyond this a well-lighted and empty street. Then you think happily that this is your country—unique, mysterious and vast. One has no such feelings in airplanes, airports and the trains of other nations.

A train arrives, a passenger departs and is met by a real-estate agent named Hazzard, for who else will know the exact age, usefulness, value and well-being of the houses in the town. "Welcome to Bullet Park. We hope you'll like it well enough to join us here." Mr. Hazzard does not happen to live in Bullet Park. His name, like that of every other licensed real-estate dealer, is nailed to the trees in vacant lots, but he transacts his business in a small office in the next village. The stranger has left his wife in the Hotel Plaza, watching television. The search for shelter seems to him to go on at a nearly primordial level. Prices are high these days and nothing is exactly what one wants. The scuffed paint and discarded portables of earlier owners seem as alive and demanding as the clothing and papers one sorts out after a death in the family. The house or the flat that he looks for, he knows, will have had to have appeared at least twice in his dreams. When it is all over, when the gardens are planted and the furniture is settled, the rigors of the journey will have been concealed; but on this evening the blood-memory of travel and migrations courses through his veins. The people of Bullet Park intend not so much to have arrived there as to have been planted and grown

there, but this of course was untrue. Disorder, moving
vans, bank loans at high interest, tears and desperation
had characterized most of their arrivals and departures.

"This is our commercial center," says Hazzard. "We
have all sorts of plans for its improvement. There's Powder Hill," says Hazzard, nodding towards a lighted hill
on their right. "There's a property there I'd like to show
you. The asking price is fifty-seven thousand. Five bedrooms, three baths . . ." The lights of Powder Hill twin-
kled, its chimneys smoked and a pink plush toilet-seat
cover flew from a clothesline. Seen at an improbable distance by some zealous and vengeful adolescent, ranging
over the golf links, the piece of plush would seem to be
the imprimatur, the guerdon, the accolade and banner of
Powder Hill behind which marched, in tight English
shoes, the legions of wife-swapping, Jew-baiting, booze-
fighting spiritual bankrupts. Oh damn them all, thought
the adolescent. Damn the bright lights by which no one
reads, damn the continuous music which no one hears,
damn the grand pianos that no one can play, damn the
white houses mortgaged up to their rain gutters, damn
them for plundering the ocean for fish to feed the mink
whose skins they wear and damn their shelves on which
there rests a single book—a copy of the telephone direc-
tory, bound in pink brocade. Damn their hypocrisy,
damn their cant, damn their credit cards, damn their dis-
counting the wilderness of the human spirit, damn their
immaculateness, damn their lechery and damn them
above all for having leached from life that strength, mal-

odorousness, color and zeal that give it meaning. Howl, howl, howl.

But the adolescent, as adolescents always are, would be mistaken. Take the Wickwires, for instance, whose white house (estimated resale price: $65,000) Hazzard and the traveler were passing. If the social customs of Powder Hill were to be attacked by the adolescent the Wickwires would make a splendid target. They were charming, they were brilliant, they were incandescent, and their engagement calendar was booked solid from Labor Day to the Fourth of July. They were quite literally social workers—celebrants—using their charm and their brilliance to make things go at a social level. They were people who understood that cocktails and dinner in their time and place were as important to the welfare of the community as the village caucus, the school board and the municipal services. For a community that had so few altars—four to be exact—and none of them sacrificial, they seemed, as serious and dedicated celebrants, to have improvised a sacrificial altar on which they had literally given up some flesh and blood. They were always falling downstairs, bumping into sharp-edged furniture and driving their cars into ditches. When they arrived at a party they would be impeccably dressed but her right arm would be in a sling. He would support a game leg with a gold-headed cane and wear dark glasses. She had sprained her arm in a fall. He had broken his leg in the winter and the dark glasses concealed a mouse that had the thrilling reds and purples of a late winter moon,

6

cloud-buried and observed by some yearning and bewildered youth. Their brilliance was not diminished by their injuries. In fact they almost always appeared with some limb in a sling, some extremity bandaged, some show of court plaster.

Their brilliance, their ardor as celebrants, is serious. After any common weekend when they have lunched and dined out for three days running the seriousness of their role can best be estimated when the light of Monday morning shines on them as they sleep. When the alarm rings he mistakes it for the telephone. Their children are away at school and he concludes that one of them is sick or in trouble. When he understands that it is the alarm and not the telephone he puts his feet onto the floor. He groans. He swears. He stands. He feels himself to be a hollow man but one who has only recently been eviscerated and who can recall what it felt like to have a skinful of lively lights and vitals. She whimpers in pain and covers her face with a pillow. Feeling himself to be a painful cavity he goes down the hall to the bathroom. Looking at himself in the mirror he gives a loud cry of terror and revulsion. His eyes are red, his face is scored with lines, his light hair seems clumsily dyed. He possesses for a moment the curious power of being able to frighten himself. He soaks his face with water and shaves his beard. This exhausts his energies and he comes back down the hall to the bedroom, says that he will take a later train, returns to bed and pulls the blankets over his face to shut out the morning. She whimpers and cries.

7

She then leaves the bed, her nightgown hooked up over her comely backside. She goes to the bathroom but she shuts her eyes as she passes the mirror. Back in bed she covers her face with a pillow and they both lie there, groaning loudly. He then joins her on her side of the bed and they engage in a back-breaking labor of love that occupies them for twenty minutes and leaves them both with a grueling headache. He has already missed the 8:11, the 8:22 and the 8:30. "Coffee," he mutters, and gets out of bed once more. He goes downstairs to the kitchen. Stepping into the kitchen he lets out another cry of pain when he sees the empties on the shelf by the sink.

They are ranged there like the gods in some pantheon of remorse. Their intent seems to be to force him to his knees and to wring from him some prayer. "Empties, oh empties, most merciful empties have mercy upon me for the sake of Jack Daniels and Seagram Distillers." Their immutable emptiness gives them a look that is cruel and censorious. Their labels—scotch, gin and bourbon—have the ferocity of Chinese demons, but he definitely has the feeling that if he tried to placate them with a genuflection they would be merciless. He drops them into a wastebasket, but this does not dispose of their force. He puts some water on to boil and feeling for the wall like a blind man makes his way back to the bedroom where he can hear his wife's cries of pain. "Oh I wish I were dead," she cries, "I wish I were dead." "There, there, dear," he says thickly. "There, there." He sets out a clean suit, a shirt, a tie and some shoes and then gets back into bed again and pulls the blankets over his face. It is now close to nine and the garden is filled with light. They hear the schoolbus at the corner, sounding its horn for the Marsden boy. The week has begun its splendid procession of days. The kettle begins to whistle.

He gets out of bed for the third time, returns to the kitchen and makes some coffee. He brings a cup for them both. She gets out of bed, washes her face without examining it and then returns to bed. He puts on some underwear and then returns to bed himself. For the next hour they are up and down, in and out, struggling to rejoin the stream of things, and finally he dresses and racked by vertigo, melancholy, nausea and fitful erections he boards his Gethsemane—the Monday-morning 10:48.

There was nothing hypocritical about the Wickwires' Monday mornings, and so much for the adolescent.

The stranger might observe that the place seems very quiet; they seem to have come inland from the sounds of wilderness—gulls, trains, cries of pain and love, creaking things, hammerings, gunfire—not even a child practices the piano in this precinct of disinfected acoustics. They pass the Howestons (7 bedrooms, 5 baths, $65,000) and the Welchers (3 bedrooms, 1½ baths, $31,000). The wind draws through the beam of their headlight some yellow elm leaves, a credit card, potato chips, bills, checks and ashes. Are there songs for this place, the stranger might wonder; and there are. Songs sung to children and by children, songs for cooking, songs for undressing, water songs, ecclesiastical doggerel (We throw our crowns at

Your feet), madrigals, folk songs, and a little native music. Mr. Elmsford (6 bedrooms, 3 baths, $53,000) dusts off his tarnished psalter which is something he never mastered and sings: "Hotchkiss, Yale, an indifferent marriage, three children and twenty-three years with the Universal Tuffa Corporation. Oh, why am I so disappointed," he sings, "why does everything seem to have passed me by." There is a rush for the door before he starts his second verse but he goes on singing. "Why does everything taste of ashes, why is there no brilliance or promise in my affairs." The waiters empty the ashtrays, the bartender locks an iron screen over the bottles and they finally turn off the lights, but he goes on singing, "I tried, I tried, I did the best I knew how to do so why should I feel so sad and blue?" "This place is shut, mister," they tell him, "and you're the guy who shut it." Then there are the affirmative singers: "Bullet Park is growing, growing, Bullet Park is here to stay, Bullet Park shows great improvement, every day in every way . . ."

Vital statistics? They were of no importance. The divorce rate was way down, the suicide rate was a secret; traffic casualties averaged twenty-two a year because of a winding highway that seemed to have been drawn on the map by a child with a grease pencil. The winters were too inclement for citrus fruit but much too clement for the native white birch.

Hazzard drew his car up in front of a white house with lighted windows. "This is the property I had in mind for you," he said. "I hope she won't be in. She's not much of a

10

saleswoman. She said she was going out." He rang the bell but Mrs. Heathcup opened the door. It appeared that she was preparing to go out but had not quite made it. She was a stocky woman with skewered silver-gilt hair, wearing a bathrobe. On the tip of one of her silk slippers there was a cloth rose; on the other there was none. "Well you're welcome to look," she said in a hoarse, carrying voice. "I hope you'll like it well enough to buy it. I'm getting a little tired of having people track mud through the place and then decide on something else. It's a lovely house and everything works—you'll have to take my word for that—but I've known people around here to sell houses with dangerous wiring, backed-up septic tanks, obsolete plumbing and leaky roofs. There's nothing like that here. Before my husband passed away he saw that everything was in apple-pie order and the only reason I'm selling is because there's nothing here for me, now that he's gone. Nothing at all. There's nothing in a place like this for any single woman. Speaking of tribes, it's like a regular tribe. Widows, divorcées, single men, the tribal elders give them all the gate. Fifty-seven is my price. That's not my asking price, it's my final price. We put twenty thousand into the place and my husband painted it every single year before he passed away. In January he'd paint the kitchen. Saturdays and Sundays and nights, that is. Then he'd paint the hallway and the living room and the dining room and the bedrooms and then next January he'd start all over again in the kitchen. He was painting the dining room the day he passed away.

I was upstairs. When I say that he passed away I don't want you to think that he died in his sleep. While he was painting I heard him talking to himself. 'I can't stand it any longer,' he said. I still don't know what he meant. Then he went out into the garden and shot himself. That was when I found out what kind of neighbors I had. You can look all over the world but you won't find neighbors as kind and thoughtful as the people in Bullet Park. As soon as they heard about my husband passing away they came over here to comfort me. There must have been ten or twelve of them and we all had something to drink and they were so comforting that I almost forgot what had happened. I mean it didn't seem as though anything had happened. Well here's the living room. Eighteen by thirty-two. We've had fifty guests here for cocktails but it never seems crowded. I'll sell you the rug for half of what I gave for it. All wool. If your wife wants the curtains I'm sure we can work something out. Do you have a daughter? This hallway would be a beautiful place for a wedding. I mean when the bride throws down her bouquet. Now the dining room . . ."

The dinner table was set for twelve with soup plates, wine glasses, candlesticks and wax flowers. "I always keep my table set," said Mrs. Heathcup. "I haven't entertained for months but Mr. Heathcup hated to see an empty table and so I always keep it set, sort of in memory. An empty table depressed him. I change the setting once or twice a week. There are four churches in the village. I suppose you know about the Gorey Brook

Country Club. It has a good eighteen-hole course designed by Pete Ellison, four en tout cas courts and a pool. I hope you're not Jewish. They're very strict about that. I don't have a pool myself and frankly it's something of a limitation. When people start talking about pool chemicals and so forth you'll find yourself left out of the conversation. I've had an estimate made and you can have one put in the back garden for eight thousand. Maintenance comes to around twenty-five a week and they charge a hundred to open and close it. The neighbors, as I've said, are wonderful people although they take some knowing. You might think Harry Plutarch, who lives across the street, a little odd unless you knew the whole story. His wife ran off with Howie Jones. What she did was to have a moving van come to the house one morning and take everything out of the place except a chair, a single bed and a parrot cage. When he came home from work he found an empty house and he's been living with a chair, a bed and a parrot ever since. Here's a copy of the evening paper. It might give you some idea of what the place is like . . ."

As Mrs. Heathcup flushed toilets, opened and shut doors, the stranger, whose name was Hammer, felt a lack of interest in her house increase until it seemed like a kind of melancholy, but the tragic and brightly lighted place was commodious and efficient and one lived in such places. There was the ghost of poor Heathcup, but every house has a ghost. "I think it's what we want," he said. "I'll bring Mrs. Hammer out tomorrow and let her decide."

Hazzard drove him back to the railroad station then and left him there. Suburban waiting rooms are not maintained and the place had been sacked. Broken windows let in the night wind. The clock face was smashed. The hands of the clock were gone. The architect, so many years ago, had designed the building with some sense of the erotic and romantic essence of travel, but all his inventions had been stripped or defaced and Hammer found himself in a warlike ruin. He opened the paper and read: "The Lithgow Club had its annual dinner on Thursday evening at Harvey's restaurant. The program began with a parade of sweethearts—wives of the members—which was followed by a demonstration of the hula given by Mrs. Leonard A. Atkinson who was accompanied by her husband on the ukelele . . .

"Seventeen debutantes were presented to society at the Gorey Brook Country Club . . .

"Mr. Lewis Harwich was burned to death last night when a can of charcoal igniter exploded and set fire to his clothing during a barbecue party in the garden of his home at 23 Redburn Circle . . .

"School taxes expected to increase."

He caught the 7:14.

II

Holy Communion. Sexagesima. Nailles heard a cricket in the chancel and the noise of a tin drum from the rain gutters while he said his prayers. His sense of the church calendar was much more closely associated with the weather than with the revelations and strictures in Holy Gospel. St. Paul meant blizzards. St. Mathias meant a thaw. For the marriage at Cana and the cleansing of the leper the oil furnace would still be running although the vents in the stained-glass windows were sometimes open to the raw spring air. Abstain from fornication. Possess your vessel in honor. Jesus departs from the coast of Tyre and Sidon as the skiing ends. For the crucifixion a bobsled stands stranded in a flowerbed, its painter coiled among the early violets. The trout streams open for the resurrection. The crimson cloths at Pentecost and the miracle of the tongues meant swimming. St. James and Revelations fell on the first warm days of summer when you could smell the climbing roses by the window and when an occasional stray bee would buzz into the house of God and buzz out again. Trinity carried one into summer, the dog days and the drought, and the parable of the Samaritan was spoken as the season changed and the gentle sounds of the night garden turned as harsh as hardware. The flesh lusteth against the spirit to the smoke of leaf fires as did the raising of the dead. Then one was back again with St. Andrew and the snows of Advent.

This division of Nailles's attention during worship had begun when, as a young boy, he had spent most of his time in church examining the forms captured in the grained-oak pews. In certain lights and frames of mind they seemed quite coherent. There was a charge of Mongol horsemen in the third pew on the right, next to the font. In the pew ahead of that there appeared to be a broad lake—some body of water—with a lighthouse on a peninsula. In the pew across the aisle there was a clash of arms and in the pew ahead of that there seemed to be a herd of cattle. This lack of concentration did not distress Nailles. He did not expect to part with his flesh or his memory in the narthex. His concerns in church remained at least partially matter-of-fact, and on this winter morning he noticed that Mrs. Trencham was carrying on her particular brand of competitive churchmanship. Mrs. Trencham was a recent convert—she had been a Unitarian—and she was more than proud of her grasp of the responses and courtesies in the service; she was bellicose.

At the first sound of the priest's voice in the vestarium she was on her feet and she fired out her amens and her mercies in a stern and resonant voice, timed well ahead of the rest of the congregation as if she were involved in a sort of ecclesiastical footrace. Her genuflections were profound and graceful, her credo and confession were letter-perfect, her Lamb of God was soulful, and if she was given any competition, as she sometimes was, she would throw in a few signs of the cross as a proof of the superiority of her devotions. Mrs. Trencham was a winner.

There were chrysanthemums on the altar. The cloth was purple. Only the two candles that represent the flesh and the spirit burned. Charlie Stuart came in and took a forward pew. Something about his appearance perplexed Nailles. His clothing hung on him loosely. He must have lost weight; but how much? Forty pounds. Fifty pounds. The voluminousness of his jacket gave him a shocking, wasted and decrepit look. Cancer, Nailles wondered. But their wives were good friends and if it had been cancer he would have heard. Truths and rumors of cancer moved through the neighborhood as freely as the wind. The sight of his stricken friend forced onto him some heavy thoughts about the mysteriousness of infirmity and death. Thoughts of death brought him around to the fact that Charlie's father had died in an airplane crash in South America six months ago and this brought him around to the cheerful conclusion that Charlie was wearing his father's suits. How simple it all was! He beamed at this triumph of practicality over death. Then the strangers came in.

The handful of men and women who attended Holy Communion were all well known to Nailles. New communicants were seldom seen, and his curiosity was legitimate. They were perhaps in their forties—the man's hair was brown—superior products of heterosexual monogamy. She genuflected deeply, curtsied in fact. He gave the cross a stiff nod. At the mention of the Virgin Mary in the Credo she genuflected again while he remained standing. She had been a very pretty woman and would probably never lose the authority this good fortune had given her when she was younger. His face was scrubbed, decent and bright. But for its brightness it might have seemed commonplace. They spoke the responses in a clear voice.

She was, Nailles thought, in her grace and loveliness one of those women who seem to bask in the extraordinary and visionary state of holy matrimony. Regret, he thought, had not left a line on her face. She would excel in all her roles—ardent, clever, sage and loving. Matrimony seemed invented for her kind; indeed her kind might have had a hand in its invention. Someone less sympathetic than Nailles would have singled him out as one of those men who, at the summit of their perfection, would be discovered to have embezzled two million dollars from the accounts entrusted to him in order to finance the practice and blackmail of his savage and unnatural sexual appetites. The same critic would imagine her to be bored, vindictive, a secret sherry drinker who dreamed nightly of being debauched in a male harem.

But to Nailles, on this rainy morning, they seemed invincible. Their honor, passion and intelligence were genuine. Their lives would not be undangerous but they would bring to their disappointments and their successes an immutable brand of common sense.

When the peace that passes understanding was dispersed among them, the priest left the altar and muttered a prayer from the vestarium. The sounds of muttered prayer seemed to Nailles to have an organic antiquity; to fall on his ear like the grating sound of a wave. The acolyte extinguished the lights of the flesh and the spirit, Nailles finished up his devotions and went down the aisle behind the strangers.

"We're the Hammers," the stranger said to the priest.

Nailles did not think this funny, anticipating the fact that almost everyone else in the neighborhood would. How many hundreds or perhaps thousands of cocktail parties would they have to live through, side by side: Hammer and Nailles. Nailles claimed not to be a superstitious man but he did believe in the mysterious power of nomenclature. He believed, for example, that people named John and Mary never divorced. For better for worse, in madness and in saneness they seemed bound together for eternity by the simplicity of their names. They might loath and despise one another, quarrel, weep and commit mayhem, but they were not free to divorce. Tom, Dick and Harry could go to Reno on a whim, but nothing short of death could separate John and Mary. How much worse was Hammer and Nailles.

"Welcome to Christ's Church," the priest was exclaiming. "Welcome to Bullet Park. Father Frisbee did write to me about you." Father Frisbee had probably not gone into their finances, but Father Ransome, at a glance, guessed them to be good for at least five hundred a year; although he had experienced many disappointments. The Follansbees, for instance, who kept saddle horses and went to Europe every summer, dropped a dollar into the plate whenever they came to church and let it go at that. On top of this they very likely claimed a tax exemption of a thousand. Live and learn. "Mr. and Mrs. Hammer," he said, "may I present your neighbor Mr. Nailles." He laughed.

The look they exchanged was deeply curious and in some ways hostile. The stranger evidently anticipated the unwanted union that the sameness of their names would enforce in such a place. Nailles, who detested genealogy, crests, idle investigations into the elegance of time gone, spoke from a conflict of feeling when he said: "Our name used to be de Noailles."

"I've never looked into the history of our name," said the stranger. He could have been unfriendly. He took his wife's arm and left the church.

"Tell me," the priest asked Nailles, "what's happened about Tony and the confirmation class."

"He's playing varsity basketball," said Nailles quite loudly. The Hammers were still within hearing. "He's the only member of his form on the varsity squad and I hate to ask him to give it up."

"Oh well," said Father Ransome, "the bishop will come

again in the spring but I suppose he'll be playing baseball then."

"I'm afraid you're right," said Nailles, yielding his
place to Mrs. Trencham, who hinted at a curtsy and
would probably have kissed the priest's ring had he
worn one, but his fingers were bare.

Driving away from church Nailles turned on his windshield wiper although the rain had let up. The reason for
this was that (at the time of which I'm writing) society
had become so automative and nomadic that nomadic
signals or means of communication had been established
by the use of headlights, parking lights, signal lights and
windshield wipers. The evening paper described the issues involved and the suitable signals. Hang the child
murderer. (Headlights.) Reduce the state income tax.
(Parking lights.) Abolish the secret police. (Emergency
signal.) The diocesan bishop had suggested that church-
goers turn on their windshield wipers to communicate
their faith in the resurrection of the dead and the life of
the world to come. He drove on through a neighborhood
where all the houses stood on acre or half-acre lots. All
the houses were white. His own place was at the western
edge of the town. He had three acres. At the edge of his
property was a sign that said: "No dumping. $50 fine.
Violators will be prosecuted." Below the sign were a
gutted automobile, three defunct television sets and a
soiled mattress. The night population of Bullet Park was
sparse but its most inscrutable and mysterious members
were the scavengers' opposite—the dumpers. Four or five

times a year Nailles would find on his property a collection of broken refrigerators, television sets, maimed and
unidentifiable automobiles and always a few mattresses,
rent, stained, human and obscene. The mattresses were
ubiquitous. The town clerk had explained to him that the
cost and inconvenience of legitimate dumping out-
weighed the scrap value of the rubbish. It was cheaper
and easier to drive up to Bullet Park from the city and
dump your waste than to have some professional haul it
away. No violator had ever been caught and prosecuted.
The problem for Nailles was merely emotional—Nellie
would call the clerk and a truck would haul the stuff
away in the morning—but his anger at seeing his land
disfigured and his sadness and unease at the human allu-
sions of this intimate and domestic rubbish disturbed
him.

Nailles's house (white) was one of those rectilinear
Dutch Colonials with a pair of columns at the door and
an interior layout so seldom varied that one could, standing in the hallway with its curved staircase, correctly
guess the disposition of every stick of furniture and almost every utility from the double bed in the northeast
master's room through the bar in the pantry to the washing machine in the laundry basement. Nailles was met in
the hall by an old red setter named Tessie whom he had
trained and hunted with for twelve years. Tessie was getting deaf and now, whenever the screen door slammed,
she would mistake this for the report of a gun and trot
out onto the lawn, ready to retrieve a bird or a rabbit.

Tessie's muzzle, her pubic hair and her footpads had turned white and it was difficult for her to climb stairs. In the evening, when he went to bed, Nailles would give her a boost. She sometimes cried out in pain. The cries were piteous and senile and the only such cries (or the first such cries) the house had heard since Nailles had bought the place. Nailles spoke to the old bitch with a familiarity that could seem foolish. He wished her good morning and asked her how she had slept. When he tapped the barometer and looked out at the sky he asked her opinion on the weather. He invited her to have a piece of toast, talked with her about the editorials in the *Times* and urged her, like some headmaster, to have a good day when he left for the train. When he returned in the evening he gave her some crackers or peanuts while he mixed the cocktails and often lighted a wood fire as much for her pleasure as anything else. He had decided that should a time come when she would have to be killed he would take her out behind the rose garden and shoot her himself. As she had grown old she had developed two common frailties. She was afraid of heights and thunderstorms. When the first peal of thunder sounded she would seek out Nailles and stay at his side until the violence had definitely gone into the next county. Nailles still hunted with her in the autumn.

Nellie was frying bacon in the kitchen and he kissed her and embraced her passionately. Nailles loved Nellie. If he had a manifest destiny it was to love Nellie. Should Nellie die he might immolate himself on her pyre, al-

23

though the thought that Nellie might die had never occurred to him. He thought her immortal. The intenseness of his monogamy, the absoluteness of his belief in the holiness of matrimony, was thought by a surprising number of people to be morbid, aberrant and devious. In the course of events many other women were made available to Nailles but when some ardent divorcée, widow or wayward housewife attacked him, his male member would take a painful attitude of disinterest. It would seem to summon him home. It was a domesticated organ with a love of home cooking, open fires and the thighs of Nellie. Had he any talent he would have written a poem to the thighs of Nellie. The idea had occurred to him. He sincerely would have liked to commemorate his spiritual and fleshly love. The landscapes that he beheld when he raised her nightgown made his head swim. What beauty; what incredible beauty. Here was the keystone to his love of the visible world.

They ate breakfast in the dining room. Nailles went to the hallway and shouted up the stairs to his son: "Breakfast's ready, Tony."

"But he isn't here, darling," Nellie said. "He's at the Pendletons'. You drove him over on your way to church."

"Oh yes," said Nailles, but he seemed bewildered. He never seemed quite to understand that the boy was free to move in and out of his house, in and out of his orbit and his affections. Knowing that the boy was away, having in fact driven him to an airport and put him on a plane, he would then return home and look for him in the garden. The love Nailles felt for his wife and his only son seemed like some limitless discharge of a clear amber fluid that would surround them, cover them, preserve them and leave them insulated but visible like the contents of an aspic.

Sitting at their breakfast table Nailles and Nellie seemed to have less dimension than a comic strip, but why was this? They had erotic depths, origins, memories, dreams and seizures of melancholy and enthusiasm. Nailles sighed. He was thinking of his mother. She had suffered a stroke four months ago and had never quite regained consciousness. She was a patient in a nursing home in the west end of the village. Nailles visited her every Sunday and remembered uneasily his visit of a week ago.

The nursing home was one of those large places, the favorite of undertakers, that had been made obsolete by the disappearance of a servant class. There was a crystal chandelier and a marble floor in the vestibule but the furniture seemed to have been gathered from some ancient porch and the flowers on the table were made of wax. The director was a Swede and must have been a prosperous Swede since his rates began at one hundred and fifty dollars a week; but he did not spend his money on clothes. His trousers shone and he wore a shapeless brown jacket of cotton. He spoke without an accent but in the pleasant, singing way of Scandinavians. "Dr. Powers was here yesterday," he sang, "but he had nothing to report. Her blood pressure is a hundred and seventy-two. Her heart is damaged but still very strong. She is getting twenty-two cc.'s of PLM six times a day and the usual anticoagulants." The director had received no medical education but he displayed the medical information that had rubbed onto him with the same flair with which a green soldier will display his military nomenclature. "The hairdresser came on Wednesday but I didn't have her hair touched up. You asked me not to."

"My mother never dyed her hair," Nailles said.

"Yes, I know," the director said, "but most of my clients like to see their parents looking well. I call them my dolls," he said, speaking with genuine tenderness. "They look like people and yet they're really not." Nailles wondered darkly if the director had played with dolls. How else could he have hit on this comparison. "We dress them. We undress them. We have their hair arranged. We talk with them but of course they can't answer. I think of them as my dolls."

"Could I see her," Nailles asked.

"Certainly."

The director led him up the marble stairs and opened the door to his mother's room. It was a small bedroom with a single window. It would have been a child's bedroom when the house contained a family. "She spoke last Thursday," the director said. "The nurse was feeding her. She said, 'I'm living in a foxhole.' Of course her speech was blurred. Now I'll leave you alone." He closed the door and Nailles said: "Mother, Mother . . ."

Her white hair was thin. Her teeth were in a glass on a

table by the bed. She breathed lightly and moved her left hand on the covers. Nailles had pled with the doctor to, as he put it, let her die, but the doctor had said that it was his responsibility to save lives. Inert, uncomprehending, the emaciated figure still had for him an immense emotional power. She had been in all things a fair woman—kindly, decent and loving—and that she should be so cruelly smitten and left so close to death challenged Nailles's belief in the fitness of things. She should, he thought, have been rewarded for her excellence by a graceful demise. He took the deathly wages of sin quite literally. The wicked were sick, the good were robust; although her inertness made these the opinions of a simpleton. Her hand moved and he noticed then that she wore her diamond rings. Some nurse, playing doll, must have slipped them onto her fingers. "Mother," he asked, "Mother, is there anything I can do for you? Would you like Tony to come and visit you? Would you like to see Nellie?" He was talking to himself.

Nailles then thought of his father. The old man had been a crack shot, a lucky fisherman, a heavy drinker and the life of his club. Nailles remembered returning from college in his freshman year. He had brought his roommate with him. He admired his roommate and presented him proudly to his father at the railroad station, but the old man raked the stranger with an instantaneous look of scorn and rejection and gave a perceptible shake of his head at the incredible bad taste his son had displayed in the choice of a companion. Nailles had thought they would go home for dinner but his father took them instead to a hotel where there was a band and dancing. When he began to order the dinner Nailles saw that his father was very drunk. He joked with the waitress, made a grab at her backside and spilled his water. When the band began to play "I'm Forever Blowing Bubbles" he left the table, made his way through the dancers, took the baton away from the conductor and led the band. Everyone in the restaurant was amused but Nailles who, had he possessed a pistol, would have shot his father in the back.

The old man shook his white head, weaved, bobbed, called for fortissimo and pianissimo and gave a hilarious impersonation of an orchestral conductor. It was one of his most successful acts at the club. The band laughed, the conductor laughed, the waitresses put down their trays to watch and Nailles sank deeper and deeper into his abyss of misery and unease. He could leave the place and take a taxi home but the already touchy relationship between himself and his father would only worsen. He excused himself and went to the toilet, where he leaned on a washbasin. It was the only way he had to express his grief. When he returned to the table the performance was over and his father was having a third or fourth drink. They finally got some dinner and in the taxi on the way home his father fell into a drunken sleep. Nailles had helped him up the steps to the house, grateful to be able to play out this much of his role as a son. He ardently wanted to love the old man but this was his only filial opportunity. His father went on up to his room and Nailles was greeted by his mother's faint, pained, knowledgeable and winsome smile.

A fresh pillow lay on the only other chair in the room. He could, by taking a step, lift it, press it to her face firmly and end her pain in a few minutes. He took the step, he lifted the pillow off the chair and returned to his seat, but suppose she struggled, suppose, in spite of her pain and her cavernous loss of consciousness she still instinctively and tenaciously loved what remained of her life; suppose she regained consciousness long enough to see that her son was a matricide. These were Nailles's memories at the breakfast table.

Nellie was not the sort of hostess who, greeting you at a dinner party, would get her tongue halfway down your throat before you'd hung up your hat. She was winsome. She wore lace that morning and smelled of carnations. She was a frail woman with reddish hair whose committee work, flower arrangements and moral views would have made the raw material for a night-club act. She was interested in the arts. She had painted the three pictures in the dining room. The canvas came printed with a maze of blue lines like a geodetic survey map. The areas within the lines were numbered—one for yellow, two for green and so forth—and by following the instructions carefully she was able to raise, on the lifeless cloth, the depth and brilliance of an autumn afternoon in Vermont or (over the sideboard) Gainsborough's portrait of the daughters of Major Gillespie. This was vulgar and she guessed as much, but it pleased her. She had recently enrolled—genuinely curious and anxious to be informed—in a class on the modern theater. One of her assignments had been to go to New York and report on a play that was being performed in the Village. She had planned to go with a friend but her friend was taken sick and she made the journey alone.

The play was performed in a loft before a small audience. The air was close. Towards the end of the first act one of the cast took off his shoes, his shirt, his trousers and then, with his back to the audience, his underpants. Nellie could not believe her eyes. Had she protested by marching out of the theater, as her mother would have done, she would seem to be rejecting the facts of life. She intended to be a modern woman and to come to terms with the world. Then the actor turned slowly around, yawning and stretching himself unself-consciously. It was all true to life but some violent series of juxtapositions, concepts of propriety and her own natural excitability threw her into an emotional paroxysm that made her sweat. If these were merely the facts of life why should her eyes be riveted on his thick pubic brush from which hung, like a discouraged and unwatered flower, his principal member. The lights faded. The cast remained dressed for the rest of the play but Nellie was unnerved. When she left the theater it was rainy and humid. She crossed Washington Square to catch a bus. Some students from the university were circling the pool carrying picket signs on which were written Fuck, Prick

and Cunt. Had she gone mad? She watched the procession until it wound out of sight. Shit was the last placard
she saw. She was weak. Boarding the bus she looked
around for the reassuring faces of her own kind, looked
around desperately for honest mothers, wives, women
who took pride in their houses, their gardens, their flower
arrangements, their cooking. Two young men in the seat
in front of her were laughing. One of them threw his arm
around the other and kissed him on the ear. Should she
thrash them with her umbrella? At the next stop what
she was looking for—an honest woman—took the seat
beside her. She smiled at the stranger, who returned the
smile and said, wearily: "I've been looking everywhere
for English cretonne, good English cretonne, and there
doesn't seem to be a yard of it available in the city of
New York. I have good English things and an English-
type house and nubbly, stretchy reps look completely out
of place in my decorating scheme, but nubbly, stretchy
reps are all you can get. I suppose there must be some
cretonne somewhere but I haven't been able to find it.
My old cretonne is perfectly beautiful but it's showing
signs of wear. Iris, peonies and cornflowers on a blue
background. I have a sample here." She opened her bag
and took out a scrap of printed linen.

It was what Nellie had wanted, but while the stranger
went on talking about stuffs the words printed on the
picket signs—Fuck and Prick—seemed to burn in her
consciousness with a lingering incandescence and she
could not forget the actor's pubic brush and his un-

watered flower. She seemed unable to return to where she had been. The stranger had begun to describe her things and Nellie's reaction shifted from boredom to irritability. How contemptible was a life weighted down with rugs and chairs, a consciousness stuffed with portables, virtue incarnate in cretonne and evil represented by rep. It seemed more contemptible than the amorous young men in front of her and the asininity of the students. She seemed to have glimpsed an erotic revolution that had left her bewildered and miserable but that had also left her enthusiasm for flower arrangements crippled. She walked east to the station in the rain, passed several newsstands that seemed to specialize in photographs of naked men. Boarding the train was a step in the right direction. She was going home and she would, in the space of an hour, be able to close her door on that disconcerting and rainy afternoon. She would be herself again, Nellie Nailles, Mrs. Eliot Nailles, honest, conscientious, intelligent, chaste, etc. But if her composure depended upon shutting doors, wasn't her composure contemptible? Contemptible or not, she felt, as the train moved, the symptoms of restoration. When she left the train at her stop and walked through the parking lot to her car she had arrived back at herself. She drove up the hill; opened the door. The cook was stewing mushrooms in butter and the living room smelled of this. "Did you have a nice day," the cook asked.

"Yes, thank you. Very nice. It was disappointing to have it rain but we do need rain for the reservoirs, don't

32

we?" She found the utter artificiality of her sentiments galling, but how close could she come to the truth? Could she say shit to the cook and describe what she had seen on the stage? She climbed the stairs to her pleasant room and took a pleasant bath, but falsehood, confinement, exclusion and a kind of blindness seemed to be her only means of comprehension. She did not tell Nailles about the experience.

After breakfast Nailles climbed the stairs to his son's room. Nailles had sat up the night before with his son when he and Nellie had come in from a party and found the young man reading.

"Did you have a good time?" Tony had asked.

"Pretty good."

"You going to have a nightcap," Tony asked.

"Sure. Why not. Do you want a beer?"

"Yes. I'll get them."

"I'll get them," Nailles said, not sternly but finally. He did not like to see a man his son's age tending bar. Some of his friends and neighbors allowed their children to pass drinks and mix drinks. Nailles thought this inefficient and unsuitable. The children usually got the proportions wrong and lost, he thought, through this performance, some desirable innocence. He got the beer and the whiskey and returned to his chair. He seemed intensely absorbed in his thoughts and frowned at the air above the rug. There was between the two men, preparing to speak but still silent, that sense of sanctuary that is the essence of love.

Nailles described the party to Tony, who knew most of the guests. The boy wondered if his mother would have fallen asleep and if he would be spared the carnal demands, encouragements, exclamations and cheers that he heard so often from his parents' bedroom. He hoped his mother had fallen asleep. There was some preference in the air, some enjoyable and yet self-conscious sense that they were playing out the roles written for them as a Father and a Son. Love was definitely what Nailles felt, and where a more demonstrative man in another country would have embraced his son and declared his love, Nailles would not. Nailles lighted a cigarette and coughed. The cough was racking, phlegmatic, it shook him pitilessly and brought the blood to his face. It declared, much more than anything else, the difference in their ages. Tony wondered why he didn't stop smoking. If he stopped smoking he might stop coughing. In the discord of his father's cough, in its power to briefly enfeeble him, the boy was reminded unsentimentally of the facts of sickness, age and death. But his father, he thought proudly, looked and acted much younger than his age; much younger than Don Waltham's father or Henry Pastor's father and Herbert Matson's father. His father played no game admirably but he could still knock his way through a brief ice-hockey scrimmage, score occasionally at touch football and ski intermediate trails. He was forty-two. This time of life seemed to Tony bewildering, antique and hoary. The thought of having lived for so long excited him as an archaeologist is excited by a Sumerian or a Scythian relic. But his hair was thick and there was no gray in it, his face was lined but it was not puffy, he held himself well and he had a flat stomach. His father was unusual, Tony thought, and went on to think, complacently, that he would inherit this unusualness; he would be the unusual son of an unusual father spared the usualness of gray hair, baldness, obesity and fussiness.

Nailles put a record on the player. It would, Tony knew, be *Guys and Dolls*. Nailles almost never went to the theater and he was uninterested in music, but for some reason that no one remembered clearly now, it was all so long ago, he had been given a pair of tickets for the opening night of *Guys and Dolls*. Some friend had been taken sick or called out of town. Nailles wanted to pass the tickets on to someone else, he so disliked musicals and had never heard of Loesser or Runyon, but Nellie had a new dress she wanted to wear and for this reason they went to the theater. He listened suspiciously to the overture but his rapture seems to have begun with the opening fugue and to have mounted, number by number. On the final chorus he got to his feet and began to smash his hands together, roaring, "Encore, encore." When the house lights went on he continued to clap and shout and he was one of the last people to leave the theater.

He thought that he had seen that night the writing of theatrical history and he had evolved some sentimental theory about the tragedy of the sublime. He got Frank Loesser all mixed up with Orpheus and when he read in the paper that Loesser had divorced he thought—sadly —that this had something to do with the perfection of *Guys and Dolls*. He had no interest in going to any of Loesser's other shows since he was convinced that they would be tragically inferior. No man—no artist—could repeat such a triumph. He seemed to feel that Loesser, like the architect of St. Basil's, should have plucked out his eyes. That opening night seemed to him to have had the perfection of a midsummer day whose sublimity hinted at the inevitability of winter and death.

He began to sing along with the recording. He had bought the recording immediately after the opening and had not replaced it, so that its tonal values were faded. He didn't care. He dispensed with the words and substituted a series of inchoate noises (dadadadad) but on "Luck Be a Lady Tonight" he got to his feet, smashed his fist into his palm and sang the verses he remembered. On the last chorus he made a groping gesture to illustrate a man reaching for stars and when the last note had been played he sighed and said: "That's a great show, really great. It's too bad you never saw it. Well, good night."

Now on this Sunday morning he seemed to be looking for the boy. Tony's room was cold. The boy kept the heat turned off and slept with both windows open. The cold made the room seem to have been emptied for more than the morning. He might have been gone for a year, Nailles felt, but why? He looked around with love at the intimate and common clutter: rucked and cleated football shoes, a football sweater, a pile of books including Stephen Crane, Somerset Maugham, Samuel Butler and Hemingway. Sometime earlier, looking for a dictionary, he had taken one from his son's bookcase and as he opened the dictionary fifty or more printed photographs of naked women slipped and cataracted to the floor. He had been provoked, it had been his principal reaction. He examined the photographs, bringing his very limited knowledge of women to this gallery of lewd strangers. The paper was cheap and he guessed that the pictures had been cut from those nudist magazines that one finds in some shoeshine parlors and barber shops. He was not in the least dismayed that his beloved son had chosen to collect these pictures instead of stamps, Indian arrowheads, geological specimens or numismatic rarities. He dropped the pictures into a wastebasket and looked up the spelling of the word that had concerned him. Sometime later, perhaps a month later, the boy asked: "Have you been using my dictionary?"

"Why yes," Nailles said, "and I threw away all those pictures."

"Oh," the boy said and neither of them said anything more.

On the table by the window was a tape recorder he had given the boy as a birthday present. He would no more have switched it on than he would have opened the boy's mail. His sense of these aspects of privacy was scrupulous and immutable; but had he turned on the recorder he would have heard his son's voice, lowered half an octave by reproduction, saying: "You dirty old baboon, you dirty old baboon. For as long as I can remember it seems to me that whenever I'm trying to go to sleep I can hear you saying dirty things. You say the dirtiest things in the whole world, you dirty, filthy, horny old baboon." However he didn't turn on the recorder.

He changed out of the business suit he wore to church into work clothes. He had once suggested to the vestry that early communicants be encouraged to attend church in the sports and work clothing most of them wore on Sunday, but Father Ransome had countered by asking if he would be expected to serve the sacraments in tennis shorts. He went to the cellar, where he fueled the chain saw with gasoline and oil. South of the house was a small valley in which a grove of twelve elms had been lingeringly destroyed by the elm beetle. Nailles spent his weekends felling the dead trees and cutting and splitting the wood into fireplace lengths. The trees had preserved no trace of their lachrymose beauty. They had dropped their upper branches and shed their bark and the wood shone like bone in the winter light, half truncated and ungainly, the landscape for some nightmare or battlefield. He chose a tree and planned his cut. He was proud, in fact complacent, about his expertness with a chain saw and enjoyed maneuvering the howling, screaming engine and its murderous teeth. The valley was protected and was, that morning, so unseasonably warm that the dead wood had released some fragrance—a smell of spice that reminded him of the cold churches in Rome. Spring. He heard the belling of a wood dove or an owl. The air was soft but seemed much less than idyllic—a troubled soft-ness—the unease of all change. Sexagesima. The Epistle? What was it? Then he remembered. "Of the Jews five times received I forty stripes save one. Thrice was I beaten with rods, once was I stoned, thrice I suffered shipwreck, a night and a day I have been in the deep; in journeyings often, in perils of waters, in perils of robbers, in perils by mine own countrymen, in perils by the heathen, in perils in the city, in perils in the wilderness, in perils in the sea, in perils among false brethren; in weariness and painfulness, in watchings often, in hunger and thirst, in fastings often, in cold and nakedness."

Nellie then heard the howling of the saw.

III

One morning Tony refused to get out of bed.

"I'm not sick," he said when his mother took his temperature. "I just feel terribly sad. I just don't feel like getting up."

His parents decided to let him take the day off.

Five days later he was still in bed.

Nellie was to think of the three doctors who came to treat him as suitors in some myth or legend where a choice of three caskets—Gold, Silver and Lead—was offered to the travelers. In one of the caskets there would be the key to some great fortune—jewels and a bride. It was the element of guesswork that reminded her of the legendary princes. One by one they stood over her son trying to divine or guess the force that had stricken him. Gold? Silver? Lead? The first to come was the general practitioner.

Dr. Mullin came unwillingly since at this time doctors

never visited their patients at home. When critical illness struck, the victim was taken to the hospital in an ambulance where residents and interns performed the final rites. Dr. Mullin urged Nellie to bring Tony to the office. It was difficult for Nellie to explain that Tony refused to get out of bed. When this was finally made clear Mullin agreed to come to the house at noon.

He arrived in an unwashed Volkswagen with a dented fender. He was a young man—younger than Nellie—with an optimism, a brightness, that seemed untouched and uninformed by what he must have learned about the inalienable power of sickness, disease and death. This had actually harmed his practice, since patients, faced with the grave, did not like a healer so inexperienced in grief. He was not a blustering man and he was not a fool but the forcefulness of his optimism was a kind of disturbance like those sudden winds that fling open doors and scatter papers. Nellie showed him up to Tony's room and waited downstairs. She could hear Mullin's resonant and cheerful voice and Tony's quiet replies.

"There's absolutely nothing wrong with him," the doctor said when he came down. "I've taken a specimen and some blood and I'll have the laboratory check these. If he gets up tomorrow I'll give him a cardiogram but I'm pretty sure there's nothing wrong. As a matter of fact I haven't seen as perfect a specimen in a long time. Of course he's a young man but he's certainly enjoying all the benefits of his time of life. This doesn't get him out of bed but it may be a passing depression. If he doesn't get out of bed tomorrow I'll give you some pills that ought to do the trick." He wrote a prescription and smiled at Nellie. Our relationships with healers are swift, intimate and in some ways tender, and for a moment Nellie loved the doctor. He asked her to call him in the morning at around eleven and she did.

"He wouldn't get up again," Nellie said. "He's been in bed six days now. I gave him one of the pills in a glass of orange juice at about ten. A little later I heard him get up and take a shower and then he came down into the kitchen. He was dressed but I saw right away that something was wrong. He was staggering a little and laughing and the pupils of his eyes were like pinpoints. I asked if he wanted some breakfast and he said he wanted six fried eggs and six slices of toast and a quart of milk. He said he'd never been so hungry in his life. He was very restless. He wandered around the kitchen laughing and once he bumped into a table like a drunken man. After he'd eaten all his breakfast he said: 'I feel strong. I've never felt so strong in my life. I'd better get out of the house before I tear it down.' That's what he said. Then he went out of the kitchen door and started running up the path towards Courtland. It's an old bridle path that cuts through the woods there for about six miles. He used to run it when he was on the track team. Well, I couldn't keep up with him of course so I drove around to Route 64 where the path comes out. I waited there for about an hour, I guess, and then he came running along the path. He seemed to have sweated out the drug because he didn't seem drunk any more but he seemed to have lost his memory. He couldn't remember eating breakfast and he didn't seem very clear in his mind about how he'd gotten out to Route 64. I drove him home. He went to sleep in the car. Then he took another shower and went back to bed."

"Well I guess we won't try that again," Dr. Mullin said. "I've heard of bad side effects from that drug but I thought we'd take a chance. I don't really know what to tell you Mrs. Nailles unless you want to try psychotherapy. I work with Dr. Bronson who has an office in the village if you want to call him."

The psychiatrist was even more reluctant than the general practitioner to leave his office, but when Nellie made the situation clear he finally agreed to come. Nellie was standing at the window when he drove up at three. His car was a bright-blue sports convertible with a peculiarly long hood, determined, it seemed, to give an impression of bestiality and expensiveness. It confused Nellie that a man whose profession was to cure melancholy and sorrow should have such a worldly car, but when the doctor climbed out of his racer he seemed unworldly. He seemed a little browbeaten and indecisive. He closed the door, wrung his hands and examined the car from end to end with a deeply worried and suspicious frown. Then he climbed the stairs and rang the bell.

He carried no bag, of course—no identification of any sort. He had, she thought, some of the occupational mannerisms of a dentist. His manner was weary and kindly and he wrung his hands. While she described what had happened he circled the living-room floor as if a dentist chair stood in the middle of the rug. He was a little stooped as if he were accustomed to spending his time in the company of prone patients and his voice had a sad and a healing tone. Nellie led him upstairs to Tony's bedroom and closed the door. Fifty minutes later he was back in the living room.

"I'm afraid he's quite sick, Mrs. Nailles, and the worst of it is that he's uncooperative. I think you may have to send him to a hospital."

"What hospital?"

"Well there's a sanatorium called Stonehenge in the next town where I often send patients. He might respond to electric shock."

"Oh, no," Nellie said. She began to cry.

"Electric shock isn't fatal, Mrs. Nailles. After the first treatment he won't know what's happening. The treatment does not build up anxiety."

"Oh, no," Nellie said. "Please."

"Well he's deeply troubled, Mrs. Nailles. It would take months of intense therapy, with his cooperation, to begin to understand what's gone wrong. Men of his generation, coming from environments of this sort, very often present us with problems that resist analysis. I suppose you give the boy everything he wants?"

"Within reason," Nellie said. "He doesn't have a car."

"I see that he has a tape recorder, a record player, a closet full of expensive clothes."

"Yes."

"There is a tendency in your income group to substitute possessions for moral and spiritual norms. A strict sense of good and evil, even if it is mistaken, is better than none."

"Eliot goes to church nearly every Sunday," Nellie said.

How poor and transparent the fact seemed now that she had stated it. She knew the lassitude of Eliot's prayers, the indifference of his devotions, and that it was habit, superstition and sentimentality that got him up for Holy Communion. "We don't tell lies," she went on. "I think Tony's never told a lie." The doctor gave her an offensively thin smile. "We don't read one another's mail. We don't cheat. We don't gossip. We pay our bills. Eliot loves me. We drink before dinner. I smoke a good deal . . ."

Was that all? It seemed like a poor show but what else was expected of her? Prophets with beards, fiery horsemen, thunder and lightning, holy commandments inscribed on tablets in ancient languages? "We are honest and decent people," she said angrily, "and I'm not going to be made to feel guilty about it."

"I don't intend to make you feel guilty, Mrs. Nailles. There is nothing reprehensible about honesty and decency, but the fact is that your son is very sick."

The telephone rang and when Nellie answered it someone asked to speak with the doctor. "I will not sell that property for less than fifty thousand dollars," the doctor said. "If you're looking for a cheaper place I have a nice modern ranch on Chestnut Street. I *know* the property is assessed at thirty thousand but that assessment was made eight years ago. Fifty thousand dollars is my final price. Excuse me," he said to Nellie.

"Certainly," Nellie said, but the conversation had nettled her. Did this healer sell real estate on the side or was the healing of madness his sideline?

"Will you come again?" Nellie asked.

"Not unless he asks for me," the doctor said. "It would simply be a waste of your money and my time."

When the doctor had gone Nellie climbed the stairs and asked Tony how he felt.

"About the same," he said. "I still feel terribly sad. I feel as if the house were made of cards. When I was a little kid and sick you used to make me card houses and I'd blow them over. This is a nice house and I like it but I feel as if it were made of cards."

The third to come was a specialist on somnambulatory phenomena. He came by train and taxi and looked to Nellie like a mechanic. He carried a suitcase and a larger case filled with instruments. When she asked if Tony might be harmed he assured her that he had nothing but gentle electrodes that recorded body temperatures. She showed him up to the guest room and was about to introduce him to Tony when he said: "I think I'll take a little nap. You see, I'll be up most of the night."

"Is there anything I can get you," Nellie asked.

"Oh no thank you. I'll just lie down." He closed the door.

When he came down at five Nellie offered him a drink. "Not me," he said, "no thanks. I'm AA. I've been off it for a year and a half now. Oh, you should have seen me. I weighed two hundred and fifty pounds, most of it gin. The first group I joined was in the Village. That wasn't much help. I mean they were all freaks. Then I switched to a group in the East Sixties and believe me, Mrs. Nailles, there's not a clinker in that crowd. All important businessmen. Lawyers. Doctors. We get our kicks out of talking about withdrawal symptoms. What it feels like to hit bottom. It's like talking about a trip to hell. We've all been there and we talk just like travelers talk about places where they've been. It's a great crowd. Then when the meeting's over we say a prayer. I suppose," he said, "that ministers and priests think about God all the time. I suppose they think about God when they wake up and I suppose everything they see during the day reminds them about God and of course they say their prayers before they go to sleep. It was just like that with me except that I didn't think about God; I thought about the hootch. I thought about hootch the first thing in the morning, I thought about hootch all day long and I always went to bed with a skinful. Hootch was just like God to me, I mean it was everywhere the way God is supposed to be. The clouds reminded me of hootch, the rain reminded me of hootch, the stars reminded me of hootch. I used to dream about girls before I got on the hootch but after that I just used to dream about hootch. I mean dreams are supposed to come from some very deep part of your mind like sex but with me it was hootch. I'd dream that I had a glass in one hand and a bottle in the other. Then I'd dream that I poured two or three inches into the glass. Then I'd drink it and dream about that wonderful feeling I used to get as if I were beginning a new life. I used to dream about bourbon and scotch and gin and vodka. I never dreamed about rum. I never liked rum. Just sitting there drinking and watching comics on TV I'd feel as if I was sliding down a greased pole, just sliding and sliding so nice and easy. Then in the morning I'd wake up with the shakes and the blues and start thinking about hootch again."

The specialist tried to explain his profession at dinner but his vocabulary was so highly technical that neither Nellie nor Eliot was very clear about what to expect. At eight o'clock he carried his case of instruments upstairs and said: "Time to get to work." He closed the door. When he came down for breakfast his eyes were red and he seemed to have been up all night. Nailles drove him to the station and he mailed them his findings at the end of the week. The report read: "The patient suspended consciousness at 9:12 with a corresponding drop in body temperature. He slept in the Fanchon position—that is on his abdomen with his right knee bent. At 10:00 he had a two-minute dream sequence that raised his body temperature and generally relaxed his cardiovascular tensions. At 10:03 he changed to the nimbus position, that is he crooked his left leg. His next dream sequence was at 1:15 and lasted three minutes. This caused him to have an erection which woke him briefly but he then shifted to the prenatal position and fell asleep again. His body temperature remained constant. At 3:10 he returned to the Fanchon position and began to snore. The snoring was both oral and nasal and continued for eight and one half minutes. . . ." The report was five typewritten pages and attached to it was a bill for five hundred dollars.

IV

Nailles thought of pain and suffering as a principality, lying somewhere beyond the legitimate borders of western Europe. The government would be feudal and the country mountainous but it would never lie on his itinerary and would be unknown to his travel agent. Now and then he received postcards from this distant place. There would be a view of the statue of Aesculapius in the public gardens with some snowy mountains in the distance and on the back of the card this message: "Edna is under sedation most of the time and has about three weeks to live but she would like a letter from you." He wrote entertaining letters to the dying and mailed them off to that remote and quaint capital where the figures on the Rathaus Glockenspiel were crippled, where the statues in the park were the grotesques pain can extort from the imagination, where the palace had been converted into a hospital and rivers of blood foamed under the arched bridges. He was not meant to travel here and he was surprised and frightened to wake from a dream in which he had seen, out of a train window, that terrifying range of mountains.

When Tony had been in bed for twelve days Nailles's inexperience with grief was ended. He would not have gone so far as to say that fortune was dealt out like the peanuts at the end of a child's birthday party, but he felt vaguely that one had one's share of brute pleasure, hard work, money and love and that the rank inequities that he saw everywhere were mysteries that did not concern him. Lucky Nailles! Now his son lay close to death. This did not come like a new fact in his life. It was to be his life and he was to learn the obsessiveness of suffering. When he woke in the morning his first thought was that he might hear Tony's step on the stairs. Whatever occupied him—drink, play, work or money—was merely a distraction from the consuming image of his lost son, gripping a pillow. Having observed the obsessiveness of pain he went on to observe the gross jealousy of a man who feels that his luck has run out. Why, of all the young men in Bullet Park, should Tony have been singled out to suffer a mysterious and incurable disease? It was not a question that he asked himself but a question forced onto him pitilessly by the world as it appeared to him from the first thing in the morning until dark. Cheerful and thoughtless laughter on the station platform merely made Nailles wonder angrily and bitterly why the sons of his friends were free to walk and run in the light while his son lay imprisoned. Lunching with friends who spoke inevitably about the successes of their sons would provoke in him such sadness and misgiving that he would seem physically alienated from the company. Seeing a young stranger run down the street he wanted to call after him: "Stop, stop, stop, stop. Tony was once as strong and swift as you." Having been a patriot about his way of life he found himself involved in subversion, espionage and vengefulness.

"Do you know anyone named Hammer," Nellie asked one evening. Nailles explained that he had met the Hammers in church. "Well she called this afternoon," Nellie said, "and asked us to dinner. I don't approve of asking strangers to dinner but perhaps they come from some part of the world where this goes on."

"It does seem strange, doesn't it," Nailles said. "We just said hello on the porch. Perhaps they're lonely . . ." He was not thinking of the Hammers' probable aloneness but of his own. It was the image of Tony in bed that broke down his rigid sense of social fitness. Tony was sick, Nailles was sad, there was more suffering in life than he had been led to believe and mightn't it be generous to overlook Mrs. Hammer's importunity and accept her invitation. "If we're not doing anything else why don't we go," he said. "It would be neighborly and we can leave early." A few nights later then they drove up to Powder Hill. It was a starry night—Venus blazed like a light bulb, and going up the walk to the house Nailles bent and kissed his wife. Hammer let them in and introduced them to his wife and the other guests. Marietta Hammer seemed absentminded, unenthusiastic or perhaps drunk. One of Nailles's great liabilities was an inability to judge people on their appearance. He thought all men and women honest, reliable, clean and happy and he was often surprised and disappointed. He could see at once that the optimistic estimate of the Hammers that he had made in church might have to be overhauled. There were three other couples—the Taylors, the Phillipses and the Hazzards. There seemed to be no maid. Hammer mixed the drinks in the pantry and Marietta excused herself and went into the kitchen.

"Have you known the Hammers for long," Eliot asked the others.

"I don't really know them at all," Mr. Taylor said. "I have the Ford agency in the village and when he came in to buy a car he asked me for dinner. I figure they'll be a two-car family—everybody on Powder Hill is—so I'm really here on business."

"I sold them their deep freeze," said Mr. Phillips.

"I sold them the house," said Mr. Hazzard.

"Isn't it a lovely house," said Mrs. Hazzard. "The Heathcups lived here until he passed away."

"He was such a nice fellow," said Mr. Hazzard. "I've never understood why he did it."

"Let's see," Hammer said, coming in from the pantry. "Bourbon for you. Scotch and water . . ."

"What business are you in, Mr. Hammer," asked Mr. Hazzard.

"I'm president of Paul Hammer Associates," Hammer said. "We do just about everything."

Marietta Hammer laughed. Her laughter was meant to discountenance her husband. It was a musical laugh—half an octave—but it was, Eliot thought, the kind of laughter one hears in women's clubs, at bridge parties and in those restaurants that feature rich desserts. It had no power of sexual arousal as laughter often does. Her blond hair, her earrings and her dress were all long and she had a definite beauty—the kind of beauty you might see on a magazine cover, but it would be an old cover in a dentist's anteroom, a little worn and dating from the year before last. She went into the pantry and helped herself to more whiskey. Taylor did not conceal the fact that he was there on business and during cocktails he spoke of the interesting discounts he could offer Hammer when the time came to buy his second car. The dinner, as things went in Bullet Park, wasn't much. There was some kind of goulash or stew and Marietta picked at it with such obvious distaste that Eliot wondered if Hammer hadn't cooked the meal. "Well I don't suppose you've been in Bullet Park long enough to form any judgments but we do hope you like the place. I've always found it a very nice community."

"We've only been here two weeks," Hammer said.

"If you want my opinion," Marietta said, "I'll be happy to give you one. I think it stinks. It's just like a masquerade party. All you have to do is to get your clothes at Brooks, catch the train and show up in church once a week and no one will ever ask a question about your identity."

"Please darling," Hammer said. "Not tonight."

"Oh what's wrong with you," she asked. "What are you so cross about? You've been cross all week. Are you sore because I bought this dress? Is that your trouble? Do you think I ought to buy my clothes at Macy's or Alexander's or someplace like that? Do you think I ought to make my own clothes, for Christ's sake. So it cost four hundred dollars but it looks good on me and I need something to wear. And I don't have many clothes. Well I don't have very many clothes. All right I *do* have a lot of clothes and I've said something stupid and now you're going to gloat over it. Oh Jesus, I wish you could see your face. You make me laugh."

"You can get nice couturier dresses at Ohrbach's," Mrs. Taylor said.

"Not tonight, sweetheart," Hammer said.

"You're a doormat," she went on. "You're a henpecked doormat and don't try and blame me for it. You're the kind of a man who thinks that someday, someday, some slender, well-bred, beautiful, wealthy, passionate and intelligent blonde will fall in love with you. Oh God, I can imagine the whole thing. It's so disgusting. She'll have long hair and long legs and be about twenty-eight, divorced, but without any children. I'll bet she's an actress or a night-club singer. That's about the level of your imagination. What do you do with her, chump, what do you do with her besides tying on a can. What is a henpecked doormat up to. Do you take her to the theater? Do you buy her jewelry? Do you travel? I'll bet you travel. That's your idea of a big thing. Ten days on the *Raffaello*, tying on a can morning, noon and night and drifting into the first-class bar at seven in your beautifully cut dinner jacket. What a distinguished couple! What crap. But I guess it would be the *France*, someplace where you can show off your lousy French. I suppose you'd drag her around Paris in her high heels, showing her all your old haunts. I feel sorry for her, I really do. But get this straight, chump, get this straight. If this blonde showed up you wouldn't have the guts to take her to bed. You'd just moon around, kissing her behind pantry doors, and finally decide not to be unfaithful to me. That's if a blonde showed up, but no blonde is going to show up. There isn't any such blonde. You're going to be lonely for the rest of your life. You're a lonely man and a lonely man is a lonesome thing, a stick, a stone, a bone, a doormat, an empty gin bottle . . ."

"I think we'd better go," said Mrs. Taylor.

"Yes," said the Phillipses, and there was a rush for the door.

"Good night."

"Good night."

"Good night."

Lying in bed that night Nailles thought: Hammer and Nailles, spaghetti and meatballs, salt and pepper, oil and vinegar, Romeo and Juliet, block and tackle, thunder and lightning, bacon and eggs, corned beef and cabbage, ham and cheese, curb and snaffle, shoes and socks, line and sinker, true and false, sharp and flat, boots and spurs, snorkel and flipper, fish and chips, white tie and tails, bride and groom, dog and cat, sugar and cream, table and chair, pen and ink, stars and moon, ball and chain, tears and laughter, Mummy and Dad, war and peace, heaven and hell, good and evil, life and death, love and death, death and taxes . . . He slept and dreamed.

He dreamed that they were in a small country church that they sometimes attended in the summer. The church was cruciform and had a threadbare green carpet. There was a sharp and depressing smell of ecclesiastical varnish. The occasion was a funeral and the coffin stood before the chancel but he could not remember whose soul it was they had come to pray for and he looked around the congregation to discover who was missing. Charlie Estabrooke? But he was on the left with his wife. Bailey Barnes? Bailey was on the right with his whole family. Alex Kneeland? Eddie Clapp? Jim Randolph? Sam Farrar? Dave Poor? Rick Rhodes? Jim Stesse? And Roger Cromwell? When he saw that the congregation was intact he realized that the funeral must be his own.

V

When Tony had been in bed for seventeen days there was a spell of fine weather and Nailles woke one morning feeling wonderful. It was about six. The sun had not yet risen but the sky was brilliant. He shaved and bathed and bounded into Nellie's side of the bed and taking her in his arms he thought she seemed a much younger woman than he knew her to be. They seemed in their loving and being loved to have put down the accumulations of time, as if their baser qualities, like some stern presence, had gone off for an hour or so, leaving them free to sport and revel. When he went to the window the land that he saw looked like a paradise. It was not, he knew. Septic drain fields lay under the grass and that flock of cardinals in the fir trees might have lice, but while the brilliance of their plumage and the clarity of their singing had nothing to do with peace on earth, love or bank deposits, it gave him such a feeling of exaltation he threw his arms apart as if he were going to embrace the landscape and the birds. "Oh I feel so wonderful," he said. "Something seems to have happened while I slept. I feel as though I'd been given something, some kind of a present. I feel that everything's going to be the way it was when it was so wonderful. Tony will get up today or perhaps tomorrow and go back to school. I just know that everything's going to be wonderful."

Nailles ate a big breakfast and then went up to Tony's room. That neither he nor his wife nor his son had ever been ill made the reek of a sickroom, as it flew up to his nose, cutting and strange. The shades were drawn. Tony slept. He slept in his underpants and his shoulders were bare. His skin was a liverish color. His hair was mussed and had not been cut for a month. He embraced his pillow with desperation. "Wake up, Tony," Nailles said. "Wake up. It's a marvelous, marvelous morning. Wake up and take a look." He raised the shades and a brilliant light poured into the sickroom. "Look, Tony, see how bright everything is. Nobody can stay in bed on a day like this. It's like a challenge, Tony. Everything's ahead of you. Everything. You'll go to college and get an interesting job and get married and have children. Everything's in front of you, Tony. Come to the window."

He took his son by the hand and drew him out of bed to the window and stood there with an arm around his shoulder. "See, Tony, how bright it all is. Doesn't it make you feel better?" Tony dropped to his knees on the floor. "Tomorrow, Daddy," he sobbed. "Maybe tomorrow."

Nailles felt, like some child on a hill, that purpose and order underlay the roofs, trees, river and streets that composed the landscape. There was some obvious purpose in his loving Nellie and the light of morning but what was the purpose, the message, the lesson to be learned from his stricken son? Grief was for the others; sorrow and pain were for the others; some terrible mistake had been made. Tony was sobbing violently and then he spoke—he howled:

"Give me back the mountains."

"What, Sonny, what did you say?"

"Give me back the mountains."

"What mountains, Sonny," Nailles asked. "Do you mean the mountains that we used to climb? The White Mountains. They're not really white, are they? Remember how we used to climb from Franconia to Crawford? That was fun, wasn't it? Are those the mountains you mean?"

"I don't know," Tony said. He got back into bed.

"Well I have to go or I'll miss the train," Nailles said. "I'll see you tonight."

Nailles, waiting that morning for the 7:56, fended off any questions about his son's health by saying that he had mononucleosis. He stood on the platform between Harry Shinglehouse and Hammer. Nailles and Hammer read the *Times*. Shinglehouse read the *Wall Street Journal*. Since the dinner party Nailles and Hammer had said good morning but not much more. They sometimes took the same train in the morning but Nailles had only once seen his neighbor on the 6:32 home, when Hammer was asleep, either drunk or weary or both. He had a black dispatch case in his lap and was humped unconscious over this in a position that seemed desperate and abject. What is the pathos of men and women who fall asleep on trains and planes; why do they seem forsaken, poleaxed and lost? They snore, they twist, they mutter names, they seem the victims of some terrible upheaval although they are merely going home to supper and to cut the grass. Nailles watched his neighbor and when he did not wake up at Bullet Park he shook his shoulder and said: "Time to get up." "Oh thank you," said Hammer. It had been their only conversation.

This morning they nodded to one another and read their folded papers as down the tracks came the Chicago express, two hours behind schedule and going about ninety miles an hour. Nailles grabbed for his hat, folded his paper and shut his eyes because the noise and commotion of the express was like being in the vortex of some dirty wind tunnel. When the express had passed he opened his eyes and saw the train helling off into the distance, gaily waving a plume of steam like a pig's tail. He had started to read the *Times* again when he noticed that Harry Shinglehouse had vanished. He swung around to see if Harry had changed his position but he was not on the platform. Looking back to the tracks he saw a highly polished brown loafer lying on the cinders. "My God," he finally said. "That fellow. What's his name. He was sucked under the train."

"Hmmmmm," said Hammer, lowering his paper.

"Shinglehouse. He's gone."

"By Jesus, so he has," said Hammer.

"Shinglehouse," Nailles shouted. "He's dead. I mean he was killed."

"What'll we do," said Hammer.

"I'll call the police," Nailles said. "I'd better call the police."

There was a telephone booth at the end of the platform and he ran to this and got the police.

"Patrolman Shea speaking," said a voice.

"Look," Nailles said. "This is Eliot Nailles. I'm at the station. The Chicago train just came through and Shinglehouse was sucked under the train."

"I don't get it," said the patrolman. Nailles had to repeat his story three times. The 7:56 came in and everyone but Hammer and Nailles boarded it. A few minutes later they heard the siren and saw the lights of a police car. Two policemen ran out onto the platform. "He was standing right there," Nailles said. "There's his loafer. He was standing right there and the train came through and he was gone."

"Where's the body?"

"I don't know," Nailles said.

"Well I guess you two had better come back to the stationhouse with me for questioning."

"But we have to go to work," Hammer said. "I have a meeting."

"So have I," Nailles said, "and anyhow we don't know anything about it. Why don't you call the railroad police?" This was a shot in the dark but someone had to do something to make that moment continuous and the police seemed grateful for the suggestion. One of them picked the shoe off the tracks and they went back to the patrol car. Suddenly Hammer began to cry. "There," Nailles said. "There. It's all right. Was he a friend of yours?"

"No," Hammer sobbed. "I didn't know the poor bastard."

"There, there," Nailles said, putting an arm around Hammer. They were merely acquaintances but the casualty had thrust them into an intimate relationship. Hammer controlled his sobbing but Nailles kept an arm around his shoulders and this curious couple were seen by the passengers of the 8:11. Nailles and Hammer rode into the city together, stunned by the mysteriousness of life and death.

The evening paper carried the story. The vanished man had been unemployed and had left a wife and three children. He had once run for town council on the Republican ticket and had formerly been in advertising. Nailles wanted to call the widow but he could think of nothing to say.

The next morning was dark and rainy. He overslept and missed the express train that usually took him to his office. The local that he traveled on made twenty-two stops between Bullet Park and Grand Central Station. The dirty train windows and the overcast sky seemed to have eclipsed his spirits. He remembered Shinglehouse's loafer. He felt peculiar. He read his *Times* but the news in the paper, with the exception of the sporting page, seemed to be news from another planet. A maniac with a carbine had massacred seventeen people in a park in Dallas, including an archbishop who had been walking his dog. The usual wars were raging. The Musicians' Union, Airplane Pilots, Firemen, Circus Performers and Deckhands were all threatening to strike. The White House secretary denied rumors of a fistfight between the President, the Secretary of State and the Secretary of Defense. Drought threatened the wheat crop. An unidentified flying object had been seen in Ohio. A hairdresser in Linden, New Jersey, had shot his wife, his four children, his poodle and himself. A three-day smog in Chicago had paralyzed most transportation and closed many businesses. Nailles felt uncheerful and tried the naïve expedient of bolstering his spirits by assessing his good fortune. Had he been indicted for grand larceny? No. Had he been murdered in a park? No. Had he been trapped in a burning building, lost on a glacier, bitten by a rabid dog? No. Then why wasn't he more cheerful?

The train stopped at Tremont Point, Greenacres, Lascalles, Meadowvale and Clear Haven. The trip seemed intolerable, but why? He had made it a thousand times. Why should this link between his home and his office seem torturous? His breathing was heavy, his palms were wet, there was a quaking feeling in his gut and the dark rain seemed to beat upon his heart. When the train reached Longbrook, Nailles suddenly grabbed his raincoat, pushed his way past the oncoming passengers and left the car. The train coasted on and he found himself alone in a suburban railway station at half past eight in the morning.

Nailles's sense of being alive was to bridge or link the disparate environments and rhythms of his world, and one of his principal bridges—that between his white house and his office—had collapsed. He stepped out of the rain into the waiting room. What he needed was guts but where could he find them? He could not summon them, that much was clear. Could he develop them in a gymnasium, win them in a lottery, buy them from a mail-order house or receive them as a heavenly dispensation? There was another local in fifteen minutes and commuters had begun to gather for this. Nailles boarded it, trying to sell himself a specious brand of cheerfulness. He stayed on that local for two more stops and got off again. Station by station he made a cruel pilgrimage into the city.

After dinner that night Nailles poured a strong whiskey and took it up to Tony's room. He sat in a chair beside Tony's bed as he had done so many times in the past when he used to read to the boy *Treasure Island*.

"How do you feel, Sonny?"

"About the same."

"Did you eat any supper?"

"Yes."

"There was a long thing in the paper on Sunday about how your generation thinks the world is terribly compromised. Do you think the world is terribly compromised?"

"No, I don't think it's compromised."

"You don't think this has anything to do with your trouble?"

"I love the world. I just feel sad, that's all."

"Well I suppose there's plenty to be sad about if you look around, but it makes me sore to have people always chopping at the suburbs. I've never understood why. When you go to the theater they're always chopping at the suburbs but I can't see that playing golf and raising flowers is depraved. The living is cheaper out here and I'd be lost if I couldn't get some exercise. People seem to make some connection between respectability and moral purity that I don't get. For instance, the fact that I wear a vest doesn't necessarily mean that I claim to be pure in heart. That doesn't follow. All kinds of scandalous things happen everywhere but just because they happen to people who have flower gardens doesn't mean that flower gardens are wicked. For instance, Charlie Stringer was indicted last year for sending pornography through the mails. He claims to be some kind of a publisher and I guess dirty pictures is his business. He lives in one of those Tudor houses on Hansen Circle and he has a pretty wife and three children. Flower gardens. Trees. A couple of poodles. The critics would say: Look, look, look what a big façade he's constructed to conceal the fact that he deals in obsceneness and corruption, but what's the point? Why should a man who deals in filth have to live in a cesspool? He's a bastard for sure but why shouldn't a bastard want to water his grass and play softball with the kids?

"We talk an awful lot about freedom and independence. If you were going to define our national purpose I don't guess you could avoid using words like freedom and independence. The President is always talking about freedom and independence, the army and navy are always fighting to defend freedom and independence and on Sundays at church Father Ransome thanks God for our freedom and independence but you and I know that the blacks who live in those firetraps down along the river don't have any freedom or independence in the choice of what they do and where they live. Charlie Simpson is really a great fellow but he and Phelps Marsden and a half a dozen other prominent and wealthy men around here make their money in deals with Salazar, Franco, Union Minière and all those military juntas. They talk about freedom and independence more than anybody else but they furnish the money and the armaments and the technicians to crush freedom and independence whenever it appears. I hate lying and I hate falsehoods and when you get a world that admits so many liars I suppose you've got something to be sad about. I don't, as a matter of fact, have as much freedom and independence as I'd like myself. What I wear, what I eat, my sex life and a lot of my thinking is pretty well regimented but there are times when I like being told what to do. I can't figure out what's right and wrong in every situation.

"The newspapers are sometimes very confusing. They keep running photographs of soldiers dying in jungles and mudholes right beside an advertisement for a forty-thousand-dollar emerald ring or a sable coat. It would be childish to say that the soldier died for emeralds and sables but there it is, day after day, the dying soldier and the emerald ring. And homosexuality. You read a lot about that these days and it bothers me. I wish it didn't exist. Before I joined the Chemists Club I used to have to pump ship in Grand Central and I almost never went into those choppers without getting into trouble. Once when I was going up the stairs this guy came along and took my arm. I had on a Brooks suit and a Locke hat and Peal shoes and the reason I had all this stuff on was to make my intentions clear. So I walked away from him. I didn't hit him. I didn't see his face. I've never seen any of their faces. The only reason I joined the Chemists Club was so that I could have a place in midtown where I could pump ship without getting into a moral crisis. Of course I'm not really a chemist and pushing mouthwash isn't a very inspiring life but when you think of the things we need you realize that someone has to make them. I mean razor blades and soap and bacon and eggs and gasoline and train tickets and shoes. Somebody has to make all that stuff. Tony? Tony?" Tony slept.

Nailles finished his drink and looked lovingly at his mysterious son. Tony was born in Rome, where Nailles had worked as a chemist for FAOU. Nailles had taken Nellie to the international hospital across the river late one afternoon. The doctor was a very fat man. He timed

Nellie's pains and told Nailles to return to the hospital
at half past ten. When Nailles returned he was taken
into an office to have his blood typed. There was no explanation. Later a friend appeared with a bottle of scotch
and a package of American cigarettes, both of which
were difficult to get at the time. The nuns seemed to have
no objection to their drinking; in fact they brought them
glasses and ice. Nailles's friend left at midnight. The
doctor came in at three. He was sweating and seemed
worried. "Is she in danger," Nailles asked. "Yes," the
doctor said harshly, "she is in danger. Life is dangerous.
Why do Americans want to be immortal?"

"Please tell me," Nailles said.

"I will tell you that when this is over I would advise
her not to have any more children."

There were some peacocks in a park across the street.
They began to shriek as the sun rose. This sounded to
Nailles portentous. The doctor came in again at eight.
"Take a walk," he said to Nailles. "Divert yourself.
Breathe some fresh air." Nailles walked down the hill to
St. Peter's and said his prayers. Then he climbed the
stairs to the roof where all the gigantic saints and apostles
stood with their backs to him. He had liked the city of
Rome. Now it seemed sinister; the city of the wolf. Rome
would kill Nellie. The bloody history of the place seemed
to have some bearing on her life. Rome would murder
Nellie.

He walked across the city on foot, trying to sweat out
his pain. In some back street he encountered an old man
selling phallic symbols and death's heads. He walked to

the zoo and had a Campari at the café. Beside the café
was a cage of carnivorous birds, tearing at raw meat.
Leaving the café he saw a hyena; then a cage of wolves.
When he got back to the hospital a nun told him that he
had an eight-pound son and that his wife was out of
danger. He howled with relief and banged drunkenly
around the waiting room. He saw Nellie and his son that
night and Tony seemed to him then to be brilliant, impetuous and strong. Much later they had discussed the possibility of adopting a brother or sister for Tony, but a found-
ling would have challenged Tony's sovereignty and this
was something they did not want.

He had no way of judging his worth as a father.
They had quarreled. When Tony was nine. He had
suddenly given up all his athletics and friendships
and settled down in front of the television set. The
night of the quarrel was rainy. Nailles came into the
house by the kitchen door. Nellie was cooking. Nailles
kissed her on the back of the neck and raised her skirts
but she demurred. "Please darling," she said. "It makes
me feel as if I were in a burlesque skit. Tony's report card
is on the table. You might want to take a look at it." Nailles
mixed a drink and read the report. The marks were all C's
and D's. Nailles walked through the dining room, crossed
the dark hall to the living room where Tony was watching
a show. The tube was the only light, shifting and submarine, and with the noise of the rain outside the room
seemed like some cavern in the sea.

"Do you have any homework," Nailles asked.

"A little," Tony said.

"Well I think you'd better do it before you watch television," Nailles said. On the tube some cartoon figures were dancing a jig.

"I'll just watch to the end of this show," Tony said. "Then I'll do my homework."

"I think you'd better do your homework now," Nailles said.

"But Mummy said I could see this show," Tony said.

"How long has it been," said Nailles, "that you've asked permission to watch television?" He knew that in dealing with his son sarcasm would only multiply their misunderstandings but he was tired and headstrong. "You never ask permission. You come home at half past three, pull your chair up in front of the set and watch until supper. After supper you settle down in front of that damned engine and stay there until nine. If you don't do your homework how can you expect to get passing marks in school?"

"I learn a lot of things on television," Tony said shyly. "I learn about geography and animals and the stars."

"What are you learning now?" Nailles asked.

The cartoon figures were having a tug of war. A large bird cut the rope with his beak and all the figures fell down.

"This is different," Tony said. "This isn't educational. Some of it is."

"Oh leave him alone, Eliot, leave him alone," Nellie called from the kitchen. Her voice was soft and clear. Nailles wandered back into the kitchen.

"But don't you think," he asked, "that from half past

three to nine with a brief interlude for supper is too much time to spend in front of a television set?"

"It is a lot of time," Nellie said, "but it's terribly important to him right now and I think he'll grow out of it."

"I know it's terribly important," Nailles said. "I realize that. When I took him Christmas shopping he wasn't interested in anything but getting back to the set. He didn't care about buying presents for you or his cousins or his aunts and uncles. All he wanted to do was to get back to the set. He was just like an addict. I mean he had withdrawal symptoms. It was just like me at cocktail hour but I'm thirty-four years old and I try to ration my liquor and my cigarettes."

"He isn't quite old enough to start rationing things," Nellie said.

"He won't go coasting, he won't play ball, he won't do his homework, he won't even take a walk because he might miss a program."

"I think he'll grow out of it," Nellie said.

"But you don't grow out of an addiction. You have to make some exertion or have someone make an exertion for you. You just don't outgrow serious addictions."

He went back across the dark hall with its shifty submarine lights and outside the noise of rain. On the tube a man with a lisp, dressed in a clown suit, was urging his friends to have Mummy buy them a streamlined, battery-operated doll carriage. He turned on a light and saw how absorbed his son was in the lisping clown.

"Now I've been talking with your mother," he said, "and we've decided that we have to do something about your television time." (The clown was replaced by the cartoon of an elephant and a tiger dancing the waltz.) "I think an hour a day is plenty and I'll leave it up to you to decide which hour you want."

Tony had been threatened before but either his mother's intervention or Nailles's forgetfulness had saved him. At the thought of how barren, painful and meaningless the hours after school would be the boy began to cry.

"Now crying isn't going to do any good," Nailles said. The elephant and the tiger were joined by some other animals in their waltz.

"Skip it," Tony said. "It isn't your business."

"You're my son," Nailles said, "and it's my business to see you do at least what's expected of you. You were tutored last summer in order to get promoted and if your marks don't improve you won't be promoted this year. Don't you think it's my business to see that you get promoted? If you had your way you wouldn't even go to school. You'd wake up in the morning, turn on the set and watch it until bedtime."

"Oh please skip it, please leave me alone," Tony said. He turned off the set, went into the hall and started to climb the stairs.

"You come back here, Sonny," Nailles shouted. "You come back here at once or I'll come and get you."

"Oh please don't roar at him," Nellie asked, coming out of the kitchen. "I'm cooking veal birds and they smell nice and I was feeling good and happy that you'd come home and now everything is beginning to seem awful."

"I was feeling good too," Nailles said, "but we have a

problem here and we can't evade it just because the veal birds smell good."

He went to the foot of the stairs and shouted: "You come down here, Sonny, you come down here this instant or you won't have any television for a month. Do you hear me? You come down here at once or you won't have any television for a month."

The boy came slowly down the stairs. "Now you come here and sit down," Nailles said, "and we'll talk this over. I've said that you can have an hour each day and all you have to do is to tell me which hour you want."

"I don't know," Tony said. "I like the four-o'clock show and the six-o'clock show and the seven-o'clock show . . ."

"You mean you can't confine yourself to an hour, is that it?"

"I don't know," Tony said.

"I guess you'd better make me a drink," Nellie said. "Scotch and soda."

Nailles made a drink and returned to Tony. "Well if you can't decide," Nailles said, "I'm going to decide for you. First I'm going to make sure that you do your homework before you turn on the set."

"I don't get home until half past three," Tony said, "and sometimes the bus is late and if I do my homework I'll miss the four-o'clock show."

"That's just too bad," Nailles said, "that's just too bad."

"Oh leave him alone," Nellie said. "Please leave him alone. He's had enough for tonight."

"It isn't tonight we're talking about, it's every single

night in the year including Saturdays, Sundays and holidays. Since no one around here seems able to reach any sort of agreement I'm going to make a decision myself. I'm going to throw that damned thing out the back door."

"Oh no, Daddy, no," Tony cried. "Please don't do that. Please, please, please. I'll try. I'll try to do better."

"You've been trying for months without any success," Nailles said. "You keep saying that you'll try to cut down and all you do is to watch more and more. Your intentions may have been good but there haven't been any noticeable results. Out it goes."

"Oh please don't, Eliot," Nellie cried. "Please don't. He loves his television. Can't you see that he loves it?"

"I know that he loves it," Nailles said. "That's why I'm going to throw it out the door. I love my gin and I love my cigarettes but this is the fourteenth cigarette I've had today and this is only my fourth drink. If I sat down to drink at half past three and drank steadily until nine I'd expect someone to give me some help." He unplugged the television set with a yank and picked the box up in his arms. The box was heavy for his strength, and an awkward size, and in order to carry it he had to arch his back a little like a pregnant woman. With the cord trailing behind him he started for the kitchen door.

"Oh, Daddy, Daddy," Tony cried. "Don't, don't, don't," and he fell to his knees with his hands joined in a conventional, supplicatory position that he might have learned from watching some melodrama on the box.

"Eliot, Eliot," Nellie screamed. "Don't, don't. You'll be sorry, Eliot. You'll be sorry."

Tony ran to his mother and she took him in her arms. They were both crying.

"I'm not doing this because I want to," Nailles shouted. "After all I like watching football and baseball when I'm home and I paid for the damned thing. I'm not doing this because I want to. I'm doing this because I have to."

"Don't look, don't look," Nellie said to Tony and she pressed his face into her skirts.

The back door was shut and Nailles had to put the box on the floor to open this. The rain sounded loudly in the yard. Then, straining, he picked up the box again, kicked open the screen door and fired the television out into the dark. It landed on a cement paving and broke with the rich, glassy music of an automobile collision. Nellie led Tony up the stairs to her bedroom, where she threw herself onto the bed, sobbing. Tony joined her. Nailles closed the kitchen door on the noise of the rain and poured another drink. Fifth, he said.

All of this was eight years ago.

VI

Tony had gone out for football and had made the second squad in his junior year. He had never been a good student—he got mostly C's—but in French his marks were so low they were scarcely worth recording. One afternoon when he was about to join the squad for practice it was announced over the squawk box that he should report to the principal. He was not afraid of the principal but he was disturbed at the thought of missing any of the routines of football practice. When he stepped into the outer office a secretary asked him to sit down.

"But I'm late," Tony said, "I'm late for practice already."

"He's busy," the secretary said.

"Couldn't I come back some other time? Couldn't I do it tomorrow?"

"You'd be late for practice tomorrow."

"Couldn't I see him during class time?"

"No."

Tony glanced at the office. In spite of the stubborn and obdurate facts of learning, the place had for him a galling sense of unreality. A case of athletic trophies stood against one wall but this seemed to be the only note of permanence. Presently he was let into the principal's office and given a chair.

"You've failed first-year French twice, Tony," the principal said, "and it looks as if you're going to fail it again. Your parents expect you to go on to college and you know you have to have a modern-language credit. Your intelligence quotient is very high and neither Miss Hoe nor I can understand why you fail."

"It's just that I can't say French, sir," Tony said. "I just can't say any French. My father can't either. I just can't say French. It sounds phony."

The principal switched on the squawk box and said into it: "Could you see Tony now, Miss Hoe?" Her affirmative came through loud and clear. "Certainly." "You go down and see Miss Hoe now," said the principal.

"Couldn't I see her after class tomorrow, sir? I'm missing football practice."

"I think Miss Hoe will have something to say about that. She's waiting."

Miss Hoe was waiting in a room whose bright lights and pure colors did nothing to cheer him. It would soon be getting dark on the playing field and he had already missed passing and tackle. Miss Hoe sat before a large poster showing the walls of Carcassonne. It was the only traditional surface in the room. The brilliant, fluorescent lights in the ceiling made the place seem to be a cavern of incandescence, authoritative in its independence from the gathering dark of an autumn afternoon; and the power to light the room came from another county, well to the north, where snow had already fallen. The chairs and desks were made of brightly colored plastic. The floor was waxed Vinylite.

"Sit down, Tony," she said. "Please sit down. It's time that we had a little talk."

She might have been a pretty woman—small-featured and slender—but her skin was sallow and in the brightness of the light one saw that she had a few chinwhiskers. Her waist was very slender and she seemed to take some pride in this. She always wore belts, cinctures, chains or ribbons around her middle and she sometimes wore a girlish ribbon in her brown hair. Her mouth, considering the strenuous exercise it got in French vowels, was very small. She wore no perfume and exhaled the faint unfreshness of humanity at the end of the day.

She lived alone, of course, but we will grant her enough privacy not to pry into the clinical facts of her virginity or to catalogue the furniture, souvenirs, etc. with which her one-room apartment was stuffed. As a lonely and defenseless spinster she was prey to the legitimate anxieties of her condition. There were four locks on the door to her apartment and she carried a vial of ammonia in her handbag to throw into the eyes of assailants. She had read somewhere that anxiety was a manifestation of sexual guilt and she could see, sensibly, that her aloneness and her virginity would expose her to guilt and repression. However, the burden of guilt must, she felt, be somewise divided between her destiny and the news in the evening paper. It was not her guilt that had caused the increase in sexual brutality. She had come to feel that some disorganized conspiracy of psychopaths was developing. Weekly, sometimes daily, women who resembled her were debauched, mutilated and strangled. Alone in the dark she was always afraid. Since she frequently dreamed that she was being debauched by some brute in a gutter she had to include guilt along with terror.

"When were you born, Tony," she asked.

"May twenty-seventh."

"Oh, I knew it," she said. "I knew it. You're Gemini."

"What's that?"

"Gemini is the constellation under which you were born. Gemini determines many of your characteristics and one might say your fate; but Gemini men are invariably good linguists. The fact that you are Gemini proves to me that you can do your work and do it brilliantly. You can't dispute your stars, can you?"

He looked past her through the window to the playing field. There was still enough light in the air, enough color in the trees to compete with the incandescence of their cavern; but in another ten minutes there would be nothing to see in the window but a reflection of Miss Hoe and himself. He knew nothing about astrology beyond the fact that he thought it to be a sanctuary for fools. He supposed that she might have read in the stars (and he was right) that it was her manifest destiny to be unloved, unmarried, childless and lonely. She sighed and he was suddenly conscious of her breathing, its faint sibilance and the rise and fall of her meager front. It seemed intimate—sexual—as if they lay in one another's arms, and he moved his chair back suddenly, scraping the legs on the Vinylite. The noise restored him.

"I've talked this over with Mr. Northrup, Tony, and we've reached a decision. Since you seem unable to manage your own time with any efficiency we are going to give you a little assistance. We are going to ask you to give up football."

He had not anticipated this staggering injustice. He would not cry but there was a definite disturbance in his eyeducts. She didn't know what she was saying. She knew, poor woman, much less about football than he knew about French. He loved football, loved the maneuvers, the grass work, the fatigue, and loved the ball itself —its shape, color, odor and the way it spiraled into the angle of his elbow and ribcage. He loved the time of year, the bus trips to other schools, he loved sitting on the bench. Football came more naturally to him than anything else at his time of life and how could they take this naturalness away from him and fill up the breach with French verbs?

"You don't know what you're saying, Miss Hoe."

"I'm afraid I do, Tony. I've not only talked with Mr. Northrup. I've talked with Coach."

"With Coach?"

"Yes, with Coach. Coach thinks it will be better for you, better for our school, better perhaps for our football team if you spent more time at your studies."

"Coach said this?"

"Coach said that you were enthusiastic but he doesn't think that in any way you're indispensable. He thinks perhaps that you're wasting your time."

He stood. "You know what, Miss Hoe?" he asked.

"What, Tony," she said. "What, dear?"

"You know I could kill you," he said. "I could kill you. I could strangle you."

She stood, hurling her chair against the walls of Carcassonne, and began to scream. Her screaming brought Mr. Graham, the Latin teacher, and Mr. Clark (science) running. She stood at her desk, her arm outflung, pointing at Tony. "He tried to kill me," she screamed. "He threatened to kill me."

"There, there, Mildred," said Mr. Graham. "There, there."

"I want a policeman," she screamed. "Call the police." Mr. Clark called the office through the squawk box and asked for the secretary to call the police. Mr. Clark picked up Miss Hoe's chair and she sat in it, trembling and breathing heavily but sternly as if she were about to upbraid an unruly class. Tony simply stared at his hands. Then in the distance they heard the sound of a police siren that seemed, excited and grieving, not to come from the autumn twilight but from some television drama in which they were the actors or combatants, playing out nothing so simple as poor French marks and a mistaken threat. Tony was Miss Hoe's long-lost brother who had just returned from his travels with the news that their beautiful mother was a well-known communist spy. The science teacher would have been Miss Hoe's husband—a dreary failure whose business misadventures and drinking bouts had brought her to the brink of a nervous breakdown—and Mr. Clark came from the FBI. Thus, juxtaposed for a moment by the sound of the siren, they seemed about to have their dilemma interrupted by an advertisement for painkillers or detergents, until the police came in, asking, "What's up, what's going on here?" Vandalism had been their guess, although it was the wrong time of day—but vandalism was the usual complaint. Why did kids want to rip the lids off desks and break windows. Miss Hoe raised her head. Her poor face, shining with tears, was ugly. "He tried to kill me," she said. "He tried to kill me."

"Now Mildred," said Mr. Clark. "Now Mildred."

"Don't I have any protection at all," she cried angrily. "Are you all going to stand around and defend this murderer until I'm found some night with a broken neck? How do you know he doesn't have a knife. Has anyone searched him? Has anyone even asked him a question?"

"You got a knife, Sonny," one of the police asked.

"No," said Tony.

"You try to kill this lady?"

"No, sir," said Tony.

"You try to kill this lady?"

"No, sir. I got angry at her and said that I'd like to but I didn't touch her. I wouldn't ever touch her."

"I want something done about this," Miss Hoe said. "I am entitled to some protection."

"You want to file charges against him lady? Felonious assault, I guess."

"I do," Miss Hoe said.

"All right. I'll take him down to the station and book him. Come on, Sonny."

The corridor was crowded by this time with teachers, secretaries and janitors, none of whom knew what had happened and all of whom were asking one another what it was. Tony and the police had gotten to the end of the corridor and were about to turn out of sight when Miss Hoe cried: "Officer, Officer." It was a frightened voice and they turned quickly.

"Could you take me home, will you drive me home?"

"Where do you live?"

"Warwick Gardens."

"Sure."

"I'll just be a minute."

She got her coat, turned off the lights and locked the door to her classroom. She came swiftly down the hall, through the crowd, to where they waited. She got into the back seat of the car and Tony sat in front between the two police. "It's very kind of you to take me home," Miss Hoe said. "I do appreciate it, but I'm terribly afraid of the dark. When I go into the cafetorium for my lunch the first thing I think of is that it will get dark in four hours. Oh, I wish it would never get dark—never. I

suppose you know all about that lady who was mis-
treated and strangled on Maple Street last month. She
was my age and we had the same first name. We had the
same horoscope and they never found the murderer . . ."

One of the police walked her to the door of the Warwick Gardens and then they drove to the police station in
the center of town. Tony explained that his mother was
in the city but that his father usually came out on the
6:32. "Well, the judge won't be here until eight or later,"
one of the police said, "and we can't book you without
the judge but you don't look very desperate to me and I'll
remand you in the custody of your father as soon as he
comes home. The lady seemed a little hysterical . . ."

It was, of course, the first time Tony had been in the
police station. It was a new building, not in any way
shabby, but definitely grim. Fluorescent tubing shed a
soulful, grainy and searching light and an extraordinarily
harsh and unnatural voice was coming from a radio.
"Five foot eight," said the voice. "Blue eyes. Crooked
teeth. A scar on the right side of the jaw. A birthmark at
the back of the neck. Weight one hundred and sixty
pounds. Wanted for murder . . ." They took down Tony's
name and address and invited him to sit down. The only
other civilian in the place was a shabbily dressed man
who wore a stained, white silk scarf around his neck. His
clothing was greasy and threadbare, his hands were
black but the white silk scarf seemed like a declaration of
self-esteem. "How long do I have to stay here," he asked
the lieutenant at the desk.

"Until the judge comes in."

"What did I do wrong?"

"Vagrancy."

"I hitched a ride on Twenty-seven," the vagrant said. "I asked this guy to stop the car so I could take a piss and as soon as I got out of the car he drove away. Why would he do a thing like that?" The lieutenant coughed. "Well you don't have long for this world," the vagrant said. "You don't have long for this world with a cough like that. Ha. Ha. A doctor told me that twenty-eight years ago and you know where the doctor is now? Six feet under. Pushing up daisies. He died a year later. The secret of keeping young is to read children's books. You read the books they write for little children and you'll keep young. You read novels, philosophy, stuff like that and it makes you feel old. You fish in the river?"

"Some," said the lieutenant, putting as much disinterest into the sound as he could. The vagrant offended his nose, his sight and his sense of the fitness of things, not because of his manifest eccentricity but because he had heard the story so many times. They were all alike, the roadside vagrants, they suffered a sameness greater than the intellectual and sumptuary sameness of the businessmen who rode the 6:32. They all had theories, travels, diets, colorful pasts, studied conversational openings, and they usually wore some piece of soiled finery like the white silk scarf.

"Well, I hope you don't eat the fish," the vagrant said. "That river's nothing but an open toilet. All the shit from New York City comes up the river twice a day on the tides. You wouldn't eat the fish you found in a toilet, would you? Would you?"

Then he turned to Tony and asked: "What you here for, Sonny."

"Don't tell him," said the lieutenant. "He's not here to ask questions."

"Well, can't I be friendly," the vagrant asked. "Perhaps if we had a little conversation we might discover that we have some interests in common. For instance I've made a study of the customs and history of the Cherokee Indians and a great many people find this interesting. I once lived with them on a reservation in Oklahoma for three months. I wore their clothes, observed their customs and ate their food. They eat dogs, you know. Dogs are their favorite food. They boil them mostly although sometimes they roast them. They . . ."

"Shut up," said the lieutenant.

At quarter to seven they called Nailles, who answered and said that he would be right over. When he strode into the station and found his son there his first impulse was to embrace the young man but he restrained himself. "You can take him home," the lieutenant said. "I don't think anything much will come of this. He'll tell you what happened. The complainant seems to have been a little hysterical."

Tony told his father what had happened as they drove home. Nailles had no counsel, advice, censure, experience or any other paternal qualities to bring to that crazy hour. He understood the boy's deep feelings about being dropped from the squad and he seemed to have shared in his son's felonious threatening of Miss Hoe. A little wind was blowing and as they drove, leaves of all colors—but mostly yellow—blew through the shaft of their headlights and what he said was: "I love to see leaves blowing through the headlights. I don't know why. I mean they're just dead leaves, no good for anything, but I love to see them blowing through the light."

VII

It was an autumn afternoon. Saturday.

Below the house, near the grove of dead elms, there was a swamp where a flock of red-winged blackbirds nested each spring. According to the law of their species they should have turned south in the autumn but the number of bird-feeding appliances in the neighborhood, overflowing with provender, had rattled their migratory instincts and they now spent the autumn and winter in Bullet Park in utter confusion. Their song—two ascending notes and a harsh trill like a cicada—was inalienably associated with the first long nights of summer but now one heard it in the autumn, one heard it in the snow. To hear this summery music on one of the last clement days of the year was like some operatic reprise where the heroine, condemned to death, hears in her dark cell (Orrido Carcere) the lilting love music that was first sung at the beginning of Act II. The wind that day was westerly and after lunch one heard the thump-thump-thump of a base drum from the football field where the band was warming up for a home game.

Tony, after having been dropped from the squad, did not, of course, spend his spare time studying irregular verbs. Instead he read poetry as if he shared, with the poets, the mysterious and painful experience of being forced into the role of a bystander. He had not read poetry before. Nailles was not so obtuse as to protest but he was uneasy. He might say that poetry was one of the most exalted of the arts but he could not cure himself of the conviction that poetry was the demesne of homely women and morbidly sensitive men.

As soon as Tony heard the bass drum that afternoon he went upstairs and lay down on his bed. Nailles was worried and called up the stairs: "Tony, hey Tony, let's do something, shall we? Let's go for a ride or something."

"No thank you, Daddy," Tony said. "What I think I'll do is to go into New York if you don't mind. I'll go to a movie or maybe see the basketball game."

"That's fine," Nailles said. "I'll drive you to the train."

At three the next morning Nailles woke. He got out of bed and started down the hall towards Tony's room. He felt very old, as if while he slept he had put down the dreams of a strong man—snow-covered mountains and beautiful women—in exchange for the anxieties of some decrepit octogenarian who feared that he had lost his false teeth. He felt frail, wizened, a shade of himself. Tony's bed was empty. "Oh, my God," he said loudly.

"Oh, my God." His only and dearly beloved son had been set upon by thieves, perverts, prostitutes, murderers and dope addicts. He was, in fact, not so much afraid of the pain his son might know as of the fact that should his son endure any uncommon pain he, Nailles, would have no resources to protect him from the terror of seeing his beloved world—his kingdom—destroyed. Without his son he could not live. He was afraid of his own death.

He went back down the hall, closed the door to the room where Nellie slept and went downstairs, where he telephoned the New York City bureau of missing persons. There was no answer. He then called the central police office but they had no record of anyone like Tony. He gave them his number and asked them to call if there was any news. He drank half a glass of whiskey and then walked around the living room saying, "Oh, God, oh, God, oh, God." Then he went upstairs, took a Nembutal, got into bed and lost consciousness a few minutes later.

Nailles woke at half past seven and went back to Tony's room, which was empty. He then woke Nellie and told her the boy was missing. He telephoned the missing persons bureau but there was still no answer and when he telephoned the police they had no news. The next train from New York was the 8:10 and having absolutely nothing else to go on he settled for a kind of specious, single-minded hopefulness. Tony would be on that train. He felt that if he hoped strenuously enough for the boy's return the boy would appear. He drove to the station and when the train came in Tony appeared, surrounded by that mysterious company of men and women who travel on Sunday mornings and who invariably carry paper bags. Nailles embraced his son, embraced him until his bones cracked, and asked: "Oh my God, why didn't you telephone, why didn't you tell us."

"It was too late, Daddy. I didn't want to wake you up."

"What happened?"

"Well, I was feeling blue about football and I thought I'd buy a book of poetry so I went into a bookstore and there was this nice lady—Mrs. Hubbard—and we talked and then I asked her if she'd have dinner with me and she said why didn't I come to her apartment—she called it her flat—and she'd cook me dinner and so I did."

"Did you spend the night with her?"

"Yes."

Nailles knew that his son was a mature male and he had no reason to protest that the boy had acted as one; but what sort of a woman would pick up a young man in a bookstore and hustle him home to bed?

"Was she a slut?"

"Oh, no, Daddy, she's very nice. She's a widow. She graduated from Smith. Her husband was killed in the war."

This irritated Nailles. She had given her husband to her country and thus he must give his son to her. He somehow thought it the responsibility of war widows to remarry hastily and not to parade their forlornness throughout society, stressing the inequities of warfare. If she was attractive, intelligent and clean why hadn't she remarried?

"Well, we can't tell your mother. It would kill her. We'll have to make up some story. You went to a basketball game and it went overtime and you spent the night at the Crutchmans'."

"But I've asked her to lunch."

"Who."

"Mrs. Hubbard."

"Oh, my God," said Nailles. "Why did you do that?"

"Well, she's lonely and doesn't seem to have many friends and you've always told me that I should ask people to the house."

"All right," Nailles said. "This is our story. You went into a bookstore and you met a lonely war widow and you asked her to lunch. Then you got some dinner somewhere and you went to a basketball game and you spent the night at the Crutchmans'. Right?"

"I'll try."

"You'd damned well better."

Nellie embraced her son tenderly. He said that he had invited a widow for lunch and Nailles explained that Tony had spent the night at the Crutchmans'. The boy might possibly dissemble but he was incapable, Nailles knew, of a forthright lie.

"How are the Crutchmans," Nellie asked. "I haven't seen them for so long. Do they have a nice guest room? They've always urged us to use it but I always like to come home. I suppose we ought to send them something.

Do you think we ought to send them flowers? I could write them a note."

"Oh, don't bother," Nailles said. "I'll send them something."

After breakfast Nailles asked Tony if he wanted to cut wood but the boy said he thought he'd do his homework. The word "homework" touched Nailles—it seemed to mean innocence, youth, purity, simple things—all lost in the bed of a sluttish war widow. He felt sad. He cut wood until it was time to bathe and dress and then he made a drink. Nellie was cooking a leg of lamb and this humble and innocent smell filled the kitchen. He looked at Nellie for some trace of suspiciousness, reflection or misgiving but she seemed so unwary, so truly innocent that he went to the stove and kissed her. Then he went to the living room window and waited.

Tony parked the car in the driveway and opened the door for Mrs. Hubbard, who got out laughing. She wore a gray Chesterfield with a velvet collar and carried an umbrella, which she swung in a broad arc, striking the ground like a walking stick. Her right arm was hooked rakishly in Tony's and she seemed propelled forward partly by Tony, partly by the umbrella. She was shorter than he and looked up into the young man's face with a flirtatiousness that angered Nailles. She wore no hat and her hair was a nondescript reddish color, obviously dyed. Nailles, at a glance, put her age at thirty. Her heels were very high and this made the calves of her legs bulge a little. Her face was round and flushed and Nailles wondered. Indigestion? Alcohol? He opened the door and welcomed her politely and she said:

"It's simply heavenly of you to take pity on a poor widow."

"We're delighted to have you," said Nailles. Tony took her coat.

"How do you do," said Nellie. "Won't you please come in." She was in the living room to the right of the hall, where a fire was burning. The pleasure she took in presenting her house, her table, to someone who was lonely shone in her face.

"What a divine house," said Mrs. Hubbard, keeping her eyes on the rug. Nailles guessed that she needed glasses. "Can I get you a Manhattan," Nailles asked. "We usually drink Manhattans on Sunday."

"Any sort of drinkee would be divine," said Mrs. Hubbard, and Nailles made for the pantry. Tony asked if he could help and Nailles thought that he could help by throwing her out the door but he said nothing.

"Did you find the train trip boring," Nellie asked.

"Not really," said Mrs. Hubbard. "I had the great good luck to find an interesting traveling companion—a young man who seems to have some real-estate interests out here. I can't remember his name. I think it was Italian. He had the blackest eyes . . . Hmm," she said of a novel on the table. "O'Hara."

"I'm just leafing through it," Nellie said. "I mean if you know the sort of people he describes you can see how distorted his mind is. Most of our set are happily married and lead simple lives. I much prefer the works of Camus." Nellie pronounced this Camooooo. "We have a very active book club and at present we're studying the works of Camus."

"What Camus are you studying?"

"Oh, I can't remember all the titles," Nellie said. "We're studying *all* of Camus."

It was to Mrs. Hubbard's credit that she did not pursue the subject. Tony got her an ashtray and Nailles looked narrowly at his beloved son and this stray. His manner towards her was manly and gentle. He didn't at any point touch her but he looked at her in a way that was proprietory and intimate. He seemed contented. Nailles did not understand how, having debauched this youth, she had found the brass to confront his parents. Was she totally immoral? Did she think them totally immoral? But his strongest and strangest feeling, observing the boy's air of mastery, was one of having been deposed, as if, in some ancient legend where men wore crowns and lived in round towers, the bastard prince, the usurper, was about to seize the throne. The sexual authority that Nailles imagined as springing from his marriage bed and flowing through all the rooms and halls of the house was challenged. There did not seem to be room for two men in this erotic kingdom. His feeling was not of a contest but of an inevitability. He wanted to take Nellie upstairs and prove to himself, like some old rooster, that the scepter was still his and that the young prince was busy with golden apples and other impuissant matters.

"How did you lose your husband, Mrs. Hubbard," Nellie asked.

"I really can't say," said Mrs. Hubbard. "They don't go in terribly much for detail. They simply announce that he was lost in action and that you are entitled to a pension. Oh, what a divine old dog," she exclaimed as Tessie came into the room. "I adore setters. Daddy used to breed and show them."

"Where was this," Nailles asked.

"On the island," said Mrs. Hubbard. "We had a largish place on the island until Daddy lost his pennies and I may say he lost them all."

"Where did he show his dogs?"

"Mostly on the island. He showed one dog in New York—Aylshire Lassie—but he didn't like the New York show."

"Shall we go in to lunch," asked Nellie.

"Could I use the amenities," asked Mrs. Hubbard.

"The what?" said Nellie.

"The john," said Mrs. Hubbard.

"Oh, of course," said Nellie. "I'm sorry . . ."

Nailles carved the meat and absolutely nothing of any interest or significance was said until about halfway through the meal when Mrs. Hubbard complimented Nellie on her roast. "It's so marvelous to have a joint for Sunday lunch," she said. "My flat is very small, as are my means, and I never tackle a roast. Poor Tony had to make do with a hamburger last night."

"Where was this," Nellie asked.

"Emma cooked my supper last night," Tony said.

"Then you didn't spend the night at the Crutchmans'?"

"No, Mother," Tony said.

Nellie saw it all; seemed to be looking at it. Would she rail at the stranger for having debauched her cleanly son? Bitch. Slut. Whore. Degenerate. Would she cry and leave the table? Tony was the only one then who looked at his mother and he was afraid she would. What would happen then? He would follow her up the stairs calling: "Mother, Mother, Mother." Nailles would telephone for a taxi to take dirty Mrs. Hubbard away. Nellie, her lunch half finished, lighted a cigarette and said: "Let's play I packed my grandmother's trunk. We always used to play it when Tony was a boy and things weren't going well."

"Oh, let's," said Mrs. Hubbard.

"I packed my grandmother's trunk," said Nellie, "and into it I put a grand piano."

"I packed my grandmother's trunk," said Nailles, "and into it I put a grand piano and an ashtray."

"I packed my grandmother's trunk," said Mrs. Hubbard, "and into it I put a grand piano, an ashtray and a copy of Dylan Thomas."

"I packed my grandmother's trunk," said Tony, "and into it I put a grand piano, an ashtray, a copy of Dylan Thomas and a football."

"I packed my grandmother's trunk," said Nellie, "and into it I put a grand piano, an ashtray, a copy of Dylan Thomas, a football, and a handkerchief."

"I packed my grandmother's trunk," said Nailles, "and

into it I put a grand piano, an ashtray, a copy of Dylan Thomas, a football, a handkerchief and a baseball bat . . ."

They got through lunch and when this was over Mrs. Hubbard asked to be taken to the station. She thanked Nailles and Nellie, got into her Chesterfield, went out the door and then returned saying: "Oops, I nearly forgot my bumbershoot." Then she was gone.

Nellie cried. Nailles embraced her, saying: "Darling, darling, darling, darling." She went upstairs and when Tony returned Nailles said that his mother was resting. "For God's sake," said Nailles, "please don't ever do anything like that again."

"I won't, Daddy," said Tony.

VIII

On the night but one before Tony was stricken with what Nailles insisted was mononucleosis, Nailles and Nellie had gone to a dinner party at the Ridleys'.

The Ridleys were a couple who brought to the hallowed institution of holy matrimony a definitely commercial quality as if to marry and conceive, rear and educate children was like the manufacture and merchandising of some useful product produced in competition with other manufacturers. They were not George and Helen Ridley. They were "the Ridleys." One felt that they might have incorporated and sold shares in their destiny over the counter. "The Ridleys" was painted on the door of their station wagon. There was a sign saying "The Ridleys" at the foot of their driveway. In their house, matchbooks, coasters and napkins were all marked with their name. They presented their handsome children to their guests with the air of salesmen pointing out the merits of a new car in a showroom. The lusts, griefs, exaltations and shabby worries of a marriage never seemed to have marred the efficiency of their organization. One felt that they probably had branch offices and a staff of salesmen on the road. They were very stingy with their liquor and when they got home Nailles made a nightcap for Nellie and himself.

Nailles put on eyeglasses to measure the whiskey. Now and then his glasses flashed a double beam of light. He seemed, to Nellie, fussy that night as he measured out the ice and soda and she noticed a large lipstick stain along the side of his mouth. He would have exchanged an innocent kiss behind a pantry door and this did not worry her but the streak of crimson made him look ridiculous. His procreative usefulness was over—she thought —but his venereal itch was unabated—he scratched himself while she watched—and she wondered if there wasn't some massive obsolescence to the overly sensual man in his forties; some miscalculation in nature that left him able to populate a small city with his unwanted progenerative energies. Later, when Nailles lurched over to Nellie's side of the bed she didn't actually kick him but she made it clear that he was unwelcome.

Now Nailles had no use for men who were afraid of women. He had grown up with a man who suffered from this terrible infirmity. His name was Harry Pile and Pile had been afraid of women all his life. This had begun quite naturally with his mother—a large, big-breasted, impetuous woman who fired out contradictory commands, broke her husband's spirit and thrashed her only son with a thorny walking stick. When Pile was eight or nine years old he fell in love with a girl named Janet Forbes. She was intelligent and responsive and yet in some way formidable. Her shoulders were broad, her voice was a little gruff for a girl and her uncle, Wilbert Forbes, had discovered a mountain in Alaska that bore his name. That Harry's beloved shared her name with a mountain seemed to hint at some snowcapped massiveness, some inaccessibility that both pleased and frightened him. In school and college he invariably fell in love with women distinguished by their independence and intractability. He first married a high-spirited and beautiful young woman who gave him three daughters and then ran off with an Italian waiter. This deepened his fears. For his second wife he chose a woman so preternaturally demure, wistful and shy that it seemed he had outmaneuvered his fears but she turned out to be a heavy drinker and another source of anxiety. In the meantime the three daughters of his first marriage had grown up into argumentative, robust and determined young women and when he once tried to correct the eldest she picked up a china lamp and smashed it over the top of his head. It was Pile who swept up the pieces and retired in defeat. Pile was afraid of his secretary, afraid of his receptionist, afraid of strange women approaching him on the sidewalk. In his thirties he was taken ill and when Nailles went to visit him in the hospital he found, of course, that Pile was afraid of the nurses, afraid even of those kindly and maternal volunteers who sell cigarettes and newspapers. He failed rapidly and when Nailles last saw him he was emaciated and barely able to speak. When Nailles asked if there was anything he wanted he shook his head. When Nailles asked if there was any friend he would like to see he merely sighed. When he finally spoke it was in a hoarse whisper. "Do you think God will be a woman?" he asked. It was one of the last things or perhaps the last thing he said, since he died that night.

Nailles was *not* afraid of Nellie but he bothered her no more. Frustrated, angry and indignant he went into the guest room and slept there.

If you met Nailles on a train or a plane or a bus or a boat and asked him what he did he would describe himself as a chemist. If you questioned him further he would say that he worked for the Saffron Chemical Corporation but that was all you would get out of him. He had majored in chemistry at college but he had not taken a graduate degree and his chemistry was dated. He worked for Monsanto in Delaware for five years and then he worked for three years analyzing chemical fertilizers for the Food and Agricultural Offices of the United Nations in Rome. Saffron hired him when he returned to the United States. Saffron operated a small laboratory in Westfield but it was basically a manufacturing firm that produced a patent floor mop called Moppet, a line of furniture polish called Tudor, and Spang, a mouthwash. Nailles was principally occupied with the merchandising of Spang and he was definitely restive about this. It seemed to reflect on his dignity. He had argued with himself frequently on this score. Would he be more dignified if he had manufactured mattresses, depilatories, stained-glass windows or toilet seats? No. In the TV commercials for Spang, boxers in the ring objected to one another's bad breath. Bad breath came between young lovers, friends, husbands and wives. In a sense this was all true, he told himself. Bad breath was a human infirmity like obeseness and melancholy and it was his simple task to cure it. Sexual compatibility was the keystone to any robust marriage and bad breath could lead to divorce, alimony and custody suits. Bad breath could sap a man's self-esteem, posture and appearance. Suspecting himself to be a sufferer, the victim would mumble into his shirt, hoping to divert the fumes downward. Bad breath recognized no class. Nailles had read in the paper that bad breath came between Lord Russell and his love. Bad breath could come between the priest and his flock, Nailles had observed when Father Ransome breathed on him as he reached for the chalice. In Nailles's mythology the nymphs complained among themselves about the bad breath of Priapus. Bad breath drove children away from home. The wise statesman in his councils was not heeded because his breath was noxious. Bad breath was a cause of war.

Saffron was a paternal organization. A kindly old man named Marshman was president and majority stock owner and in the last year his son Michael had graduated from college and joined the firm. He was energetic, full of ideas and detestable. He had the products appraised by a firm of motivational psychologists. They concluded that the formula for Spang was too bland. Cleanliness was associated—so they claimed—with bitterness, and the sales of Spang would increase if its taste was more unpleasant. The laboratory had been asked to work up a new formula and on the day after the Ridleys' dinner Nailles drove to Westfield to test mouthwash. It was a pointless day. He rinsed and spat, rinsed and spat. His taste was not especially keen and when he chose a formula it was guesswork. He started back to Bullet Park at about four. His mouth was stinging and he stopped at a bar on the road for a drink.

There was nothing to recommend the place from the outside. It was shabby but when he stepped into the dark room he found himself in one of those quiet bars where the customers sit in a palpable atmosphere of sanctuary. The bartender wore a rented yellow jacket. Four men at the bar were drinking whiskey. One of them was feeding potato chips to a mongrel dog. "I never get any further than Southwark," one of them said. "Southwark is the only place I ever get to any more." There seemed to be some metric regulation to the pace of the talk. It was emotional, intimate, evocative and as random as poetry. They had come from other places and would go to other places but sitting against the light at four in the afternoon they seemed as permanent as the beer pulls. "I'll buy a free drink for anyone that can tell me what kind of dog my dog is," said the man with the potato chips. There were no takers and so he answered the question himself. "My dog is half beagle," he said, "and half Irish setter."

Nailles ordered a martini, which marked him as a traveler and a stranger.

"I had this girl who used to say hello," one of the men said. "You ever know a girl like that?" There was no answer and he went on. "She used to say hello all the time. I used to go over there on Thursday nights after supper. Her husband bowled on Thursdays. She was usually in a bathrobe or something like that and she'd give me a big kiss and start saying hello. So then when I was getting undressed she'd kiss my ears and everything and keep saying hello, hello, hello. She'd keep saying hello all through the preliminaries and then when we came to the main feature she'd keep on saying hello only louder and louder and finally she'd sort of yell hello, hello. Then afterwards she'd light me a cigarette and get me a drink of whiskey—she always did that—and she'd keep kissing me and saying hello. Then when I got dressed and kissed her good night she'd keep on saying hello. I suppose she must have said something else but I honestly can't remember her saying anything but hello."

"The things my wife used to say," the fourth man said, "I wouldn't want to repeat. She was very gentle-spoken and everything but when she got into bed she'd say anything. Worse than a whore. I used to wonder who taught her to speak like that. I mean it wasn't me. It used to make me jealous and I have a very jealous nature. She was a beautiful woman and she loved to put it out and if she wanted to two-time me she had every chance. I mean I was away from seven in the morning until half past six and when she wouldn't put it out I figured she must be getting it somewheres else. I suffered awfully from jealousy. I wouldn't hire a detective or follow her around or anything like that but I just wanted to be sure, if you know what I mean. So then I hit on this idea. The Thing. Has she got the Thing on. If she's got the Thing on she's planning to put it out. She kept the Thing in the medicine cabinet and it was very easy for me to find out where it was. So, one night I came home and washed my face and I chanced to look in the medicine cabinet and I saw that the Thing wasn't there. I thought I had her. So I went downstairs, very angry, and I asked her what kind of a day she'd had and she said she went shopping. She didn't buy anything but she spent the afternoon looking at dresses. So then I said it struck me she was looking at something else. She went on cooking and I asked her where the Thing was, why did she have to wear the Thing in order to go shopping. So then I hollered at her and called her names and she cried and cried and said she had the Thing on because we did it in the morning and you know she had me there because I couldn't remember whether or not we did it in the morning. So then I apologized and she stopped crying and we had dinner but she wouldn't let me touch her and I was still suspicious. Jealous, I mean. So about a week later she was going to visit her sister in Detroit. Her sister is very immoral. I drove her out to the airport and kissed her goodbye and when I got home that night I opened the medicine cabinet and there was the Thing. So I met her at the airport when she came home and everything was fine but that night while I was brushing my teeth I opened the medicine cabinet and I saw two Things. I figured she'd left one Thing at home to deceive me and bought another Thing in Detroit. So then I asked her why she had to buy a Thing in Detroit and she began to cry and said she'd bought a new Thing that afternoon because there was a hole in the old Thing. So then I asked her if she'd bought it at the drug store and she said yes and I said I'm going to find out the truth and I called the drug store and asked them if she'd bought a Thing that afternoon. They told me they didn't keep a record of those purchases and that the afternoon clerk had gone home so I asked for his telephone number, the number of the clerk, and they gave it to me and I called him and he said he couldn't remember, it was a busy afternoon and he couldn't remember every purchase that was made. She was still crying and naturally I felt a little cheap but I still wasn't sure about what was going on. Well, about a week later she was sleeping late and I was getting dressed to go to work and a button pulled off my jacket and I went to this box where she keeps needles and threads and I opened it up and there was another Thing. So I took it into the bedroom and I showed it to her and I asked her how the hell many Things did she have to have and she pulled the blankets up over her face and didn't say anything and I went to work with a button off my jacket. About a week after that they put the pill on the market and she threw away all her Things and started taking the pill and so, of course, I never knew. We got divorced six, seven months later."

Nailles had a second drink and went back to the road. The conversation at the bar had disconcerted more than it had amused him. What about the man on the bowling team? Did he know or care how his wife spent her Thursday nights? Nailles was monogamous—incurably so— and the existence of promiscuity bewildered him. He had fallen in love with Nellie the first time he met her and the success of his marriage was not an affair of the heart—it was a matter of life and death. He remembered a recent Saturday afternoon when she had fallen asleep in his arms. Holding her he had experienced a sense of being fused as heady as total drunkenness—a sense of their indivisibility for better or for worse, an exalting sense of their oneness. Her breathing was a little harsh and he was supremely at peace. She was his child, his goddess, the mother of his only son. When she woke she asked: "Did I snore?" "Oh, terribly," he said, "you sounded like a chain saw." "It was a nice sleep," she said. "It was nice to have you in my arms," he said, "that was very nice. . . ." When he got home that afternoon he mixed them both a drink and going upstairs to wash his face he opened the medicine cabinet for the same obscene and detestable purpose as had the stranger in the bar. Then he went downstairs and asked Nellie what sort of a day she'd had. "I went shopping," she said. "I didn't buy anything. I just looked at dresses. Everything was the wrong size or the wrong color."

"Would you come into the living room for a minute. There's something I want to ask you." She followed him into the living room and he shut the double doors into the hall so their voices wouldn't be heard by Tony.

In the natural course of events and in a society whose sexual morals were empirical, Nellie, as an attractive woman, had been approached by a number of men. The following things had happened. One Saturday night at the club the Fallows had introduced her to a young house guest named Ballard. He asked her to dance and when he took her in his arms she felt a galvanic flash of sexuality, much stronger than anything she had ever felt for Nailles. She could tell that he was equally disturbed. They moved absentmindedly over the floor. If he asked her to go out with him to his car she could not have refused and why should she? She was in the throes of the most profound sexual attraction of her life. He didn't ask her to go out. He didn't have to. They were both pale. He simply gave her his arm and they walked off the floor but as they passed the bar someone shouted: "Fire, fire, fire!" The bar began to fill up with smoke and the drinkers poured out into the corridor, jostling the lovers. Then down the hall came Nailles, carrying a brass fire extinguisher, and plunged into the smoke-filled room. The band went on playing but all of the dancers left the floor and crowded in the doorways. The fire department was there in a few minutes and the bartenders, coughing and weeping, began to carry the bottles out into the hallway, two by two. A white canvas firehose was dragged along the crimson carpet but they got the fire under control without having to inundate the place. When Nailles finally came out of the gutted room, smeared with soot, Nellie ran to his side and said: "Oh, my darling. I was worried about you." Then they went home and she never saw or thought of Ballard again.

Among the village libertines was a man named Peter Spratt although he was naturally known as Jack. His wife was a heavy drinker and there was endless speculation about whether his philandering had begun with her drinking or vice versa. At parties he often took Nellie aside and spoke about what he would do if they were ever left alone. She was not offended and was sometimes provoked. He borrowed Nailles's hedge clipper on Saturday. At Monday noon he rang the bell. Nellie answered the door. He stepped into the hall, put the hedge clipper onto a chair and giving Nellie an amorous and penetrating look that made her head swim said: "Now I've got you alone." Whether or not Nellie could have resisted him will never be known because Nailles was upstairs in bed with a bad cold. "Who's there, dear," he asked, "who's there, sweetheart." He appeared at the head of the stairs in his bathrobe and pajamas. "Why Jack," he said, "why aren't you working."

"I thought I'd take a day off," Jack said.

"Well have a drink, come in and have a drink." Nellie

got the ice and the two men had a drink. Spratt never tried again.

Another philanderer in the neighborhood—Bob Harmon—had several times asked Nellie to lunch with him and at a time when she was bored with Nailles and his worries about mouthwash, she accepted. She was thirty-eight years old and what harm could there be in flirting over a restaurant table with a good-looking man? They met in a midtown bar and instead of taking her to a restaurant he took her to an apartment. Here was all the paraphernalia for a seduction, including champagne and caviar. She ate a caviar sandwich and drank a glass of wine while he began to tell her how barren his life had been until he met her. He had still not moved towards her when either the caviar sandwich or something she had eaten for breakfast started a volcanic disturbance in her insides. She asked the way to the bathroom, where she remained for the next fifteen minutes, racked with cramps. When she reappeared she was quite pale and shaken and said that she would have to go home. He seemed, if anything, glad to see her go. So her chasteness, preserved by a fire, a runny nose and some spoiled sturgeon eggs was still intact, although she carried herself as if her virtue was a jewel—an emblem—of character, discipline and intelligence.

When the extremely shabby scene in the living room ended, Nellie went upstairs and washed away her tears. Then she served dinner so that Tony would not suspect there was anything wrong. At the end of dinner Nailles asked: "Have you done your homework?"

"It's all done," Tony said. "I had two study halls."

"Shall we play some golf?"

"Sure."

Nailles got some putters and balls out of the hall closet and they drove to a miniature golf links off Route 64. The links, Nailles guessed, had been built in the thirties. There were deep water traps, bridges and a windmill. The place had long ago gone to seed and had then been abandoned. The water traps were dry, the windmill had lost its sails and the greens were bare concrete but most of the obstacles were intact and on summer nights men and boys still played the course although there were no-trespassing signs all over the place. There were no lights, of course, but that was a summer night and there was light in the sky. A little wind was blowing from the west and there was thunder across the river. When Nailles described the scene to himself, as he would a hundred times or more, his description followed these lines.

"I was ashamed of having quarreled with Nellie and I kept blaming the whole thing on psychological motives and mouthwash. If I hadn't gone to Westfield none of this would have happened. Tony led off and I remember feeling very happy to be with him. I taught him how to putt and he has a nice stance. I gave up golf four years ago but I thought I might take it up again. We would play together. I know he isn't handsome—his nose is too big and he has a bad color—but he's my son and I love him.

Well, it was windy and there was some thunder on the other side of the river. I remember the thunder because I remember thinking how much I liked the noise of thunder. It seems to me a very human sound, much more human than the sound of jet planes, and thunder always reminds me of what it felt like to be young. We used to belong to the country club when I was a kid and I went to all the dances—assemblies—and when I hear the music we used to dance to—'Rain' and 'The Red, Red Robin'—and so forth I remember what it felt like going to dances when you're seventeen and eighteen, but thunder refreshes my memory much better. It isn't that I feel young when I hear thunder, it's just that I can remember what it felt like to be young. We shot the second hole at par and on the third hole you're supposed to make your ball loop the loop through an old automobile tire. I had some trouble with this. Tony made it in par but I was two over and still trying when Tony said: 'You know what, Dad?' and I said, 'What?' and he said 'I'm going to leave school.'

"Well this got me off-guard. It really spilled me. The idea had never crossed my mind. The first thing I figured out was that I mustn't lose my temper. I must be reasonable and patient and so forth. He was only seventeen. I worked out a reasonable and a patient character like a character in a play. Then I tried to act the part. What it really felt like was that patience was this big woolly blanket and I was wrapping myself up in it but it kept slipping. So I said very patiently, 'Why, Tony?' and he said because he wasn't learning anything. He said that French was all grief and English was even worse because he read more than the teacher. Then he said that astronomy was just a gut course and that his teacher was senile. He said that whenever the teacher turned off the lights for a film strip everybody took naps and threw spitballs and that once the teacher cried when they piled out of the class in the middle of a sentence. He said that when he got to the door he looked back and saw the teacher crying. So he went up to him and explained that they didn't mean to be rude, they just didn't want to be late for the next class, and then he said that the teacher said that nobody understood him, that he loved his students, he loved them all. Then Tony said he didn't think too much of a teacher who cried. Well, then we played the fifth hole where you have to get your ball through a gate. I did this in par but he was three over and we went on talking. I said that he had to get his diploma. I asked him what he was planning to do without a diploma and he said he thought he might do some social work in the slums. He said there was this place for children with disturbed parents and he thought he might work there. Well, I was having trouble with my patience, my woolly blanket. It kept slipping. I said that if he wanted to do social work that was all right with me and I felt sure it would be all right with his mother but first he had to get his diploma. I said I guessed that social work like everything else needed training and preparation and that after he got his diploma I and his mother would be happy to send him on to some college where he could get training as a social worker. So then he said he couldn't see what was the good of a diploma if he wasn't learning anything. He said it was just a phony, just a phony scrap of paper like a phony treaty. Then I said that phony or not you had to observe some of the rules of the game. I said that trousers, for instance, weren't perhaps the most comfortable form of clothing but it was one of the rules of the game that you wear trousers. I asked him what would happen if I went to the train bare-ass and he said he didn't care if I went to the train bare-ass. He said I could go to the train bare-ass as far as he was concerned. By this time we'd stopped playing and that was when these other men, men or boys, asked if they could play through and we said yes and stood aside.

"It was windy, as I say, and there was more thunder and it looked like rain and the light on the course was failing so you really couldn't see the faces of the men who played through. They were high school kids, I guess, slum kids, hoods, whatever, wearing tight pants and trick shirts and hair grease. They had spooky voices, they seemed to pitch them in a way that made them sound spooky, and when one of them was addressing the ball another gave him a big goose and he backed right into it, making groaning noises. It isn't that I dislike boys like that really, it's just that they mystify me, they frighten me because I don't know where they come from and I don't know where they're going and if you don't know anything about people it's like a terrible kind of darkness. I'm not afraid of the dark but there are some kinds of human ignorance that frighten me. When I feel this I've noticed that if I can look into the face of the stranger and get some clue to the kind of person he is I feel better but, as I say, it was getting dark and you couldn't see the faces of any of these strangers as they played through. So they played through and we went on talking about his diploma and the rules of the game. I said that whatever he wanted to do he had to train himself for it, he had to prepare himself. I said that even if he wanted to be a poet he had to prepare himself to be a poet. So then I said to him what I've never said before. I said: 'I love you, Tony.'

"So then he said, 'The only reason you love me, the only reason you think you love me is because you can give me things.' Then I said this wasn't true, that the only reason I was a generous father was because my own father hadn't given me very much. I said that because my own father had been so tight was why I wanted to be generous. So then he said: 'Generous, generous, generous, generous.' He said he knew I was very generous. He said that he heard about how generous I was practically every day in the year. So then he said, 'Maybe I don't want to get married. I wouldn't be the first man in the world who didn't want to get married, would I? Maybe I'm queer. Maybe I want to live with some nice, clean faggot. Maybe I want to be promiscuous and screw hundreds and hundreds of women. There are other ways of doing it besides being joined in holy matrimony and fill-ing up the cradle. If having babies is so great why did you only have one? Why just one?' I told him then that his mother had nearly died when he was born. 'I'm sorry,' he said. 'I didn't know that.' So then he said that I had got to understand that he might not want to come home at dusk to a pretty woman and play softball with a bunch of straight-limbed sons. He said he might want to be a thief or a saint or a drunkard or a garbage man or a gas pumper or a traffic cop or a hermit. Then I lost my patience, my woolly blanket, and said that he had to get off his ass and do something useful and he said: 'What? Like pushing mouthwash.' Then I lifted up my putter and I would have split his skull in two but he ducked and threw down his club and ran off the links into the dark.

"So there I was on this ruined miniature golf course having practically murdered my son but what I wanted to do then was to chase after him and take another crack at him with the putter. I was very angry. I couldn't understand how my only son, whom I love more than anything in the world, could make me want to kill him. So then I picked up his putter and walked back to the car. When I got home I told Nellie that I'd had a fight with Tony but she sympathized with him, of course, because I'd already had a fight with her. Then I had a drink and looked at television—there wasn't anything else to do. I sat there in front of the set until about midnight when he came in. He didn't speak to me and I didn't speak to him. He went upstairs to bed and I went up a little later.

"He's been in bed ever since."

IX

When Tony had been in bed twenty-two days Nellie received a letter from a cleaning woman named Mary Ashton who had once worked for her. Mary had been intelligent and industrious but she had been a thief. She had first stolen two small diamond rings that had belonged to Nellie's mother. Nellie never wore the rings and she did not accuse the maid of the theft. Good cleaning women were hard to find, Mary was poor and deserving, and Nellie thought of the diamonds as a bonus. A month or so later a pair of gold cufflinks vanished and Nellie fired the maid. She did not mention the cufflinks. The letter she received was neatly typed (had she stolen the typewriter?) on good stationery (stolen?). The letter read: "Dear Mrs. Nailles: I know that your son is sick and I am very sorry to hear this. He is one of the nicest boys I have ever known. In the village there is a guru or faith-healer who calls himself Swami Rutuola. He cured

my sister of arthritis last year. He works part time for
Percham, the carpenter, but he's usually at home in the
afternoons. He doesn't have any telephone but he lives
upstairs over Peyton's funeral parlor on Hill Street."

This combination of theft and magic disturbed Nellie.
She and Nailles gave a cocktail party that afternoon and
she didn't have a chance to show him the letter. The
party was excellent. It is difficult to praise a cocktail
party but as a hostess Nellie deserved praise. There was
no fatuity in the pride she took in her house. The pleasant rooms seemed to be partly illuminated by her graces.
The sixteen or seventeen guests were people whose company she unreservedly enjoyed. The food and liquor were
splendid and nothing banal, boring or asinine was said.
Charlie Wentworth, sitting close to Martha Tuckerman
on the sofa, shared with Martha a flash of immortal long-
ing. Looking into one another's eyes it suddenly seemed
to them both that a life together would be paradise. They
would laugh at one another's jokes, warm one another's
bones, travel to Japan. Martha left the sofa then and
joined her husband at the bar. This was the closest anyone came to adulterous passion. The only difficulty was
that Nailles had a circular driveway and without Tony—
who was, of course, in bed—to direct traffic, the parking
was haphazard. Nailles spent the last half hour of the
party either moving cars or asking people to move them.
Everyone had gone by eight. They had some scrambled
eggs and sausage in the kitchen and Nellie showed
Nailles the letter.

"Oh, my God," he said, "she was the one who stole, wasn't she? Maybe it's a ring of thieves. Maybe the Swami's an accomplice. Magic is the only thing we haven't tried but I'm not up to it."

Nailles's struggle to get into the city on the train had become so acute that he finally had gone to Dr. Mullin, who prescribed a massive tranquilizer. He took this each morning with his coffee, telling Nellie that it was a vitamin pill. The tranquilizer gave him the illusion that he floated upon a cloud like Zeus in some allegorical painting. Standing on the platform waiting for the 7:46 he seemed surrounded by his cloud. When the train came in he picked up his cloud and settled himself in a window seat. If the day was dark, the landscape wintry, the little towns they passed shabby and depressing, none of this reached to where he lay in his rosy nimbus. He seemed to float down the tracks into Grand Central, beaming a vast and slightly absentminded smile at poverty, sickness, wealth, the beauty of strange women, the rain and the snow.

On the morning after the party Nellie was waked by the sound of gunfire.

There had been riots in the slums and she wondered for a moment if the militants had decided to march out of the ghetto and take the white houses of Chestnut Lane by force. Nailles was not in bed and she went to the window. What she saw was Nailles in his underpants on their broad lawn, firing his shotgun at an immense snapping turtle. The sun had not risen but the sky was light and in this pure and subtle light the undressed man and the prehistoric turtle seemed engaged in some primordial and comical battle. Nailles raised his gun and fired at the turtle. The turtle recoiled, collapsed and then slowly raised itself up like a sea tortoise and began to lumber towards her husband. She had never seen, outside a zoo, so big a reptile, but it was Nailles, not the reptile, who seemed out of place in the early light. It was the turtle's lawn, the turtle's sky, the turtle's creation, and Nailles seemed to have wandered mistakenly onto the scene. He fired again and missed. He fired again and she saw the turtle's huge head swung to one side by the charge of buckshot. He fired again, put his gun on the grass and picked the turtle up by its jagged tail.

"Oh darling, are you sure it's dead," she called down from the window.

"Yes," he said. He seemed surprised to see her at the window. "It's dead. Its neck is broken."

"Where do you suppose it came from?"

"The bog, I guess. It must be a hundred years old. I got up to go to the bathroom and I saw it crossing the lawn. At first I thought I was dreaming. The shell must be three feet long. It could hurt a child or kill a dog. I'll bury it later."

In the bedroom Nailles, his right ear ringing from the gun and his right hand shaking a little, knocked a tranquilizer, his last, into his hand but his hand was trembling so that the tranquilizer fell to the floor and rolled under a piece of furniture. Nailles waited until Nellie had left the room. He bent a metal coathanger into the shape of a hook and lying on the floor he tried to recapture the pill. The piece of furniture—a dressing table—was flush to the floor and darkness concealed his pill. He hooked two pennies and a button. He then took the lamps off the top of the dressing table and moved it away from the wall. It was a heavy piece of furniture with loaded drawers and was a struggle to move, and when he got it away from the wall there was no pill but there was a crack in the flooring into which it must have fallen. He ran his coathanger along the crack but his only catch was dirt.

The thought of taking the train without a pill gave him all the symptoms of panic. His breathing was quick and his lips swollen. The place pain took in his memory was curious—he thought he had no memory for pain—but now the agony, confusion and humiliation of getting off at Greenacres and again at Lascalles, of getting off at Clear Haven and again at Turandot—returned to him with nearly the intensity of fact. He could not do it. Courage had nothing to do with his suffering. If he forced himself to go to the station he knew he would be unable to board the 7:46. Cold baths, self-discipline, prayer, all seemed like the moral paraphernalia of his first year in the Boy Scouts. He had to get into the city to fend for Nellie and his son. If he could not get into the city they would be defenseless and he imagined them as besieged by enemies—cold, hunger and fear—refugees from a burned city. He took a cold shower on the chance that this might help, but water had no calming effect on his image of the 7:46 as a portable abyss. He didn't know what hours the doctor kept but he knew that he had to get a new prescription before he did anything else.

The doctor's office was in a development of two-story apartments called garden apartments although there were no gardens to be seen. He rang and a man in pajamas opened the door.

"I must have the wrong address," Nailles said.

"You looking for the doctor?"

"Yes. It's terribly important. It's an emergency. It's a matter of life and death."

"You got the right place but he's not in practice any more," the stranger said. "The county medical society closed him down three weeks ago. He's doing laboratory work in the city."

"What happened?"

"Pills. He was giving out all sorts of illegal pills. But I'm right in the middle of my breakfast . . ."

"I'm sorry," Nailles said. He could drive into the city, or could he? He could take a bus. He could take a taxi. A man spoke to him from a car parked beside his. "You looking for the doctor?"

"God yes," Nailles said, "God yes."

"What was he giving you?"

"I don't know the name of it. It was for the train."

"What color?"

"Gray and yellow. It was a capsule, half gray and half yellow."

"I know what it was. You want some?"

"God yes, God yes."

"I'll meet you in the Catholic cemetery, out on Laurel Avenue. You know the one I mean. There's a statue of a soldier."

Nailles got to the cemetery before the stranger. It was an old-fashioned place with many statues, but the monument to the soldier stood a head taller than the host of stone angels and was easy to find. Gravediggers worked in the distance. Nailles had guessed that graves were dug by engines, but these men worked with a shovel and pickax. He passed an array of motley angels—some of them life-sized, some of them dwarfs. Some of them stood on the tombs they blessed with half-furled wings, some of them clung with furled wings to the cross. The soldier wore the uniform of 1918—a soup-plate helmet, puttees, baggy pants, and he held in his right hand, butt to the ground, a Springfield, bolt-action, 1912. He had been carved from a white stone that had not discolored at all but it had eroded, obscuring his features and his insignia so that he looked like a ghost. The stranger joined Nailles, holding a few tulips that he must have stolen somewhere. He put these into a container in front of the ghostly infantryman and said: "Twenty-five dollars." "I've been getting a big prescription for ten," Nailles said. "Look," the stranger said, "I can get ten years in jail for this and a ten-thousand-dollar fine." Nailles gave him the money in exchange for five pills. "You'll need some more on Monday," the man said. "Meet me at the railroad-station toilet at half past seven." Nailles put a pill into his mouth but he needed water. Rainwater had collected in one of the commemorative urns or ewers and he scooped enough up with his hand to get the pill down. Driving to the train he waited for the pill to take hold, for his cloud to gather, and by the time he got to the parking lot it had begun its wonderful work. He was moderate, calm, a little bored and absentminded. He forgot to put a quarter in the parking meter but when he had completed his painless journey into the city he telephoned Nellie and asked her to try the guru.

X

After lunch Nellie poured herself a whiskey. I should go to a shrink, she thought, until she remembered the doctor circling his invisible dentist's chair. She hated him, not for his real-estate business, but because she had always felt vaguely that in any crisis psychiatry could be counted on to work a cure, and he had taken this solace out the door with him. She remembered that the cleaning woman—the thief—had false teeth. Her favorite disinfectant had been a chemical, advertised to smell of mountain pine woods, but this imitation of the sweet mountain air was so crude, flagrant and repulsive that it amounted to an irony. Snowcapped toilet seats. Eliot had asked her to see the guru and so she went.

The slums, the oldest part of the village, were down along the banks of the river. She never had any reason to go there. She had read in the paper that women were mugged and robbed in broad daylight. There were knife fights in saloons. The rain was heavy that afternoon; the light narrow. All rain tastes the same and yet rain fell for Nellie from a diversity of skies. Some rains seemed let down like a net from the guileless heavens of her childhood, some rains were stormy and bitter, some fell like a force of memory. The rain that day tasted as salty as blood. So down into the slums went Nellie, down to Peyton's funeral parlor. This was a shabby frame building with a peaked door—a stab at holiness under which the dead (murdered in knife fights) entered and departed for the black cemetery at the edge of everything. There was a door on the left leading, she guessed, to the rooms upstairs, and she opened this onto a bare hallway with a staircase.

The strangeness of this environment disturbed her deeply as if she inhaled, in the rooms of her own house, not only the buttressed proprieties but an essence that conditioned her chromosomes and lights. The alien reek of the hallway—the immemorial reek of such places— seemed to strip her of any moral reliability. She looked around for something familiar—a fire extinguisher would have served—but there was nothing in the hallway that belonged to her. Had one of the legendary rapists she read about in the evening paper approached her she would have been helpless. She was lost. She was frightened. Her instinct was to turn and go; her duty was to climb the stairs; and the division between these two forces seemed like a broad river without bridges— seemed to give her some insight into the force of separateness in her life. She seemed to be saying goodbye to herself at a railroad station; standing among the mourners at the edge of a grave. Goodbye Nellie.

She had no role in this place and she felt it keenly. Census taker? Relief worker? An advocate for planned parenthood, distributing free pills? An adviser to unwed mothers? Lady bountiful dividing the proceeds from the church bazaar? She was none of these. She was a woman with a sick son, looking (at the advice of a thief) for a magician. I am a *good* woman, she thought. This foolishness was unintentional—compulsive—she seemed helplessly to ridicule herself. I've never once run over a squirrel on the highway. I've always kept seed in the bird-feeding station. She climbed the stairs. There was a window at the head of the stairs where someone had written on the dirty glass: "Sid Greenberg chews and smokes." There were two doors off the hall. One had a sign saying: "The Temple of Light." There was music beyond the door—singing—the voices compressed and funneled through a radio. She knocked and when there was no answer she called: "Swami Rutuola, Swami Rutuola . . ."

From behind the second door there was a loud sound of giggling—lewd or alcoholic—and then a woman imitated Nellie's accent. "Oh Swermi Rutaholah, Oh Swermi Rutaholah . . ." A man joined in the giggling. They must have been in bed. "Oh Swermi . . ." the woman said. She was nearly helpless with laughter. Nellie knocked again and a man asked her to come in. She stepped into a room

where a light-colored Negro was tacking upholstery web-
bing onto a chair frame. There was a smell of shavings.
Which came first, Christ the carpenter or the holy smell
of new wood? There was an altar in the corner. A votive
candle burned in a display of wax flowers. Wax flowers
meant death—death and Chinese restaurants. "Welcome
to the Temple of Light," he said. The voice was high,
definitely accented. Jamaican, she thought. The face was
slender and one of the eyes was injured and cast. A war,
an arrow, a stone? This eye, immovable, was raised to
heaven in a permanent attitude of religious hysteria. The
other eye was lively, bright and communicative. "I'm
Mrs. Eliot Nailles," she said. "Mary Ashton gave me your
name. My son is sick."

"Would you like me to come with you now?" he asked.
The voice was a very light singsong.

"Oh yes," she said, "if you could, if you think you can
help him."

"I can try," he said. "I'll just wash my hands. I don't
have a car and it's most difficult to find a taxi in the
rain."

She described Tony's trouble and some of its history as
they drove back to her house. The accent, she decided,
was not Jamaican. It was a rootless speech, aimed at fastidiousness or elegance. She took him up to Tony's room
and asked if he'd like a drink. "Oh no thank you," he said,
"I have something within me that's much more stimulating than alcohol."

"Is there anything I can do?"

"I would like to be sure that we won't be disturbed."

"I'll make sure of that," said Nellie and went down and poured herself another drink.

"My name is Swami Rutuola," he said to Tony, "and I've come here to help you, or that's what I hope to do. First I will tell you about my eye. When I was fifteen years old I had a most unfortunate impulse to steal a bicycle. It was a bright-red English Schwinn with three-speed gears. It was irresistible. I hid it in the cellar. When my father found it he beat me most severely and then went with me when I returned it. The father of the boy who owned the bicycle had no wish to prosecute me but my own father and mother insisted that I be taken to court. They were afraid I would become a thief if I were not punished. They were gentle people and I think I have finally come to understand them but they were very frightened of everything. I was sentenced to six months in the reform school in Livertown. Among the prisoners, as is so often the case, were some gangsters who operated a government within the prison government. They were exceedingly brutal and in order to protect myself I developed a limp. I thought that if I limped they would not subject me to their brutality but one day in the mess hall I forgot to limp and when they saw how I had deceived them they beat me up. I was two weeks in the infirmary and as a consequence of their savagery I lost the use of my left eye. I mention all of this because I have observed that when men and women talk with one another they count on communicating with their eyes almost as much as they do with their voices and since one of my eyes has no means of communication some people find it very disconcerting. I will hold my head in the shadow while we talk so that you will not be perplexed by my bad eye, but before we do anything else I would like to tidy up your room. Godliness is next to cleanliness—is that what they say—or is it the other way around?"

"I think it's the other way around," Tony said.

The swami began to gather the clothing that hung on chairs and doorknobs. He found a laundry bag in the closet and stuffed the soiled linen into this. He hung a jacket on a hanger, treed Tony's shoes, closed the closet door, and gave the chair cushions a shake. "Well that looks a little better, doesn't it," he said. "Another thing I would like to do is to burn some incense if you don't object."

"I'd like you to do everything you want to do," Tony said, "but I don't really like incense. Any kind of perfume. I never use after-shave lotion. I like to smell perfume on girls but I don't like it when it's all over the place. I don't like the way department stores smell."

"I think I know what you mean," the swami said, "but this isn't sweet or strong. It's sandalwood. It has a clean smell." He took a narrow stick of incense from his pocket and lighted it.

"That's all right," Tony said.

"I was born in Baltimore," Rutuola said, "to poor people, but the hardships of my race are well known so I won't bother you with them. I went to school until the eighth grade and I can read very well but I cannot do much arithmetic. My father was a carpenter and when I was paroled from reform school I went to work for him. It was much later that I went to New York where I found a position with the New York Central. It was not a distinguished position. What I did was to clean the toilets in Grand Central Station eight hours a night, five nights a week. I mopped the floors and so forth but what I spent most of my time doing was wiping off the walls the writing people had put there. The walls are white and you can write on them easily and after a Saturday night those walls would absolutely be covered with writing. At first I was troubled by this and then I realized that these people wrote on the walls because they had to. They hated to have the writing erased as if it seemed to be some part of them. They'd carve their messages in the wooden doors with a knife. You couldn't put them down as freaks because there were thousands of them and it gave me a very deep insight into how lonely and horny mankind is. So then one night—one morning, really—it was after three o'clock, it was closer to four—I was mopping the floor when this man came up to me and said help me, help me, help me, I think I am going to die. He was a well-dressed man but his face was very gray. So then I said a patrolman came through the concourse about now and I could go upstairs and get him and he could call an ambulance. But then he said don't leave me, I don't want to die alone, so then I said let's go up to the concourse together then, I'll help you. So then I took his arm and

we went up to the concourse very slowly—he was groaning—but when we got there there wasn't any patrolman
around, there wasn't anybody around, and he said that
he had to sit down and we sat down on some stairs. It
was very gloomy and cold and bare and empty there but
that great big colored picture that advertises cameras
was lighted. It was a picture of a man and a woman and
two children on a beach—a lake I guess—and behind
them, way off in the distance, were all these mountains
covered with snow. It was a beautiful happy picture but
it seemed more beautiful because the concourse was so
cold and bare and had nothing happy about it. So then I
told him to look at the mountain to see if he could get his
mind off his troubles. So then I said let us pray and he
said he couldn't remember any prayers and I realized I
couldn't remember many prayers myself so I said let's
make up a prayer and then I began to say valor, valor,
valor, valor, over and over again and in a little while he
joined me. So then I said some other words and he said
them along with me and then he said that he felt better
and after a little while he said he thought he'd take a cab
to a hotel and get some sleep and he said goodbye and I
never saw him again. A few weeks later I came out here
to work with Mr. Percham who is my cousin and a carpenter."

The rain lets up. Nailles comes home. Swallows and
blackbirds hunt in the early dark. The wind is out of the
northeast and coming up the steps he can distinguish the
sounds made by the different trees as the wind fills them:
maple, birch, tulip and oak. What good is this knowl-

edge for his son or himself? Someone has to observe the world. The steady twilight seems like a sustained note, perfect in pitch. Nellie tells him that the guru is upstairs but that he cannot be disturbed. Nailles drinks heavily and after dinner Nellie says she is going upstairs to lie down. She makes Nailles promise not to disturb the guru. He gives her a kiss and picks up a novel to bolster his self-control. "In the little town of Ostervogen in northern Denmark," he reads, "the following events took place in 1869. One morning in January a young man could be seen walking down the main street. The polish and elegance of his boots and the cut of his clothing suggested that they had been bought in Copenhagen or Paris. He was bareheaded and wore on his left hand an enormous signet ring, engraved with the crest of the Von Hendreichs. It had snowed during the night and the roofs of the little village were white. Maidservants were sweeping the dry snow off the walks with brooms made of twigs. The young man—it was Count Eric von Hendreichs—stopped in front of the largest residence and consulted a heavy, golden pocket watch. A moment later the bells of St. Michael's church rang eleven. As the last vibration of the bronze bells died on the cold air the young man ran lightly up the steps of the house and rang the bell. A maid wearing the apron and ribbons prescribed for servants at that time answered his ring, gave him a shy smile and dropped a deep curtsy. She was a pretty young woman but even the voluminousness of her costume could not conceal the fact that she was pregnant. He followed her down a dark hall to a large drawing room where an old lady sat by a samovar. The young count greeted his hostess affectionately in French and accepted a cup of tea. 'I can only stay a moment,' he said. 'I'm taking the stage to Copenhagen and the evening packet to Ostend.' 'Quel dommage,' said the old woman. At her side was an embroidery frame and below this a gilded basket heaped with hanks of colored yarn. She reached into the basket, extracted a small ivory-handled pistol and shot the young count through the heart . . ."

Nailles slams this book down on a table and picks up another called *Rainy Summer*. He reads the first sentence: "It was a very rainy summer and the ashtrays on the tables around the swimming pool were always filled with rainwater and cigarette butts . . ." He throws this book across the room. The doorbell rings. Nailles opens it and sees his neighbor Mrs. Harvey. Why is her face wet, he wonders. Beyond her shoulder he can see stars in the sky. Can she be crying and why is she crying? It is his turn to cry. "Please come in," Nailles says. "Please come in."

"I don't think I've been here since I solicited for the mutual fund," she says. She is crying. "I'm soliciting again." Red Cross, thinks Nailles, Muscular Dystrophy, Heart Trouble? "What is your cause tonight," Nailles asks.

"The Harvey family," she says. "I'm soliciting for Dads." She laughs; she sobs.

"Please come in and sit down," says Nailles. "Let me get you a drink."

"Well it's a long story," she says, "but I guess I'd better tell it if I expect your help. I guess you know that Charlie's a junior in Amherst. He went down to Boston and took part in a demonstration. He was arrested and spent a couple of nights in jail but they let him off with a fine and suspended sentence. Then two weeks ago the draft board changed his classification from student deferment to 1A. He was ordered to report for induction the day before yesterday. I mentioned the fact that he was going to be inducted when I was at the beauty parlor and the woman beside me—I don't really know her—told me there was a psychiatrist in the village who makes a specialty in drilling young men in how to disqualify themselves for the army. He charges five hundred dollars. I thought of speaking to Dads about this but it seemed dishonest. Charlie doesn't want to be a soldier but he doesn't want to be a liar either. I mean it seems like killing yourself in order to avoid getting killed. Anyhow I didn't mention this. He was supposed to report for induction on Thursday and on Wednesday Dads went to the savings bank and took out three thousand. It was all we had. He gave Charlie five hundred in cash and the rest in a certified check. We never once discussed his plans. After supper he went upstairs and packed a suitcase and came down and Dads drove him to the station. They didn't say anything, they didn't even say goodbye. Dads said he didn't dare say goodbye because he would start crying. I suppose he's in Canada or Sweden but we haven't heard from him. Well a day later a man came to Dads's office—a man from the government—and said that he knew Dads had taken three thousand out of the bank in order to enable his son to emigrate. Dads and I thought our bank accounts were private but evidently not. He said that he wanted to see Dads at home so Dads took an early train today and the man drove over—the government man—from the county seat where his office is. He first accused Dads of assisting a draft evader and then he said he was going to make it short and sweet and he took a cigarette out of his pocket and put it on the table and said that Dads was under arrest for the possession of dangerous drugs. The cigarette was a marijuana but it was the first one Dads had ever seen. The man explained that he was after draft evaders because he had spent a year and a half in a POW camp in Germany, eating rats and mice. He wanted the younger generation to learn what it was all about. So then Dads called the lawyer here—Harry Marchand—and they all drove over to the county seat and Dads was arrested for the possession of drugs and put into jail. They set the bail at two thousand and because this is the end of the month we simply don't have it so I'm going from house to house trying to raise it."

"I think I have two hundred upstairs," says Nailles, "if that would help."

"Oh it would help."

In the dark bedroom Nellie asks who is downstairs. "It's Grace Harvey," Nailles says. "I'll tell you about it later." When he opens the wall safe and takes out the money she asks: "Is the swami finished? Are you paying him?"

"No," Nailles says. "I'll tell you about it later."

"Would you like me to write a receipt," Grace asks.

"No. Of course not."

"I've done the mutual fund for five years," she says, "but I never thought I'd be going from door to door collecting bail for Dads."

By now Tony's room smells strongly of sandalwood. "Ever since my experience in the station," says the swami, "I have believed in prayer. As I am not a member of any organized religion you might well ask to whom it is that I pray and I would not be able to answer you. I believe in prayer as a force and not as a conversation with God and when my prayers are answered, as they sometimes are, I honestly do not know where to direct my expressions of gratitude. I have cured several cases of arthritis but my methods don't always work. I pray they will work for you.

"Your mother has informed me that you were an athlete and played football. I would like you to think of me as a spiritual cheerleader. Cheers don't make touchdowns, do they, but they sometimes help. I have all kinds of cheers. I have love cheers and compassionate cheers and hopeful cheers and then I have the cheers of place. In the place cheers I just think of someplace where I would like to be and then I keep repeating to myself a description of the place. For instance, in a place cheer I'll say that I'm in a house by the sea. Then I pick the time of day and the weather I like. I'll say that I'm in a house by the sea at four in the afternoon and it's raining. Then I'll say that I'm sitting in a kind of chair, a ladderback chair, and I have a book in my lap. Then I'll say that I have a girl I love who has gone on an errand but who will return. I say this all over and over again. I say that I'm in a house by the sea at four in the afternoon and it's raining and I'm sitting in a ladderback chair with a book in my lap and I'm waiting for a girl I love who has gone on an errand but who will return. There are all kinds of place cheers. If you have a special city you like—I like Baltimore—then you pick the time of day and the weather and the circumstances and you repeat all of this. Now will you do what I say?"

"Yes," says Tony, "I'll do anything."

"I want you to repeat after me whatever I say."

"Sure," says Tony.

"I am in a house by the sea."

"I am in a house by the sea."

"It is four o'clock and raining."

"It is four o'clock and raining."

"I am sitting in a ladderback chair with a book in my lap."

"I am sitting in a ladderback chair with a book in my lap."

"I have a girl I love who has gone on an errand but who will return."

"I have a girl I love who has gone on an errand but who will return."

"I am sitting under an apple tree in clean clothes. I am content."

"I am sitting under an apple tree in clean clothes. I am content."

"That was very good," the swami says. "Now let's try the love cheer. Repeat Love a hundred times. You don't really have to count. Just say Love, Love, Love until you get tired of saying it. We'll do it together."

"Love, Love, Love, Love, Love . . ."

"That was fine," the swami says. "That was very good. I could tell that you meant it. Let's see if you can sit up."

"It's crazy," Tony says, "I know it's crazy but I do feel much better. I'd like to try another prayer."

When Nailles hears them chanting HOPE, HOPE, HOPE, he has another whiskey. Was he a voodoo priest? Would he put a spell over Tony? Since Nailles claimed not to believe in magic why should magic have the power to frighten him? Out of the window he can see his lawns in the starlight. HOPE, HOPE, HOPE, HOPE. Their voices sound like drums. His lawns and the incantations came from different kingdoms. Nothing made any sense.

"Now try and sit up," the swami tells Tony. "Sit up and see if you can put your feet on the floor?"

Tony stands. He has lost all weight and muscle. His ribcage shows. His buttocks are wasted and there are red sores on his back.

"Take a few steps," the swami says. "Not many. Just two or three."

Tony does. Then he begins to laugh. "Oh I feel like

141

myself," he says. "I feel like myself again. I'm weak of course but I'm not sad any more. That terrible feeling has gone."

"Well why don't you put on some clothes and we'll go down and see your parents," the swami says.

Tony dresses and they go down together. "I'm all better, Daddy," Tony says. "I'm still weak but that terrible sadness has gone. I don't feel sad any more and the house doesn't seem to be made of cards. I feel as though I'd been dead and now I'm alive."

Nellie comes down the stairs in a wrapper and stands in the hall. She is crying.

"How can we thank you," Nailles asks. "Can we get you a drink?"

"Oh no thank you," says the swami in his thin singsong voice. "I have something within me that is much more stimulating than alcohol."

"You must let me pay you."

"Oh no thank you," the swami says. "You see whatever I have is a gift and I must give it away. You can however drive me home. It is sometimes most difficult to get a taxicab."

So that was it. Tony went back to school ten days later and everything was as wonderful as it had been, although Nailles, each Monday morning, continued to meet his pusher in the supermarket parking lot, the public toilet, the laundromat, and a variety of cemeteries.

PART TWO

PART
TWO

XI

My first knowledge of Nailles (Hammer wrote) was in a dentist's anteroom in Ashburnham. There was a photograph and a brief article about his promotion to head of the Mouthwash Division at Saffron. The article mentioned his years in Rome and that he was a member of the Bullet Park Volunteer Fire Department and the Gorey Brook Country Club. I didn't know then and I don't know now why I singled him out for my attentions. There was the coincidence of our names and I liked his looks. It wasn't until some months later that I made my decision. I was sitting on a beach. I had been swimming and was reading a book.

I was alone and it was at a time when the regard for domesticity had gotten so intense that the natural condition of singleness had become a sore point of suspicion. One appeared on the beach perforce with one's wife, one's children, sometimes one's parents or a brace of

house guests. One seldom saw a lonely man. It was a
beautiful beach and I remember it clearly. We tradition-
ally associate nakedness with judgments and eternity and
so on those beaches where we are mostly naked the scene
seems apocalyptic. Standing at the surf line we seem,
quite innocently, to have strayed into a timeless moral
vortex. The judgment that afternoon seemed to have
been evangelical and the only sound of sadness was the
wailing of some child who was afraid of the waves. Presently a faggot came along the strand and stopped about
ten feet from where I lay. This was a direct consequence
of my being alone. His walk was not incriminating but it
was definitely smug. His body was comely and tanned
and his trunks were exceedingly scant. He gave me an
amorous and slightly cross-eyed gaze and then hooked
his thumbs into his trunks and lowered them to show an
inch or two of backside. At the same time another man
appeared on the scene. He was a good deal older than the
faggot—forty perhaps—and had the bright sunburn of
someone whose days or hours on the beach were numbered. He was in no way muscular or comely—a conscientious desk worker with a natural stoop and a backside broadened by years of honest toil. With him were
his wife and two children and he was trying to fly a kite.
He was standing leeward on the dunes, the kite wouldn't
rise and the line was snarled. The faggot threw me another sidelong glance, gazed out to sea and gave another
absentminded pull at his trunks. I got to my feet and
joined the man with the kite. I explained that if he stood

on the crown of the beach the kite would likely fly and I helped him to unsnarl the line. At this the faggot sighed, hitched up his trunks and wandered off as I had intended that he should, but the filament of kite line in my fingers, both tough and fine, that had quite succinctly declared my intentions to the faggot seemed for a moment to possess some extraordinary moral force as if the world I had declared to live in was bound together by just such a length of string—cheap, durable and colorless. When the line was cleared I carried the kite to the crown of the beach and, holding it up, watched the wind lift it straight into the blue sky. The children were delighted. The stranger and his wife thanked me for my assistance. I returned to my book. The faggot had vanished but I longed then for a moral creation whose mandates were heftier than the delight of children, the trusting smiles of strangers and a length of kite string.

I was born out of wedlock—the son of Franklin Pierce Taylor and Gretchen Shurz Oxencroft, his one-time secretary. I have not met my mother for several years but I can see her now—her gray hair flying and her fierce blue eyes set plainly in her face like the waterholes in a prairie. She was born in an Indiana quarry town, the fourth and by far the plainest of four daughters. Neither of her parents had more than a high-school education. The hardships and boredom of the provincial Middle West forced them into an uncompromising and nearly liturgical regard for the escape routes of learning. They kept a volume of the complete works of Shakespeare on their parlor table like a sort of mace. Her father was a Yorkshireman with thick light-brown hair and large features. He was slender and wiry and was discovered, in his forties, to have tuberculosis. He began as a quarry worker, was promoted to quarry foreman and then, during a drop in the limestone market, was unemployed. In the house where she was raised there was a gilt mirror, a horsehair sofa and some china and silver that her mother had brought from Philadelphia. None of this was claimed to prove lost grandeur or even lost comfort, but Philadelphia! Philadelphia!—how like a city of light it must have seemed in the limestone flats. Gretchen detested her name and claimed at one time or another to be named Grace, Gladys, Gwendolyn, Gertrude, Gabriella, Giselle and Gloria. In her adolescence a public library was opened in the village where she lived and through some accident or misdirection she absorbed the complete works of John Galsworthy. This left her with a slight English accent and an immutable clash between the world of her reveries and the limestone country. Going home from the library one winter afternoon on a trolley car she saw her father standing under a street lamp with his lunch pail. The driver did not stop for him and Gretchen turned to a woman beside her and exclaimed: "Did you *see* that poor creature! He signaled for the tram to stop but the driver *quite* overlooked him." These were the accents of Galsworthy in which she had been immersed all afternoon, and how could she fit her father into this landscape? He would have failed as a servant or gardener. He might have passed as a groom although the only horses he knew were the wheel horses at the quarry. She knew what a decent, courageous and cleanly man he was and it was the intolerable sense of his aloneness that had forced her, in a contemptible way, to disclaim him. Gretchen—or Gwendolyn as she then called herself—graduated from high school with honors and was given a scholarship at the university in Bloomington. A week or so after her graduation from the university she left the limestone country to make her fortune in New York. Her parents came down to the station to see her off. Her father was wasted. Her mother's coat was threadbare. As they waved goodbye another traveler asked if they were her parents. It was still in her to explain in the accents of Galsworthy that they were merely some poor people she had visited but instead she exclaimed: "Oh yes, yes, they are my mother and father."

There is some mysterious, genetic principality where the children of anarchy and change are raised and Gretchen (now Gloria) carried this passport. She had become a socialist in her last year at the university and the ills, injustices, imperfections, inequities and indecencies of the world made her smart. She more or less hurled herself at the city of New York and was hired shortly as a secretary for Franklin Pierce Taylor. He was a wealthy and visionary young man and a member of the Socialist Party. Gretchen became his secretary and presently his lover. They were by all accounts very happy together. What came between them—or so my father claimed—

was that at this point her revolutionary ardor took the form of theft or kleptomania. They traveled a great deal and whenever they checked out of a hotel she always packed the towels, the table silver, the dish covers and the pillow cases. The idea was that she would distribute them among the poor although he never saw this happen. "Someone *needs* these things," she would exclaim, stuffing their suitcases with what did not belong to her. Coming into the Hay-Adams in Washington one afternoon he found her standing on a chair, removing the crystals from the chandelier. "Someone can *use* these," she said. At the Commodore Perry in Toledo she packed the bathroom scales but he refused to close the suitcase until she returned them. She stole a radio in Cleveland and a painting from the Palace Hotel in San Francisco. This incurable habit of thieving—or so he claimed—led them to bitter quarrels and they parted in New York. In the use of any utensils—toasters, irons and automobiles —Gretchen had been dogged by bad luck, and while she had been well equipped with birth-control material her bad luck overtook her again. She discovered soon after the separation that she was pregnant.

Taylor did not mean to marry her. He paid the costs of her accouchement and gave her an income and she took a small apartment on the West Side. She always introduced herself as Miss Oxencroft. She meant to be disconcerting. I suppose she saw some originality in our mutual illegitimacy. When I was three years old I was visited by my father's mother. She was delighted by the fact that I had a head of yellow curls. She offered to adopt me. After a month's deliberation my mother—who was never very consistent—agreed to this. She felt that it was her privilege, practically her vocation, to travel around the world and improve her mind. A nursemaid was gotten for me and I went to live in the country with Grandmother. My hair began to turn brown. By the time I was eight my hair was quite dark. My grandmother was neither bitter nor eccentric and she never actually reproached me for this but she often said that it had come to her as a surprise. I was called Paul Oxencroft on my birth certificate but this was thought unsatisfactory and a lawyer came to the house one afternoon to settle it. While they were discussing what to call me a gardener passed the window, carrying a hammer, and so I was named. A trust had been established to provide Gretchen with a decent income and she took off for Europe. This ended her imposture as Gloria. Her checks, endorsements and travel papers insisted that she be Gretchen and so she was.

When my father was a young man he summered in Munich. He had worked out all his life with barbells, dumbbells, etc. and had a peculiar physique that is developed by no other form of exercise. Even as an old man he was well set up and looked like one of those aging gymnasts who endorse calisthenic courses and blackstrap molasses. In Munich he posed, out of vanity or pleasure, for the architectural sculptor Fledspar who ornamented the façade of the Prinz-Regenten Hotel. He posed as one of those male caryatids who hold on their shoulders the lintels of so many opera houses, railroad stations, apartment building and palaces of justice. The Prinz-Regenten was bombed in the forties but long before this I saw my father's recognizable features and overdeveloped arms and shoulders supporting the façade of what was then one of the most elegant hotels in Europe. Fledspar was popular at the turn of the century and I saw my father again, this time in full figure holding up the three top floors of the Hotel Mercedes in Frankfurt-am-Main. I saw him in Yalta, Berlin and upper Broadway and I saw him lose caste, face and position as this sort of monumental façade went out of vogue. I saw him lying in a field of weeds in West Berlin. But all of this came much later and any ill feeling about my illegitimacy and the fact that he was always known as my uncle was overcome by my feeling that he held on his shoulders the Prinz-Regenten, the better suites of the Mercedes and the Opera House in Malsburg that was also bombed. He seemed very responsible and I loved him.

I once had a girl who kept saying that she knew what my mother must be like. I don't know why an affair that centered on carnal roughhouse should have summoned memories of my old mother, but it did. The girl had it all wrong, although I never bothered to correct her. "Oh, I can imagine your mother," the girl would sigh. "I can see her in her garden, cutting roses. I know she wears chiffon and big hats." If my mother was in the garden at all she was very likely on her hands and knees, flinging up weeds as a dog flings up dirt. She was not the frail and

graceful creature that my friend imagined. Since I have
no legitimate father I may have expected more from her
than she could give me but I always found her disappointing and sometimes disconcerting. She now lives in
Kitzbühel until the middle of December—whenever the
snow begins to fall—and then moves to a pension in the
Estoril. She returns to Kitzbühel when the snow melts.
These moves are determined more by economic reasons
than by any fondness she has for the sun. She still writes
to me at least twice a month. I can't throw the letters
away unopened because they might contain some important news. I enclose the letter I most recently received to
give you some idea of what her correspondence is like.

"I dreamed an entire movie last night," she wrote, "not
a scenario but a movie in full color about a Japanese
painter named Chardin. And then I dreamed I went back
to the garden of the old house in Indiana and found
everything the way I'd left it. Even the flowers I'd cut so
many years ago were on the back porch, quite fresh.
There it all was, not as I might remember it, for my
memory is failing these days and I couldn't recall anything in such detail, but as a gift to me from some part of
my spirit more profound than my memory. And after that
I dreamed that I took a train. Out of the window I could
see blue water and blue sky. I wasn't quite sure of where
I was going but looking through my handbag I found an
invitaton to spend a weekend with Robert Frost. Of
course he's dead and buried and I don't suppose we
would have gotten along for more than five minutes but

it seemed like some dispensation or bounty of my imagination to have invented such a visit.

"My memory is failing in some quarters but in others it seems quite tenacious and even tiresome. It seems to perform music continuously. I seem to hear music all the time. There is music running through my mind when I wake and it plays all day long. What mystifies me is the variety in quality. Sometimes I wake to the slow movement of the first Razumovsky. You know how I love that. I may have a Vivaldi concerto for breakfast and some Mozart a little later. But sometimes I wake to a frightful Sousa march followed by a chewing gum commercial and a theme from Chopin. I loathe Chopin. Why should my memory torment me by playing music that I loathe? At times my memory seems to reward me; at times it seems vindictive and, while I'm speaking of memory, I must mention little Jamsie. [Jamsie is her Border terrier.] I was waked one night last week at about three by a curious sound. As you know Jamsie sleeps beside my bed and Jamsie was making the noise. She was counting. I distinctly heard her counting. She counted from one to twelve. After this she did the alphabet. She had trouble with her s's of course but I clearly heard her go through the alphabet. I know you'll think I'm mad but if porpoises can talk why not Jamsie? When she finished the alphabet I woke her. She seemed a little embarrassed at having been caught at her lessons but then she smiled at me and we both went back to sleep.

"I suppose you think all of this foolish but at least I

don't go in for Tarot cards or astrology and I do not, as
my friend Elizabeth Howland does, feel that my windshield wiper gives me sage and coherent advice on my
stock market investments. She claimed only last month
that her windshield wiper urged her to invest in Merck
Chemicals which she did, making a profit of several
thousand. I suppose she lies about her losses as gamblers
always do. As I say, windshield wipers don't speak to me
but I do hear music in the most unlikely places—
especially in the motors of airplanes. Accustomed as I am
to the faint drone of transoceanic jets it has made me
keenly aware of the complicated music played by the old
DC-7s and Constellations that I take to Portugal and
Geneva. Once these planes are airborne the harmonics of
their engines sound to my ears like some universal music
as random and free of reference and time as the makings
of a dream. It is far from jubilant music but one would be
making a mistake to call it sad. The sounds of a Constellation seem to me more contrapuntal—and in a way less
universal than a DC-7. I can trace, as clearly as anything
I ever heard in a concert hall, the shift from a major to a
diminished seventh, the ascent to an eighth, the reduc-
tion to a minor and the resolution of the chord. The
sounds have the driving and processional sense of ba-
roque music but they will never, I know from experience,
reach a climax and a resolution. The church I attended as
a girl in Indiana employed an organist who had never
completed his musical education because of financial
difficulties or a wayward inability to persevere. He

played the organ with some natural brilliance and dexterity but since his musical education had never reached the end of things, what had started out as a forthright and vigorous fugue would collapse into formlessness and vulgarity. The Constellations seem to suffer from the same musical irresolution, the same wayward inability to persevere. The first, second and third voices of the fugue are sounded clearly but then, as with the organist, the force of invention collapses into a series of harmonic meanderings. The engines of a DC-7 seem both more comprehensive and more limited. One night on a flight to Frankfurt I distinctly heard the props get halfway through Gounod's vulgar variations of Bach. I have also heard Handel's *Water Music*, the death theme from *Tosca*, the opening of the *Messiah*, etc. But boarding a DC-7 one night in Innsbruck—the intense cold may have made the difference—I distinctly heard the engines produce some exalting synthesis of all life's sounds—boats and train whistles and the creaking of iron gates and bedsprings and drums and rainwinds and thunder and footsteps and the sounds of singing all seemed woven into a rope or cord of air that ended when the stewardess asked us to observe the No Smoking sign (Nicht Rauchen), an announcement that has come to mean to me that if I am not at home I am at least at my destination.

"Of course I know that you think all of this unimportant. It is no secret to me that you would have preferred a more conventional mother—someone who sent you baked goods and remembered your birthday—but it seems to me that in our knowledge and study of one another we are circumspect and timid to an impractical degree. In our struggle to glimpse the soul of a man—and have we ever desired anything more—we claim to have the honesty of desperation whereas in fact we set up whole artificial structures of acceptable reality and stubbornly refuse to admit the terms by which we live. I will, before I end my letter, bore you with one more observation of fact. What I have to say must be well known to most travelers and yet I would not dare confide my knowledge to an intimate friend, lest I be thought mad. Since you already think me mad I suppose no harm can be done.

"I have noticed, in my travels, that the strange beds I occupy in hotels and pensions have a considerable variance in atmosphere and a profound influence on my dreams. It is a simple fact that we impress something of ourselves—our spirits and our desires—on the mattresses where we lie and I have more than ample evidence to prove my point. One night in Naples last winter I dreamed of washing a drip-dry wardrobe which is, as you well know, something I would never do. The dream was quite explicit—I could see the articles of clothing hanging in the shower and smell the wet cloth although this is no part of my memories. When I woke I seemed surrounded by an atmosphere unlike my own—shy, earnest and chaste. There was definitely some presence in the room. In the morning I asked the desk clerk who had last occupied my bed. He checked his records and said that it had last been occupied by an American tourist—a Miss Harriet Lowell—who had moved to a smaller room but who could then be seen coming out of the dining room. I then turned to see Miss Lowell, whose white drip-dry dress I had already seen in my dreams and whose shy, chaste and earnest spirit still lingered in the room she had left. You will put this down to coincidence, I know, but let me go on. Sometime later, in Geneva, I found myself in a bed that seemed to exhale so unsavory and venereal an atmosphere that my dreams were quite disgusting. In them I saw two naked men, mounted like a horse and rider. In the morning I asked the desk clerk who the earlier tenants had been and he said: "Oui, oui, deux tapettes." They had made so much noise they had been asked to leave. After this I made a practice of deciding who the previous occupant of my bed had been and then checking with the clerk in the morning. In every case I was correct—in every case, that is, where the clerk was willing to cooperate. In cases involving prostitutes they were sometimes unwilling to help. If I found no presence in my bed I would judge that the bed had been vacant for a week or ten days. I was always correct. Traveling that year I shared the dreams of businessmen, tourists, married couples, chaste and orderly people as well as whores. My most remarkable experience came in Munich in the spring.

"I stayed, as I always do, at the Bristol, and I dreamed about a sable coat. As you know I detest furs but I saw this coat in great detail—the cut of the collar, the honey-colored skins, the yellow silk with which it was lined and in one of the silk pockets a pair of ticket stubs for the opera. In the morning I asked the maid who brought me coffee if the previous occupant of the room had owned a fur coat. The maid clasped her hands together, rolled her eyes and said yes, yes, it was a Russian sable coat and the most beautiful coat that she, the maid, had ever seen. The woman had loved her coat. It was like a lover to her. And did the woman who owned the coat, I asked, stirring my coffee and trying to seem unexceptional, ever go to the opera? Oh yes, yes, said the maid, she came for the Mozart festival and went to the opera every night for two weeks, wearing her sable coat.

"I was not deeply perplexed—I have always known life to be overwhelmingly mysterious—but wouldn't you say that I possess indisputable proof of the fact that we leave fragments of ourselves, our dreams and our spirits in the rooms where we sleep? But what could I do with this information. If I confided my discovery to a friend I would likely be thought mad and was there, after all, any usefulness in my ability to divine that my bed had been occupied by a spinster or a prostitute or by no one at all? Was I gifted or were these facts known to all travelers and wouldn't giftedness be a misnomer for a faculty that could not be exploited? I have finally concluded that the universality of our dreams includes everything—articles of clothing and theater ticket stubs—and if we truly know one another so intimately mightn't we be closer than we imagine to a peaceable world?"

XII

I grew up in Grandmother's house in Ashburnham and went to a country day school. I took my meals in the pantry until I was ten or eleven, when I was elevated to the big dinner table. There were usually guests. It was a time of life when the conversation of adults seemed painfully tiresome. I guess I was sulky. Anyhow Grandmother lectured me. "Now that you're old enough to dine at my table," she said, "I expect you to make some contribution to the conversation. When people gather in the evening they gather to dine but they also gather to exchange opinions, experiences and information. We learn something every day, don't we? We see something interesting every day. Surely during your day you learn or observe something that will be interesting to me and my guests and I want you to take a more active part in the conversation." I asked to be returned to the pantry but Grandmother didn't seem to hear me and I was nervous when I went to the table that night. The talk rattled on and then Grandmother smiled at me to signify that my turn had come. All I could remember was that walking home from school I saw a lady in the public park stealing marigolds. When she heard my footstep she hid the marigolds under her coat. As soon as I passed she went on picking flowers.

"I saw a lady in the park," I said, "stealing marigolds."

"Is that all you saw," asked Grandmother.

"I saw the basketball game."

The adults picked up the talk again but I knew I had failed and would have to prepare myself. I was taking a course in ancient history and I began each night to memorize the gist of two pages from my textbook. "Of all the Greek states," I said, "that stretched from the Black Sea to the western shores of the Mediterranean, none approached Athens, and the man responsible for this achievement was Pericles . . ." The next night we had Solon in Sardis and the night after that we had the Athenian constitution. At the end of the week Grandmother said kindly: "I guess perhaps it would be better if you listened to the conversation."

Grandmother was rich, and I won't go into this. She was a stout women with a plain face but the fact that she happened never to have worried about money had left her, even as an old woman, with an uncommon freshness. She seemed through luck and money to have missed one of the principal sources of anxiety. We were great friends although I sometimes teased her. When I was about twelve—I hadn't gone away to school—she was expecting for dinner an English earl named Penwright. Titles excited her and for some reason her excitement about the arrival of Lord Penwright put me in a bad humor. I was expected to attend the dinner. I learned that we were going to have oysters and I walked into the village and bought a large phony pearl at Woolworth's. I had Olga, the waitress, put this into one of the oysters on Lord Penwright's plate. There were maybe twelve people at the table and we were all chatting when Lord Penwright exclaimed, "Oh, my word," or "I say," and held up his pearl. It was the biggest pearl that Woolworth's had and it looked, in the candlelight, priceless. "What a charming favor," said his lordship.

"Hmmm," said Grandmother. Her face, usually quite bright, was troubled.

"I shall have it set and give it to my wife," said the lord.

"But it's my pearl," Grandmother said. "This is my house. These are my oysters. The pearl is mine."

"I hadn't quite thought of it that way," said the lord. He sighed and gave the pearl to Grandmother.

As soon as she had it in her hands she saw that it was Woolworth's and, turning to me at the end of the table, she said, "Go to your room." I went to the kitchen, had dinner and then went to my room. She never mentioned the pearl again but things between us were never the same. I was sent away to school in September.

XIII

Grandmother died in my last year at school and I had no place to go for Christmas. I had plenty of friends, as I recall, but I either didn't receive any Christmas invitations or I didn't accept any. I was left alone in the dormitory when school closed for the holidays. I was terribly lonely in the empty building and felt that my illegitimacy was a cruel injustice. Everyone else in school had at least one parent while I had none. It seemed that my father could at least buy me a beer on the Christmas holidays. That's all I wanted from him. I knew that he was married and living in Boston and I flew to Boston that night. I found his name in one of the suburban telephone directories and drove out to Dedham, where he lived. I was just going to ask him to buy me a beer. That's really all I had in mind. I rang the bell and when his wife opened the door I was surprised to see a very homely white-haired woman. Her face was sallow and her teeth were long but having so little or nothing at all to do with physical charm she seemed to have mustered another kind of charm. She seemed kindly and intelligent. Her mouth was large and thin-lipped but her smile was beautiful. I said that I was Paul Hammer and that I wanted to see Mr. Taylor. I think she knew who I was. She said he was in the city.

"He went in for a party on Wednesday," she said, "and when he goes to a party it's usually several days before he returns. He stays at the Ritz."

There was nothing long-suffering in her tone. Maybe she was happy to have him out of the house. I thanked her and drove to the Ritz. He was registered but he didn't answer the house phone and I took the elevator up to his floor. He didn't answer the doorbell either, but the door was unlocked and I went in.

There had been a party all right. The living room was full of the usual empty bottles and dirty glasses without which you can't, after all, have a party. He was in the bedroom. There were two unmade beds, both of which had seen some venereal mileage. He lay on one in a poleaxed, drunken sleep, naked. Around his neck he wore a chain of champagne corks—seventeen—which I guessed some friend had put there after he had stoned out. He was over fifty then but weight-lifting had paid off and if you couldn't see very well you might think he was a much younger man. He was lithe, really lithe, but this unseasonable litheness seemed to be obscene. He looked, hurled onto his bed by liquor, like the faded figure of some

Icarus or Ganymede that you might find painted on
the wall of some old-fashioned, second-rate Italian restaurant, flyspecked and badly drawn. I don't think he
would have waked if I'd shouted in his ears, and anyhow
he needed the sleep. I was that charitable. I was even
more charitable. He was my father, the author with some
collaboration of my heart, vitals, lights and mind, and
how far could a man go with such a creator? I could kill
him, I could abuse him and I could forgive him but I had
to do something so I settled on an uneasy brand of forgiveness and went away. My next stop was Kitzbühel. If
my father wouldn't buy me a beer maybe I could get a
cup of tea out of Mother.

We speak of travel—world travel—as if it were the
most natural human condition. "Mr. X," we read, "then
traveled from Boston to Kitzbühel." How far this is from
the truth! I got an evening plane for London at Logan
Airport. The plane was delayed and I drank five martinis
at the airport bar and crossed the Atlantic in a drunken
stupor. We got to London at daybreak, where I discovered that my bag had been lost. I wandered around the
airport until three that afternoon when my bag was
found and took a cab to the Dorchester. I tried, unsuc-
cessfully, to get some sleep and then went out to a movie
and got stoned at a pub. I had tickets for an early-
morning flight to Frankfurt-am-Main but there was a
thick fog over London that morning and when I got to
the airport everything was grounded. It was announced
at half-hour intervals that the fog was expected to lift. I

ate my complimentary breakfast. Then I ate my complimentary lunch. At three o'clock the airport was declared closed for the day. I went back to the Dorchester but there were no rooms and after trying four other hotels I ended up in a rooming house in Parkman Square where I was kept awake most of the night by noises that I do not choose to describe. In the morning it was still foggy but it seemed to be lifting and I returned to the airport. I drank a cup of abominable coffee and a glass of orange-colored water. The effect of this on my digestion was galvanic and I quick-stepped to the men's room. I had been there about fifteen minutes when I heard my flight announced. I pulled up my pants, ran the length of the airport and just caught the Frankfurt plane. My digestive troubles were not over and I spent the flight from London to Frankfurt in the toilet. Lighted signs in three languages commanded me to return to my seat but how could I? In Frankfurt, where I got a plane for Innsbruck, it was very cold. In Innsbruck I got the Transalpini to Kitzbühel, arriving at my destination at four in the afternoon, but I did not, in fact, seem to have arrived anywhere. I seemed merely to have scattered my guts and vitals a third of the way around the world.

Mother's address was the Pension Bellevue. The façade of the wooden building was decked with horns and I wondered if the Tyrolese had failed to make the connection with cuckoldry or was it that kind of a pension? When I asked to see my mother they seemed astonished. She was a Fraulein. A maid went upstairs and brought

Mother down. She cried with delight when she saw me and I took her in my arms. Her hair had begun to turn gray but she was not heavy. The color of her eyes remained a brilliant blue.

"Have you come for Christmas, Paul," she asked. "Have you come to spend Christmas with your mother? I usually go to the Estoril long before this but there hasn't been any snow this year and so I'm simply hanging on until the first flakes fall."

They gave me a room next to hers and we went upstairs together. She made some tea on a spirit lamp and poured me a cup. Then the door flew open and a bony woman flew in, exclaiming: "You've taken our sugarbowl! You borrowed our sugarbowl yesterday at teatime and you neglected to return it."

"But I did return your sugarbowl," my mother said politely. "I put it on your bookshelf. You'll find it there." When the stranger had left Mother turned to me and asked: "How is your horrid country?"

"It's not horrid, Mother," I said, "and it's your country."

"It's true that I travel on an American passport," she said, "but that's merely the sort of compromise one has to strike in dealing with a bureaucracy. It is, however, a horrid place. When I was in the Socialist Party with your father I said again and again that if American capitalism continued to exalt mercenary and dishonest men the economy would degenerate into the manufacture of drugs and ways of life that would make reflection—any sort of thoughtfulness or emotional depth—impossible. I was right." She poked a finger at me. "I see American magazines in the café and the bulk of their text is advertising for tobacco, alcohol and absurd motor cars that promise—quite literally promise—to enable you to forget the squalor, spiritual poverty and monotony of selfishness. Never, in the history of civilization, has one seen a great nation singlemindedly bent on drugging itself. I went out to California last year . . ."

"I didn't know you'd been home," I said.

"Well I was," she said. "I didn't call you."

"It doesn't matter," I said.

"I knew it wouldn't," she said harshly. "Well, to make a long story short, I went out to see some friends in Los Angeles and they took me for a ride on the freeway and here I saw another example of forgetfulness, suicide, municipal corruption and the debauchery of natural resources. I won't go back again because if I did do you know what I'd do?"

"No, Mother."

"I would settle in some place like Bullet Park. I would buy a house. I would be very inconspicuous. I would play bridge. I would engage in charities. I would entertain in order to conceal my purpose."

"What would that be?"

"I would single out as an example some young man, preferably an advertising executive, married with two or three children, a good example of a life lived without any genuine emotion or value."

168

"What would you do to him?"

"I would crucify him on the door of Christ's Church," she said passionately. "Nothing less than a crucifixion will wake that world."

"How would you crucify him," I asked.

"Oh, I haven't worked out the details," she said. Suddenly she was a gentle, gray-haired old lady again. "I suppose I'd drug him or poison him at some cocktail party. I wouldn't want him to suffer."

I went into my room to unpack. The plaster wall was thin and I could hear my mother talking through the partition. At first I thought someone had joined her after I'd left but then I could tell by the level of her voice that she was talking to herself. I could hear her clearly. "My father was a common quarry worker, often unemployed. I had read somewhere that the trajectory of a person's career could be plotted from their beginnings and given such humble beginnings I thought that if I accepted them I would end up as a waitress in a diner or at best a small-town librarian. I kept trying to tamper with my origins so that I would have more latitude for a career. Having been raised in a small town I was terrified of being confined to one . . ."

I went down the hall and opened her door. She had taken off her shoes and was lying on her bed, fully dressed, talking to the ceiling or the air.

"What in the world are you doing, Mother?"

"Oh, I'm analyzing myself," she said cheerfully. "I thought I might benefit from psychoanalysis. I went to a doctor in the village. He charged a hundred schillings an hour. I simply couldn't afford this and when I said so he suggested that I get rid of my car and cut down on my meals. Imagine. Then I decided to analyze myself. Now, three times a week, I lie down on my bed and talk to myself for an hour. I'm very frank. I don't spare myself any unpleasantness. The therapy seems to be quite effective and, of course, it doesn't cost me a cent. I still have three quarters of an hour to go and if you don't mind leaving me alone . . ." I went out and closed the door but I stood in the hall long enough to hear her say: "When I sleep flat on my back my dreams are very linear, composed and seemly. I often dream, on my back, of a Palladian villa. I mean an English house built along the lines of Palladio. When I sleep in a prenatal position my dreams are orotund, unsavory and sometimes erotic. When I sleep on my abdomen . . ."

I went back to my room and packed, the only son of a male caryatid holding up the three top floors of the Mercedes Hotel and a crazy old woman. I left her a note saying that I had suddenly gotten restless. To appear and disappear did not seem to me a dirty trick. I had the feeling that she was so wrapped up in her own eccentricities that she would hardly notice my going. I got a cab to the station and began my travels again. I was back in London that night in time for dinner. That was the twenty-third of December. After dinner I took a walk. It was snowing. I passed a theater or movie house where an evangelist, whose name I can't remember, was holding a meeting. I went in out of curiosity. The hall was about half full.

The evangelist was a plain man dressed plainly in gray—not ugly—but possessing one of those disconcerting faces that have no harmony. His nose was bulbous and red. His lips were delicate and thin. His hair and his ears seemed to have been slapped on as an afterthought. The house lights were on and I looked around at the congregation. There were plenty of rooming-house types —lonely old men and lonely old women whose devotions would be rooted in stupidity and boredom—but there were also clear faces, young faces, the faces of men and women putting up some creditable struggle for peace of mind. The ardor with which they bowed their heads in prayer and the sense of shared humanity moved me deeply. It seemed to me then that the cruel burdens of insularity, suspicion, loneliness, fear and worry had been lifted. Life was natural and we, together, were natural men and women. A man beside me seemed to plunge into the attitudes of prayer. At the end of the exhortation we were asked to come to the front of the theater, confess our sins and be forgiven. The congregation then, in small groups, went to the front of the theater and were blessed.

As they turned away, after the blessing, many of their faces were radiant, and what point would there be in my asking how long their exaltation would last? They must return, many of them, to empty rooms, the care of invalids, bankrupt marriages, contumely, ridicule and despair, but some promise had been made. I went down the aisle myself with one of the last groups. Oh Father I have sinned. I ate more than my share of the sandwiches at the picnic. I have performed every known form of carnal indecency. I left my new bicycle out in the rain. I do not love my parents. I have admired myself in a looking glass. Cleanse and forgive me most merciful Father.

Then, standing there with my head bowed, I felt completely cleansed and forgiven. Life was simple, natural, a privilege. My life had a purpose although it was not revealed to me until later. I walked happily back to the hotel.

XIV

In my sophomore year at Yale I petitioned the New Haven court to have my name changed from Paul Hammer to Robert Levy. I'm not quite sure why. Hammer, of course, was no name at all. Levy had for me a pure and simple sound and, belonging really to no community, I suppose I hoped to insinuate myself into the Jewish community. My lawyer spoke eloquently of the fact that I had been born out of wedlock and had been named for a humble and rudimentary tool that had been seen passing a window. The judge, whose name was Weinstock, refused my petition. The New Haven paper carried the story, including the origin of my name, and as a result I was dropped from the social register and lost at least a dozen friends. I have always been astonished to find that bastardy remains a threat to organized society.

I'll skip school and college. When I was twenty-four and living in Cleveland I invested fifty thousand dollars of the money Grandmother left me in a publishing house run by a man I'd known in college. We were both inexperienced and the business went poorly. At the end of a year we mortgaged our firm to a larger publishing house who, six months later, foreclosed the mortgage and copped my investment. I don't think there was any connection—I still had an adequate income—but at about this time I began to suffer from melancholy—a cafard —a form of despair that sometimes seemed to have a tangible approach. Once or twice, I think, I seemed to glimpse some of its physical attributes. It was covered with hair—it was the classical bête noire—but it was as a rule no more visible than a moving column of thin air. I decided then to move to New York and translate the poetry of Eugenio Montale. I took a furnished apartment, but I seemed to know almost no one in the city and this left me alone much of the time and much of the time with my cafard.

It overtook me on trains and planes. I would wake feeling healthy and full of plans, to be crushed by the cafard while I shaved or drank my first cup of coffee. It was most powerful and I was most vulnerable when the noise of traffic woke me at dawn. My best defense, my only defense, was to cover my head with a pillow and summon up those images that represented for me the excellence and beauty I had lost. The first of these was a mountain—it was obviously Kilimanjaro. The summit was a perfect, snow-covered cone, lighted by a passing glow. I saw the mountain a thousand times—I begged to see it—and as I grew more familiar with it I saw the fire of a primitive village at its base. The vision dated, I guess, from the bronze or the iron age. Next in frequency I saw a fortified medieval town. It could have been Mont-St-Michel or Orvieto or the grand lamasery in Tibet but the image of the walled town, like the snow-covered mountain, seemed to represent beauty, enthusiasm and love. I also saw less frequently and less successfully a river with grassy banks. I guessed these were the Elysian Fields although I found them difficult to arrive at and at one point it seemed to me that a railroad track or a thruway had destroyed the beauty of the place.

I had begun to drink heavily to lick the cafard and one morning—I had been in New York for about a month—I took a hooker of gin while I shaved. I then went back to bed again, covered my head with a pillow and tried to evoke the mountain, the fortified town or the green fields, but I saw instead a pale woman wearing a shirt with light-blue stripes. I seemed to feel for her deeply and clearly during the moment or two that I saw her but then she vanished.

I stayed in bed that day until eleven or later, when I went out to the corner drugstore and ordered some breakfast. The place had begun to fill up with the lunch-hour crowd and the noise and the smells nauseated me. I drank some coffee and orange juice and went back to my apartment and had another drink. I was drinking straight gin. This made me feel better and I had a third drink and went out once more to see if I couldn't eat something.

This time I went to a French restaurant where my alcoholic fastidiousness would not be offended. I ordered a martini, some pâté and a plate of scrambled eggs and was able to get this down. Then I returned to my apartment, undressed and got back into bed again, pulling the covers over my face. I hated the light of day, it seemed to be the essence of my cafard, as if darkness would lessen my frustrations, as if the night were a guise of forgetfulness. I stayed in bed, neither sleeping nor waking. When I dressed again and went out onto the street it was beginning to get dark. I went back to the French restaurant, where I had some snails and a beef filet, and then went to a movie. It was a spy movie and seemed so old-fashioned that it undermined my already feeble sense of time and reality. I left halfway through the movie and went back to bed again. It must have been about ten. I took a couple of sleeping pills and stayed in bed until two the next afternoon, when I dressed and went out to the restaurant and had another plate of scrambled eggs. I then returned to bed and stayed there until ten the next morning. What I wanted then was a long, long, long sleep and I had enough pills to accomplish this. I flushed the pills down the toilet and called one of my few friends and asked for the name of his doctor. I then called the doctor and asked him for the name of a psychiatrist. He recommended a man named Doheny.

Doheny saw me that afternoon. His waiting room had a large collection of magazines but the ashtrays were clean, the cushions were unrumpled and I had the feeling that perhaps I was his first customer in a long time. Was he, I wondered, an unemployed psychiatrist, an unsuccessful psychiatrist, an unpopular psychiatrist, did he wile away the time in an empty office like an idle lawyer, barber or antique dealer? He presently appeared and led me into a consultation room that was furnished with antiques. I wondered then if some part of a psychiatrist's education was the furnishing of his consultation room. Did they do it themselves? Did their wives do it? Was it done by a professional? Doheny had large brown eyes in a long face. When I sat in the patient's chair he turned the beam of his brown eye onto me exactly as a dentist turns on the light above his drills and for the next fifty minutes I basked in his gaze and returned his looks earnestly to prove that I was truthful and manly. He seemed, like some illusion of drunkenness, to have two faces and I found it fascinating to watch one swallow up the other. He charged a dollar a minute.

After our fourth or fifth consultation he asked me to masturbate when I got home and report my reactions to him. I did as he asked and reported that I had felt ashamed of myself. He was delighted with this news and said that it proved that sexual guilt was the source of my cafard. I was a repressed transvestite homosexual. I had told him about Daddy posing for Fledspar and he told me that this image of a naked man supporting hotels, palaces of justice and opera houses had intimidated me and forced me into an unnatural way of life. I told him to go to hell and said that I was through. I said that he was

a charlatan and that I was going to report him to the
American Psychiatric Society. If he wasn't a charlatan
why didn't he have diplomas hung on his wall like other
doctors? He got very angry at this, threw open his desk
drawer and pulled out a pile of diplomas. He had diplomas from Yale, Columbia and the Neurological Hospital.
Then I noticed that all these documents were made out
to a man named Howard Shitz and I asked if he hadn't
picked them up in a secondhand bookstore. He said he
had changed his name when he went into practice for
reasons that any dunce would understand. I left.

I was no better after Doheny—I was worse—and I
began to wonder seriously if the ubiquity of my father's
head and shoulders carved in limestone had not been
crippling; but if it had been what could I do? The opera
house in Malsburg and the Prinz-Regenten had been
demolished but I couldn't remove him from his position
on upper Broadway and he was still holding up the Mercedes in Frankfurt. I went on drinking—more than a
quart a day—and my hands had begun to shake terribly.
When I went into a bar I would wait until the bartender
turned his back before I tried to get the glass up to my
mouth. I sometimes spilled gin all over the bar. This
amused the other customers. I went out to Pennsylvania
one weekend with some heavy-drinking friends and
came back on a social train that got me into Penn Station
at about eleven Sunday night. The station was then being
razed and reconstructed and it was such a complex of
ruins that it seemed like a frightening projection of my

own confusions and I stepped out into the street, looking for a bar. The bars around the station were too brightly lighted for a man whose hands were shaking and I started walking east, looking for some dark saloon where my infirmity would not be so noticeable. Walking down a side street I saw two lighted windows and a room with yellow walls. The windows were uncurtained. All I could see were the yellow walls. I put down my suitcase to stare at the windows. I was convinced that whoever lived there lived a useful and illustrious life. It would be a single man like myself but a man with a continent nature, a ruling intelligence, an efficient disposition. The pair of windows filled me with shame. I wanted my life to be not merely decent but exemplary. I wanted to be useful, continent and at peace. If I could not change my habits I could at least change my environment and I thought that if I found such a room with yellow walls I would cure my cafard and my drunkenness.

The next afternoon I packed a bag and took a cab across town to the Hotel Milton, looking for that room where I could begin my illustrious life. They gave me a room on the second floor, looking out onto an airshaft. The room had not been made up. There was an empty whiskey bottle and two glasses on the bureau and only one of the two beds had been used. I called the desk to complain and they said the only other vacancy they had was a suite on the tenth floor. I then moved to this. I found a parlor, a double bedroom and a large collection of flower pictures. I ordered some gin, vermouth and a bucket of ice and got stoned. This was not what I intended to do and in the morning I moved to the Hotel Madison.

My room at the Madison was furnished with the kind of antiques Doheny had had in his consultation room. It only lacked the colored photographs of his three children. The desk, or some part of it, had once been a spinet. The coffee table was covered with leather that had been tooled, gilded and burned by many cigarettes. There were mirrors on all the walls so that I could not escape my own image. I saw myself smoking, drinking, dressing and undressing and when I woke in the morning the first thing I saw was myself. I left the next day for the Waldorf, where I was given a pleasant, high-ceilinged room. There was a broad view. I could see the dome of St. Bartholomew's, the Seagram Building and one of those yellow bifurcated buildings that has a terraced and windowed front and a flat, yellow-brick backside with no sign of life but a rain gutter. It seemed to have been sliced with a knife. Almost anywhere in New York above the fifteenth floor your view includes a few caryatids, naiads, homely water tanks and Florentine arches and I was admiring these when it occurred to me how easy it would be to escape the cafard by jumping into the street and I checked out of the Waldorf and took a plane to Chicago.

In Chicago I took a room at the Palmer House. This was on the sixteenth floor. The furniture seemed to be of some discernible period but the more I examined it the more it seemed to be an inoffensive improvisation and then I realized that it was the same furniture I had seen in my room at the Waldorf. I flipped open the venetian blinds. My window looked out into an enclosure where I could see, upwards, downwards and sidewise, a hundred, hundred windows exactly like mine. The fact that my room had no uniqueness seemed seriously to threaten my own uniqueness. I suffered an intense emotional vertigo. The fear was not of falling but of vanishing. If there was nothing in my room to distinguish it from a hundred, hundred others there might be nothing about me to set me apart from other men, and I snapped the venetian blinds shut and went out of the room. Waiting for the elevator a man gave me that bland, hopeful gaze of a faggot on the make and I thought that he might have been driven by the sameness of the hotel windows to authenticate his identity by unnatural sexual practices. I lowered my eyes chastely to the floor. Downstairs I drank three martinis and went to a movie. I stayed in Chicago two days and took the Zephyr to San Francisco. I thought a train compartment might be the environment where I could begin my new life but it was not. In San Francisco I stayed two nights at the Palace and two nights at the St. Francis and then flew down the coast and checked in at the Los Angeles Biltmore. This was the furthest from what I wanted and I moved from there to the Château Marmont. I moved from there to the Beverly Hills and a day later took a plane to London on the northerly route. I tried to get a room at the Connaught but they were full and so I went instead to the Dorchester where I lasted two days. I then flew to Rome and checked in at the Eden. My cafard had followed me around the world and I was still drinking heavily. Lying in bed in the Eden one morning with a pillow over my face I summoned up Kilimanjaro and its ancient village, the Elysian Fields and the fortified town. It occurred to me then that I had thought the town might be Orvieto. I rented a Fiat from the concierge and started north.

It was after lunch when I got into Umbria and I stopped in a walled town and had some pasta and wine. The country was wheat country, more heavily forested than most of Italy and very green. Like most travelers I kept stupidly observing the sameness of things, kept telling myself that on the evidence of what I saw I might be in New Hampshire or the outskirts of Heidelberg. What for? It was nearly seven o'clock when I came down the winding road into the broad valley that surrounds Orvieto.

I had been wrong about the towers but everything else seemed right. The city was high, its buildings seemed to be a variation of the stone butte and it looked like the place I had seen in fending off the cafard. It seemed to correspond to my vision. I was excited. My life, my sanity were involved. The papal cathedral, in its commanding position, excited, as it was meant to do, awe, admiration and something like dread as if some part of my memory was that of a heretic on my way to be questioned by the bishops. I drove through the lower town up to the city on the butte and checked in at the Hotel Nazionale where I was given a large, deluxe European room with a massive armoire and a glass chandelier. It was not the room I was looking for. I wandered around the streets and just before dark, in a building not far from the cathedral, I saw the lighted windows and the yellow walls.

I seemed, looking up at them from the sidewalk, to be standing at the threshold of a new life. This was not a sanctuary, this was the vortex of things, but this was a place where the cafard could not enter. The door of the building was open and I climbed some stairs. The pair of yellow rooms was on the second floor. They were unfurnished, as I knew they would be, and freshly painted. Everything was ready for my occupancy. There was a man putting up shelves for my books. I spoke to the man and asked him who the rooms belonged to. He said they were his. I asked if they were for sale or for rent and he smiled and said no. Then I said I wanted them and would pay whatever he asked for them but he went on smiling and saying no. Then I heard some men in the hallway, carrying something heavy. I could hear their strained voices, their breathing, and the object, whatever it was, bumping against the wall. It was a large bed, which they carried into the second of the yellow rooms. The owner explained to me then that this was his marriage bed. He was going to be married next day in the chapel of the cathedral and begin his married life here. I was still so convinced that the rooms were, spiritually at least, my property that I asked him if he wouldn't prefer to live in one of the new apartments in the lower town. I would pay the difference in the rent and was prepared to give him a large present for the wedding. He was impervious, of course. Like any groom, he had imagined so many hundreds of times the hour when he would bring his bride back to the yellow rooms that no amount of money would dislodge the memory from its place in his mind. I wished him well anyhow and went down the stairs. I had found my yellow rooms and I had lost them. I left Orvieto in the morning for Rome and left Rome the next day for New York.

I spent one night in my apartment during which I drank a quart of whiskey. The next afternoon I drove out to Pennsylvania to visit a classmate of mine—Charlie Masterson—and his wife. There were heavy drinkers and we ran out of gin before dinner. I drove into the little village of Blenville and bought a fresh supply at the liquor store and started back. I made a wrong turn and found myself on a narrow red dirt lane that seemed to lead nowhere. Then on my left, set back from the road and a little above it, I saw the yellow walls for the third time.

I turned off the motor and the lights and got out of the car. There was a brook between the road and the house and I crossed this on a wooden bridge. A lawn or a field —the grass needed cutting—sloped up to a terrace. The house was stone—rectangular—an old Pennsylvania farmhouse, and the yellow room was the only room lighted. The walls were the same color I had seen in Orvieto. I went up onto the terrace, as absorbed as any thief. A woman sat in the yellow room, reading a book. She wore a black dress and high-heeled shoes and had a glass of whiskey on a table at her side. Her face was pale and handsome. I guessed she was in her twenties. The black dress and the high-heeled shoes seemed out of place in the country and I wondered if she had just arrived from town or were just about to leave, although the size of the whiskey glass made this seem unlikely. But it was not the woman but the room I wanted—square, its lemon-yellow walls simply lighted—and I felt that if I could only possess this I would be myself again, industrious and decent. She looked up suddenly as if she sensed my presence and I stepped away from the window. I was very happy. Walking back to the car I saw the name Emmison painted on a mailbox at the end of the driveway. I found my way back to the Mastersons' and asked Mrs. Masterson if she knew anyone named Emmison. "Sure," she said. "Dora Emmison. I think she's in Reno."

"Her house was lighted," I said.

"What in the world were you doing at her house?"

"I got lost."

"Well she was in Reno. I suppose she's just come back. Do you know her?" she asked.

"No," I said, "but I'd like to."

"Well if she's back I'll ask her for a drink tomorrow."

She came the next afternoon, wearing the black dress and the same high heels. She was a little reserved but I found her fascinating, not because of her physical and intellectual charms but because she owned the yellow rooms. She stayed for supper and I asked about her house. I presently asked if she wouldn't like to sell it. She was not at all interested. Then I asked if I could see the house and she agreed indifferently. She was leaving early and if I wanted to see the place I could come back with her and so I did.

As soon as I stepped into the yellow room I felt that peace of mind I had coveted when I first saw the walls in a walkup near Pennsylvania Station. Sometimes you step into a tackroom, a carpenter's shop or a country post office and find yourself unexpectedly at peace with the world. It is usually late in the day. The place has a fine smell (I must include bakeries). The groom, carpenter, postmaster or baker has a face so clear, so free of trouble that you feel that nothing bad has ever or will ever happen here, a sense of fitness and sanctity never achieved, in my experience, by any church.

She gave me a drink and I asked again if she would sell the place. "Why should I sell my house," she asked. "I like my house. It's the only house I have. If you want a place in the neighborhood the Barkham place is on the market and it's really much more attractive than this."

"This is the house I want."

"I don't see why you're so crazy about this place. If I had a choice I'd rather have the Barkham place."

"Well I'll buy the Barkham place and exchange it for this."

"I simply don't want to move," she said. She looked at her watch.

"Could I sleep here," I asked.

"Where."

"Here, here in this room."

"But what do you want to sleep here for? The sofa's hard as a rock."

"I'd just like to."

"Well I guess you can if you want to. No monkey business."

"No monkey business."

"I'll get some bedding."

She went upstairs and came down with some sheets and a blanket and made my bed. "I think I'll turn in myself," she said, going towards the stairs. "I guess you know where everything is. If you want another drink there's some ice in the bucket. I think my husband left a razor in the medicine cabinet. Good night." Her smile was courteous and no more. She climbed the stairs.

I didn't make a drink. I didn't, as they say, need one. I sat in a chair by the window feeling the calm of the yellow walls restore me. Outside I could hear the brook, some night bird, moving leaves, and all the sounds of the night world seemed endearing as if I quite literally loved the night as one loves a woman, loved the stars, the trees, the weeds in the grass as one can love with the same ardor a woman's breasts and the apple core she has left in an ashtray. I loved it all and everyone who lived. My life had begun again and I could see, from this beginning, how far I had gone from any natural course. Here was the sense of reality—a congenial, blessed and useful construction to which I belonged. I stepped out onto the terrace. It was cloudy but some stars could still be seen. The wind was shifting and smelled of rain. I walked down to the bridge, undressed and dove into a pool there. The water was buoyant and a little brackish from the bogs in which it rose, but it had, so unlike the disinfected sapphire of a pool, a strong and unmistakably erotic emphasis. I dried myself on my shirttails and walked naked back to the house, feeling as if the earth were paved for my contentment. I brushed my teeth, turned out the light, and as I got into my bed it began to rain.

For a year or more the sound of the rain had meant merely umbrellas, raincoats, rubbers, the wet seats of convertibles, but now it seemed like some enlargement of my happiness, some additional bounty. It seemed to increase my feeling of limberness and innocence and I fended off sleep to listen to it with the attention and curiosity with which we follow music. When I did sleep I dreamed in this order of the mountain, the walled town and the banks of the river and when I woke at dawn there was no trace of the cafard. I dove into the pool again and dressed. In the kitchen I found a melon, made some coffee and fried some bacon. The smell of coffee and bacon seemed like a smell of newness and I ate with a good appetite. She came down later in a bathrobe and thanked me for having made the coffee. When she raised the cup to her lips her hand shook so that the coffee spilled. She went into the pantry, returned with a bottle of whiskey and spiked her coffee. She neither apologized or explained this but the spike steadied her hand. I asked her if she wouldn't like me to cut the grass. "Well I would frankly," she said, "if you don't have anything better to do. It's terribly hard to find anyone around here to do anything. All the young men leave home and all the old ones die. The mower's in the toolshed and I think there's some gasoline."

I found the mower and gasoline and cut the grass. It was a big lawn and this took me until noon or later. She was sitting on the terrace reading and drinking something —icewater or gin. I joined her, wondering how I could build my usefulness into indispensability. I could have made a pass at her but if we became lovers this would have meant sharing the yellow room and that was not what I wanted. "If you want a sandwich before you go there's some ham and cheese in the refrigerator," she said. "A friend of mine is coming out on the four-o'clock but I suppose you'll want to go back before then."

I was frightened. Go back, go back, go back to the greasy green waters of the Lethe, back to my contemptible cowardice, back to the sanctuary of my bed where I cowered before thin air, back to anesthetizing myself with gin in order to eat a plate of scrambled eggs. I wondered about the sex of her visitor. If it was a woman mightn't I stay on as a sort of handyman, eating my supper in the kitchen and sleeping in the yellow room? "If there's anything else you'd like me to do," I said. "Firewood?"

"I buy my firewood in Blenville."

"Would you like me to split some kindling?"

"Not really," she said.

"The screen door in the kitchen is loose," I said. "I could repair that."

She didn't seem to hear me. She went into the house and returned a little later with two sandwiches. "Would you like mustard?" she asked.

"No thank you," I said.

I took the sandwich as a kind of sacrament since it would be the last thing I could approach with any appetite until I returned to the yellow room and when would that be? I was desperate. "Is your visitor a man or a woman," I asked.

"I really don't think that concerns you," she said.

"I'm sorry."

"Thank you for cutting the grass," she said. "That needed to be done but you must understand that I can't have a strange man sleeping on my sofa without a certain amount of damage to my reputation and my reputation isn't absolutely invincible."

"I'll go," I said.

I drove back to New York then, condemned to exile and genuinely afraid of my inclination to self-destruction. As soon as I closed the door of my apartment I fell into the old routine of gin, Kilimanjaro, scrambled eggs, Orvieto and the Elysian Fields. I stayed in bed until late the next morning. I drank some gin while I shaved and went out onto the street to get some coffee. In front of my apartment house I ran into Dora Emmison. She wore black—I never saw her in anything else—and said that she had come in town for a few days to do some shopping and go to the theater. I asked if she'd have lunch with me but she said she was busy. As soon as we parted I got my car and drove back to Blenville.

The house was locked but I broke a pane of glass in the kitchen window and let myself in. To be alone in the yellow room was everything I had expected. I felt happy, peaceful and strong. I had brought the Montale with me and I spent the afternoon reading and making notes. The time passed lightly and the sense that the hands of my watch were procrustean had vanished. At six o'clock I went for a swim, had a drink and made some supper. She had a large store of provisions and I made a note of what I was stealing so that I would replace it before I left. After dinner I went on reading, taking a chance that the lighted windows would not arouse anyone's curiosity. At nine o'clock I undressed, wrapped myself in a blanket and lay down on the sofa to sleep. A few minutes later I saw the lights of a car come up the drive.

I got up and went into the kitchen and shut the door. I was, of course, undressed. If it was she I supposed I could escape out the back door. If it was not she, if it was some friend or neighbor, they would likely go away. Whoever it was began to knock on the door, which I had left unlocked. Then a man opened the door and asked softly, "Doree, Doree, you sleeping? Wake up baby, wake up, it's Tony, the old loverboy." Climbing the stairs he kept asking "Doree, Doree, Doree," and when he went into her bedroom and found the bed empty he said, "Aw shit." He then came down the stairs and left the house and I stayed, shivering in the kitchen, until I heard his car go down the road.

I got back onto the sofa and had been there for perhaps a half hour when another car came up the drive. I retired again to the kitchen and a man named Mitch went through more or less the same performance. He climbed the stairs, calling her name, made some exclamation of disappointment and went away. All of this left me uneasy and in the morning I cleaned up the place, emptied the ashtrays and drove back to New York.

Dora had said that she would be in the city for a few days. Four is what is usually meant by a few and two of these had already passed. On the day that I thought she would return to the country I bought a case of the most expensive bourbon and started back to Blenville, late in the afternoon. It was after dark when I turned up the red dirt road. Her lights were on. I first looked in at the window and saw that she was alone and reading as she had been when I first found the place. I knocked on the door and when she opened it and saw me she seemed puzzled and irritated. "Yes?" she asked. "Yes? What in the world do you want now?"

"I have a present for you," I said. "I wanted to give you a present to thank you for your kindness in letting me spend the night in your house."

"That hardly calls for a present," she said, "but I do happen to have a weakness for good bourbon. Won't you come in?"

I brought the case into the hall, tore it open and took out a bottle. "Shouldn't we taste it," I asked.

"Well, I'm going out," she said, "but I guess there's time for a drink. You're very generous. Come in, come in and I'll get some ice."

She was, I saw, one of those serious drinkers who prepare their utensils as a dentist prepares his utensils for an extraction. She arranged neatly on the table near her chair the glasses, ice bucket and water pitcher as well as a box of cigarettes, an ashtray and a lighter. With all of this within her reach she settled down and I poured the drinks.

"Chin, chin," she said.

"Cheers," I said.

"Did you just drive out from New York," she asked.

"Yes," I said.

"How is the driving," she asked.

"It's foggy on the turnpike," I said. "It's quite foggy."

"Damn," she said. "I have to drive up to a party in Havenswood and I hate the turnpike when it's foggy. I do wish I didn't have to go out but the Helmsleys are giving a party for a girl I knew in school and I've promised to show up."

"Where did you go to school?"

"Do you really want to know?"

"Yes."

"Well I went to Brearley for two years. Then I went to Finch for a year. Then I went to a country day school called Fountain Valley for two years. Then I went to a public school in Cleveland for a year. Then I went to the International School in Geneva for two years, the Parioli School in Rome for a year, and when we came back to the United States I went to Putney for a year and then to Masters for three years. I graduated from Masters."

"Your parents traveled a lot?"

"Yes. Dad was in the State Department. What do you do?"

"I'm translating Montale."

"Are you a professional translator?"

"No."

"You just do it to amuse yourself?"

"To occupy myself."

"You must have some money," she said.

"I do."

"So do I, thank God," she said. "I'd hate to be without it."

"Tell me about your marriage," I said. This might have seemed importunate but I have never known a divorced man or woman unwilling to discuss their marriage.

"Well it was a mess," she said, "an eight-year mess. He drank and accused me of having affairs with other men and wrote anonymous letters to most of my friends, claiming that I had the principles of a whore. I bought him off, I had to, I paid him a shirtful and went out to Reno. I came back last month. I think I'll have another little drink," she said, "but first I'm going to the john."

I filled her glass again. We were nearly through the first bottle. When she returned from the toilet she was not staggering, not at all, but she was walking much more lithely, with a much more self-confident grace. I got up and took her in my arms but she pushed me away —not angrily—and said: "Please don't, please don't. I don't feel like that tonight. I've been feeling terribly all day and the bourbon has picked me up but I still don't feel like that. Tell me all about yourself."

"I'm a bastard," I said.

"Oh, really. I've never known any bastards. What does it feel like?"

"Mostly lousy, I guess. I mean I would have enjoyed a set of parents."

"Well parents can be dreadful, of course, but I suppose dreadful parents are better than none at all. Mine were dreadful." She dropped a lighted cigarette into her lap but retrieved it before it burned the cloth of her skirt.

"Are your parents still living?"

"Yes, they're in Washington, they're very old." She sighed and stood. "Well if I'm going to Havenswood," she said, "I guess I'd better go." Now she was unsteady. She splashed a little whiskey into her glass and drank it without ice or water.

"Why do you go to Havenswood," I asked. "Why don't you telephone and say there's a fog on the turnpike or that you've got a cold or something."

"You don't understand," she said hoarsely. "It's one of those parties you have to go to like birthdays and weddings."

"I think it would be better if you didn't go."

"Why?" Now she was bellicose.

"I just think it would be, that's all."

"You think I'm drunk," she asked.

"No."

"You do, don't you. You think I'm drunk, you nosy sonofabitch. What are you doing here anyhow? I don't know you. I never asked you to come here and you don't know me. You don't know anything about me excepting where I went to school. You don't even know my maiden name, do you?"

"No."

"You don't know anything about me, you don't even know my maiden name and yet you have the cheek to sit there and tell me I'm drunk. I've been drinking, that's true, and I'll tell you why. I can't drive safely on the goddam Jersey Turnpike sober. That road and all the rest of the freeways and thruways were engineered for clowns and drunks. If you're not a nerveless clown then you have to get drunk. No sensitive or intelligent man or woman can drive on those roads. Why I have a friend in California who smokes pot before he goes on the freeway. He's a great driver, a marvelous driver, and if the traffic's bad he uses heroin. They ought to sell pot and bourbon at the gas stations. Then there wouldn't be so many accidents."

"Well let's have another drink then," I said.

"Get out," she said.

"All right."

I went out of the yellow room onto the terrace. I

watched her from the window. She was reeling. She stuffed some things into a bag, tied a scarf around her hair, turned out the lights and locked the door. I followed her at a safe distance. When she got to her car she dropped the keys in the grass. She turned on the lights and I watched her grope in the grass until she recovered the keys. Then she slammed the car down the driveway and clipped the mailbox post with her right headlight. I heard her swear and a moment later I heard the noise of falling glass, and why is this sound so portentous, so like a doomcrack bell? I was happy to think that she would not continue up to Havenswood but I was mistaken. She backed the car away from the mailbox post and off she went. I spent the night at a motel in Blenville and telephoned the turnpike police in the morning. She had lasted about fifteen minutes.

XV

My lawyer arranged for the purchase of the house. I was able to get the place and eight acres of land for thirty-five thousand dollars. Her mother came down from Washington and removed her personal effects and I moved into the house three weeks later, and began my orderly life. I woke early, swam in the pool, ate a large breakfast and settled down to work at a table in the yellow room. I worked happily until one or sometimes later and then ate a bowl of soup. I bought some tools and spent the afternoons clearing the woods around the house and cutting and stacking wood for the fireplace. At five I took another swim and drank the first of three daily whiskeys. After supper I studied German until half past ten when I went to bed feeling limber, clean and weary. If I dreamed at all my dreams were of an exceptional innocence and purity. I had no longer any need for the mountain, the valley and the fortified city.

I kept a cat named Schwartz, not because I like cats
but to keep the mice and shrews from overrunning the
old house. The man in the drug store in Blenville gave
me Schwartz and I knew nothing about his past. I
guessed he was a middle-aged cat and he seemed to have
a cranky disposition if such a thing is possible in an ani-
mal. I fed him canned cat food twice a day. There was a
brand of cat food he disliked and if I forgot and gave him
this he would go into the yellow room and shit in the
middle of the floor. He made his point and so long as I
fed him what he liked he behaved himself. We worked
out a practical and unaffectionate relationship. I don't
like having cats in my lap but now and then I would
dutifully pick him up and pat him to prove that I was a
good scout. With the early frosts the field mice began to
besiege the place and Schwartz bagged a victim nearly
every night. I was proud of Schwartz. At the height of his
efficiency as a mouser Schwartz vanished. I let him out
one night and in the morning he failed to return. I don't
know much about cats but I guessed they were loyal to
their homes and I supposed that a dog or a fox had killed
my friend. One morning a week later (a light snow had
fallen) Schwartz returned. I fed him a can of his favorite
brand and gave him a few dutiful caresses. He smelled
powerfully of French perfume. He had either been sitting in the lap of someone who used perfume or had been
sprayed with it. It was an astringent and musky scent.
The nearest house to mine was owned by some Polish
farmers and the woman, I happened to know, smelled

powerfully of the barnyard and nothing else. The next nearest house was shut for the winter and I couldn't think of anyone in Blenville who would use French perfume. Schwartz stayed with me that time for a week or ten days and then vanished again for a week. When he returned he smelled like the street floor of Bergdorf Goodman during the Christmas rush. I buried my nose in his coat and felt a moment's nostalgia for the city and its women. That afternoon I got into my car and drove over the back roads between my place and Blenville, looking for someplace that might house a bewitching woman. I felt that she must be bewitching and that she was deliberately tempting me by dousing my cat with perfume. All the houses I saw were either farms or places owned by acquaintances and I stopped at the drug store and told my story. "Schwartz," I said, "that cat, that mouser you gave me, he goes off every other week and comes home smelling like a whorehouse on Sunday morning."

"No whorehouses around here," said the druggist.

"I know," I said, "but where do you suppose he gets the perfume?"

"Cats roam," said the druggist.

"I suppose so," I said, "but do you sell French perfume? I mean if I can find who buys the stuff . . ."

"I don't remember selling a bottle since last Christmas," the druggist said. "The Avery boy bought a bottle for his girl friend."

"Thank you," I said.

That night after dinner Schwartz went to the door and

signaled to be let out. I put on a coat and went out with him. He went directly through the garden and into the woods at the right of the house with me following. I was as excited as any lover on his way. The smell of the woods, heightened by the dampness of the brook, the stars overhead, especially Venus, seemed to be extensions of my love affair. I thought she would be raven-haired with a marbly pallor and a single blue vein at the side of her brow. I thought she would be about thirty. (I was twenty-three.) Now and then Schwartz let out a meow so that it wasn't too difficult to follow him. I went happily through the woods, across Marshman's pasture and into Marshman's woods. These had not been cleared for some years and the saplings lashed at my trousers and my face. Then I lost Schwartz. I called and called. Schwartz, Schwartz, here Schwartz. Would anyone, hearing my voice in the dark woods, recognize it as the voice of a lover? I wandered through the woods calling my cat until a tall sapling dealt me a blinding blow across the eyes and I gave up. I made my way home feeling frustrated and lonely.

Schwartz returned at the end of the week and I seized him and smelled his coat to make sure that she was still setting out her lures. She was. He stayed with me that time ten days. A snow had fallen on the night he vanished and in the morning I saw that his tracks were clear enough to follow. I got through Marshman's woods and came, at the edge of them, on a small frame house, painted gray. It was utilitarian and graceless and might have been built by some hard-working amateur carpenter on Saturdays and Sundays and those summer nights when the dark comes late. I had seriously begun to doubt that it was the lair of a raven-haired beauty. The cat's tracks went around the house to a back door. When I knocked an old man opened the door.

He was small, smaller than I, anyhow, with thin gray hair, pomaded and combed. There was a white button in his right ear, connected to a cord. From the lines and the colorlessness of his face I would guess that he was close to seventy. Some clash between the immutable facts of vanity and time seemed to animate him. He was old but he wore a flashy diamond ring, his shoes were polished and there was all that pomade. He looked a little like one of those dapper men who manage movie theaters in the badlands.

"Good morning," I said. "I'm looking for my cat."

"Ah," he said, "then you must be the master of dear Henry. I've often wondered where Henry was domiciled when he was not with me. Henry, Henry, your second master has come to pay us a call." Schwartz was asleep on a chair. He did not stir. The room was a combination kitchen and chemistry laboratory. There was the usual kitchen furniture and on a long bench an assortment of test tubes and retorts. The air was heavy with scent. "I don't know anything about the olfactory capacities of cats but Henry does seem to enjoy perfumes, don't you Henry. May I introduce myself. I'm Gilbert Hansen, formerly head chemist for Beauregarde et Cie."

"Hammer," I said, "Paul Hammer."

"How do you do. Won't you sit down."

"Thank you," I said. "You manufacture perfume here?"

"I experiment with scents," he said. "I'm no longer in the manufacturing end of things but if I hit on something I like I'll sell the patent, of course. Not to Beauregarde et Cie, however. After forty-two years with them I was dismissed without cause or warning. However this seems to be a common practice in industry these days. I do have an income from my patents. I am the inventor of Étoile de Neige, Chous-Chous, Muguet de Nuit and Naissance de Jour."

"Really," I said. "How did you happen to pick a place like this—way off in the woods—for your experiments?"

"Well it isn't as out of the way as it seems. I have a garden and I grow my own thyme, lavender, iris, roses, mint, wintergreen, celery and parsley. I buy my lemons and oranges in Blenville and Charlie Hubber, who lives at the four corners, traps beaver and muskrat for me. I find their castors as lasting as civet and I get them for a fraction of the market price. I buy gum resin, methyl salicylate and benzaldehyde. Flower perfumes are not my forte since they have very limited aphrodisiac powers. The principal ingredient of Chous-Chous is cedar bark, and parsley and celery go into Naissance de Jour."

"Did you study chemistry?"

"No. I learned my profession as an apprentice. I think of it more as alchemy than chemistry. Alchemy is, of course, the transmutation of base metals into noble ones and when an extract of beaver musk, cedar bark, heliotrope, celery and gum resin can arouse immortal longings in a male we are close to alchemy, wouldn't you say?"

"I know what you mean," I said.

"The concept of man as a microcosm, containing within himself all the parts of the universe, is Babylonian. The elements are constant. The distillations and transmutations release their innate power. This not only works in the manufacture of perfume; I think these transmutations can work in the development of character."

I heard a woman's heels in the next room—light, swift, the step of someone young. Marietta came into the kitchen. "This is my granddaughter," he said, "Marietta Drum."

"Paul Hammer," I said.

"Oh, hello," she said. She lighted a cigarette. "Eight," she said.

"How many yesterday," he asked.

"Sixteen," she said, "but it was only twelve the day before."

She wore a cloth coat with a white thread on one shoulder. Her hair was dark blond. She was not beautiful —not yet. Something, some form of loneliness or unhappiness, seemed to mask or darken her looks. It would be a lie to say that there was always a white thread on her clothing—that even if I bought her a mink coat there would be a white thread on it—but the white thread had some mysterious power as if it were a catalyst that clarified my susceptibilities. It seemed like magic and when she picked the thread off her coat and dropped it onto the floor, the magic remained.

"Where are you going now," he asked.

"Oh, I thought I'd drive into New York," she said.

"Why? What do you want to go to New York for? You don't have anything to do in New York."

"I'll find something to do," she said. "I'll go to the Museum of Natural History."

"What about the groceries."

"I'll buy them later. I'll be back before the stores close." She was gone.

"Well, goodbye Schwartz," I said. "Come home whenever you feel like it. I always have plenty of mice. It was nice to have met you," I said to the old man. "You and your granddaughter must come over for a drink someday. I have the Emmison place."

I walked and ran through the snowy woods back to my house, changed my clothes and headed for the city. I was in love with Marietta and I recognized all the symptoms. My life was boundless—my knees were weak. This had nothing to do with the fact that I had been inhaling the aphrodisiac fumes of Étoile de Neige, Chous-Chous, Muguet de Nuit and Naissance de Jour. My sudden infatuation could be put down as immature, but the truth of the matter is that I frequently fall suddenly in love with men, women, children and dogs. These attachments are unpredictable, ardent and numerous.

205

For example, when I was still in the publishing business I had an appointment to meet a printer in New York. I telephoned from the hotel lobby and he asked me to come up to his room. When he opened the door and introduced himself I saw past him to where his wife stood in the middle of the room. She was not a beauty but she had a prettiness, a brightness, that was stunning. I talked with her only long enough for him to get his hat and coat, but during this time I seemed to fall in love. I urged her to join us for lunch but she said she had to go to Bloomingdale's and look for furniture. We said good-bye and the printer and I went out to lunch. The business conversation bored me and I had trouble keeping my mind on the contracts we were meant to discuss. All I could think of was her blondness, her trimness, the radiance with which, it seemed, she had been standing in the middle of that hotel room when he opened the door. I hurried through lunch, said that I had another appointment, and looped over to the furniture department at Bloomingdale's, where I found her reading a price tag on a chest of drawers.

"Hello," I said.

"Hello," she said, "I somehow thought you might come . . ." Then she took my arm and we left Bloomingdale's, walking on air, and went to some restaurant where she had tea and I had a drink. We seemed immersed in one another—she seemed to generate a heat and light that I needed. I don't remember much of what we said but I do remember being terribly happy and that everyone around us—the waiters and the barmen—seemed to share our happiness. They lived in Connecticut and she asked me to come out for the weekend. I walked her back to the hotel, kissed her goodbye in the lobby, and walked around the streets for an hour, so high that my ears were ringing. On Friday I went out to Connecticut and she met me at the station. There was a lot of kissing in the car. I said that I loved her. She said she loved me. That night after dinner when her husband went upstairs to the toilet we had a serious discussion about her children— they had three children—and she said that her husband had been in analysis for seven years. At this point any disruption in his affairs would be catastrophic. The pleasure his wife and I took in one another's company must have been apparent because on Saturday he began to sulk. On Sunday he was downright mean and glum. He said that he detested above all things maladjusted men who preyed on the happiness of others. He used the word parasite five times. I said I was leaving for Cleveland in the morning and she said she would drive me to the airport. He said she would not. They had a quarrel and she cried. When I left in the morning they were still sleeping and there was no one to say goodbye to but the cat.

It took me a month or so to forget her but in the meantime I had to go to London. The man with whom I shared a seat on the plane was pleasant and we began to talk. Nothing important was said but we were very sympathetic and at one point he asked if I would like to go to sleep or should we go on talking. I said that I would like to go on talking and we talked all the way across the Atlantic. We shared a cab into London. I was going to the Connaught and he was staying at the Army-Navy. When we said goodbye he suggested that we have lunch together. I had no other engagement and he met me at the Connaught for lunch. After lunch we started walking and we walked all over London—walked to Westminster and the Embankment—and when the bars reopened we went to a pub and had some drinks. He said that he knew of a good restaurant near Grosvenor Square and we went there for dinner and stayed there until about midnight when we said goodbye. We exchanged cards and promised to call one another in New York but we never did and I've never seen him again.

There was, so far as I could discern, nothing unnatural in this encounter but things are not always this simple. In the late winter I went south to Wentworth to play some golf. An amiable man in the bar the night I arrived suggested that we pair off since our scores seemed to be about the same. In the morning, at about the third or fourth hole, I noticed that he was praising my form and praising it extravagantly. There is nothing about my form that deserves praise and I began to feel that his flattery—which is what it amounted to—had in it a hint of amorousness. I then began to feel that he was losing the game to me—that his golf was better than mine but that he was chipping his shots to give me a slight advantage. We played nineteen holes and his manner grew—or so I thought—increasingly sentimental and protective. I kept my distance in the shower and when we went to the bar I definitely got the feeling that something was going on. He kept bumping into me and touching me. I was not repelled but I did not want to invest my sexuality in a one-night stand with a stranger at Wentworth and I left in the morning.

As for children I will give only one example. I went out to Maggie Fowler's for a weekend in the Hamptons. Her son—a boy of about eight or nine—was with her. He was the child of her first marriage and evidently spent most of his time with his father or away at school. He seemed a little strange with Maggie. He had that extraordinary air of privacy that some children enjoy. This may have been produced by the rigors of a divorce but I've seen it in all sorts of children. I got up early on Saturday morning and, finding him downstairs, walked with him to the beach for a swim. He held my hand on the walk—an unusual attention for a boy his age—and I guessed that he was lonely, but if I explained his conduct by this I must have been lonely myself because I enjoyed his company. He may have reminded me of my own childhood. The resonance of deep affection, some part of which is surely memory, was what I experienced. We had a good swim and had breakfast together and then he asked, very shyly, if I would like to play catch. We spent perhaps an hour on the back lawn, throwing a ball back and forth. Then the others came down and we started drinking Bloody Marys and there were the usual activities of a weekend, most of which excluded a boy his age. When we were dressing that evening to go out Maggie knocked on my door and said that her son wanted me to say good night to him. I did. When I got up on Sunday morning he was sitting on a chair outside my bedroom door and we walked again to the beach. I didn't see much of him on Sunday but I seemed aware of him—his footstep, his voice, his presence in the house. I drove back on Sunday afternoon and I've never seen or heard of him but I definitely felt something like love for him during the few hours we spent together.

As for dogs I will also confine myself to a single example. In the spring I went out to Connecticut for a weekend with the Powerses. After lunch on Saturday we decided to climb what they called a mountain. It was, in fact, a hill. They had a dirty old collie named Francey who came along. Near the summit there was a steep rock face that was too much for Francey and I picked her up in my arms and carried her to the top. She stayed at my side for the rest of the climb or walk and when we returned I carried her down the steep stretch. While we had cocktails Francey stayed at my side and I roughed the fur on her neck. I was just as pleased with her company, I think, as she was with mine. When I went upstairs to change Francey came along and lay on the floor. I went to bed at about midnight and just as I was about to close the bedroom door Francey came along the hall and joined me. She slept on my bed. Francey and I were inseparable on Sunday. She followed me wherever I went and I talked with her, fed her crackers and roughed and caressed her neck. When it was time for me to leave on Sunday, Francey, while I was saying goodbye, streaked across the driveway and got into my car. I was flattered, of course, but flattery is some part of susceptibility and all the way home I thought tenderly of the old dog as if I had left a love.

It took me an hour and a half to drive to New York and another twenty minutes to find a parking place near the museum. The odds against finding her in that labyrinth were unequal, I knew, but that it was a labyrinth, winding, twilit and cavernous, gave some fitness to my crrand and I stepped into the museum at a basement entrance with a very light heart. It was a place I had visited once or twice a year for as long as I could remember and while there had been changes there had been fewer—far fewer—than there had been outside the walls. In fifteen years the Alaskan war canoe had traveled perhaps twenty-five yards, leaving a gallery of totem poles for a vestibule. Eskimo women in glass cases were performing the same humble tasks they had been performing when I was a child, clutching Gretchen Oxencroft's hand. I decided to start at the top of the building and work my way down. I took the elevator and began my search in a gallery that contained jewels and glass constructions of molecular particles. Lighting was a problem since if the galleries had been well lighted I would, by standing in any door, have been able to see whether or not she was there; but many of the galleries were nocturnal and I had to go from exhibit to exhibit, looking for her face in the half-lights. I was able to take in the Pleistocene room in a glance—that soaring construction of prehistoric bone and the intensely human odor of wet clothing—and the room that contains the stuffed copperheads was also well lighted. I passed the Blue Whale and the stuffed Aardvark and then stepped into another dusky gallery where the only illumination came from cases of magnified Protozoa. I descended from there to the even deeper twilight of the African gallery and from there to the North American habitat groups. Here in the stale and cavernous dark was a thrilling sense of permanence. Here were landscapes, seasons, moments in time that had not changed by a leaf or a flake of snow during my life. The flamingoes flew exactly as they had flown when I was a child. The rutting mooses were still locked, antler to antler, the timber wolves still slinked through the blue snow towards the pane of glass that separated them from chaos and change, and not a leaf of the brilliant autumn foliage had fallen. The Alaska bear still reared at the end of a corridor that seemed to be his demesne and it was here that I found her, admiring the bear.

"Hello," I said.

"Oh, hello," she said.

That was quick. Then she took my arm and said: "I have the most marvelous idea. Why don't you take me to the Plaza for lunch."

We walked across the park towards the Plaza. "I don't

think I have enough money for lunch," I said, "and there's no place around here where I can cash a check." I counted the money in my wallet. I had seventeen dollars. "But seventeen is enough to take me to lunch," she said. "I mean you could miss lunch for once in your life, couldn't you?" That's what we did. She ordered a full lunch and a bottle of wine. I explained to the waiter that I had already lunched but I did drink a glass of wine. She said goodbye to me in front of the hotel. "I have to get back to Blenville in time to buy Grandfather's groceries," she said. "Back to my prison, back to my jail . . ." I had a hamburger and an orange drink at the corner and drove back to Blenville myself.

I was over there the next afternoon at around four. She answered the door. She was wearing a gray dress with a white thread on the shoulder. "Did you get anything to eat?" she asked.

"I had a hamburger."

"I'm sorry I spent all your money."

"That's all right. I've got more. Why don't you come over to my house?"

"Where do you live?"

"I bought Dora Emmison's place."

"I'll get a coat. I feel like a prisoner here."

Back at my house I lighted a fire, made some drinks and we sat in the yellow room while she told me her story. She was twenty-three and had never married. She had lived in France until she was twelve when her parents were killed in an accident and her grandfather be-

213

came her guardian. She had gone to Bennington. When her grandfather moved to the country she took an apartment and got a job as a receptionist at Macy's. She was bored and lonely in the city and had come out to Blenville in the autumn with the hope of finding a job, but the only industry in Blenville was the motel and she didn't want to be either a prostitute or a chambermaid.

While she was talking there was a loud crack of thunder. Thunder was unusual at that time of year—the late winter—and at the first explosion I thought a plane had broken the sound barrier. The second peal—rolling and percussive—was unmistakably thunder. "Dammit," she said.

"What's the matter?"

"I'm afraid of thunder. I know it's absurd but that doesn't make any difference. When I was working at Macy's and living alone I used to hide in the closet when there was a thunderstorm. I finally went to a psychiatrist to see if he could do anything and he said the reason I was afraid of thunder was because I was a terrible egocentric. He said I thought I was so important that the thunder would seek me out for extermination. All of this may be true but it doesn't keep me from trembling." She was trembling then and I took her in my arms and we became lovers before the storm had passed over my land. "That felt good," she said, "that felt very good. That was a nice thing to do."

"I've never had it better," I said. "Let's get married."

Six weeks later we were married in the church in Blenville. Marietta wore a gray suit with a white thread on the lapel. (Where did all those threads come from? Later, when we traveled in Europe, she would sometimes appear with a white thread on her shoulder.) After the wedding we flew to Curaçao and spent two weeks at St. Martha's Bay. It was lovely and when we returned to Blenville I seemed to possess everything in the world that I wanted. When I finished the Montale and took it into New York I discovered that the poetry had already been translated but for some reason this didn't disappoint me. It seemed then that nothing could. I don't know when the honeymoon ended . . . I'll settle for a night in Blenville. Eleven o'clock. Groping, I found Marietta's side of the bed empty. There was a light on in the kitchen. The shape of the lighted window stretched over the lawn. Was Marietta sick? I sleep naked and I went down the stairs into the kitchen naked. Marietta stood in the center of the floor wearing her wedding ring and nothing else. She was eating, with a bent fork, from a can of salmon. When I embraced her she pushed me away angrily and said: "Can't you see that I'm eating." The salmon gave off a sea smell, fresh and cheerful. I felt like taking a swim. When I touched her again she said: "Leave me alone, leave me alone! Can't a person get something to eat without being molested?" After that night—if that was the night—I saw more of distemper than tenderness and often slept alone; but while Marietta's distempers were strenuous they had no more permanence than the wind. They seemed at times to be

influenced by the wind. Spring and its uncertain zephyrs—
any sort of clemency—seemed to create a barometric disturbance in her nature that provoked her deepest dis-
contents. Violence, on the other hand—hurricanes,
thunderstorms and blizzards—sweetened her nature. In
the autumn when tempests with girls' names lashed the
Bermudas and moved up past Hatteras into the northeast,
she could be gentle, yielding and wifely. When snows
closed the roads and stopped the trains she was angelic,
and once, at the height of an epochal blizzard, she said
she loved me. She seemed to think of love as a universal
dilemma, produced by convulsions of nature and history.
I will never forget how tender she was the day we went
off the gold standard and her passion was boundless
when they shot the King of Parthia. (He was saying his
prayers in the basilica.) When our only mutuality was a
roof tree and some furnishings she looked at me as if I
was a repulsive brute to whom she had been sold by
some cruel slavemaster; but when the carts of thunder
rolled, when the assassin's knife struck home, when gov-
ernments fell and earthquakes blasted the city walls she
was my glory and my child.

A clinician like Shitz would have said that I had been
warned but he was wrong all along. My fault was that I
had thought of love as a heady distillate of nostalgia—a
force of memory that had resisted analysis by cybernet-
ics. We do not fall in love—I thought—we re-enter love,
and I had fallen in love with a memory—a piece of white
thread and a thunderstorm. My own true love was a
piece of white thread and that was so.

Sleeping alone then, as I often did, I found myself forced into the reveries of an adolescent, a soldier, or a prisoner. To sublimate my physical needs and cure my insomnia I fell into the habit of inventing dream girls. I know the vastness that separates revery from the realities of a robust and a sweaty fuck on a thundery Sunday afternoon, but like some prisoner in solitary confinement I had nothing to go on but my memories and my imagination. I began with my memory and pretended to be sleeping with a girl I had known in Ashburnham. I remembered her dark blondness in detail and seemed to feel her pubic hair against my naked hip. Night after night I summoned up all the girls I had ever romanced. Night after night they came singly and sometimes in pairs so that I lay happily on my stomach with a naked woman on either side. I began by summoning them but after a while they seemed to come of their own volition. Like all lonely men, I fell in love—hopelessly—with the girls on magazine covers and the models who advertise girdles. I did not go so far as to carry their photographs around in my wallet, but I was tempted to, and having fallen in love with these strangers I found that they willingly joined me in bed. Surrounded then by the women I remembered and the women I had seen photographed I was joined by a third group of comforters produced, I suppose, by some chamber in my nature. These were women I had never seen. I woke one midnight to find myself lying beside an imaginary Chinese who had very small breasts and a voluptuous backside. She was followed by a vivacious Negress and she by an amiable but very fat woman with red hair. I had never romanced a fat woman that I could recall. But they came, they solaced me, they let me sleep, and when I woke in the morning I was moderately hopeful.

I envied men like Nailles who might, I suppose, looking at Nellie, recall the number and variety of places where he had covered her. On the shores of the Atlantic and the Pacific, the Tyrrhenian and the Mediterranean, in catboats, in motorboats, in outboards, cabin cruisers and ocean liners; in hotels, motels, in castles, in tents; on beds, on sofas, on floors, on grassy hummocks, on pine needles, on stony mountain ledges warm from the sun; at every hour of the day and night; in England, in France, in Germany, Italy and Spain; while I, looking at Marietta, would remember the number of places where I had been rebuffed. In the motel in Stockbridge she had locked herself in the bathroom until I fell asleep. When I took her for a two-week cruise she forgot to pack her contraceptives and the ship's doctor had none for sale. In Chicago she kicked me in the groin. In Easthampton she defended herself with a carving knife. Her menstrual periods seemed frequent and prolonged and on most nights she would hurry into bed and cover her face with a blanket before I could get undressed. I am too tired, she would say, I am too sleepy. I have a head cold. I have a toothache. I have indigestion. I have the flu. On the beach at Nantucket she ran away from me and when I thought I had her cornered in the sailboat she dove overboard and swam to shore.

After a year or two the yellow paint on the walls had begun to crack and discolor, and Marietta called the painter in Blenville and had him bring out some samples. I had never told her about the importance of the yellow walls and so her choice of pink was not malicious but pink was the color she chose. I could have protested but my obsession with yellow had begun to seem absurd. Surely I had enough character to live with a normal spectrum and I let the painter go ahead. Two or three weeks after the painters had finished I woke with the cafard. I suffered, on getting out of bed, all the symptoms of panic. My lips were swollen, I had difficulty breathing and my hands were shaking. I dressed and had two scoops of gin before breakfast. I was drunk most of that day. I had, I knew, to change the pace of my life and on Friday we flew to Rome.

The cafard followed me throughout that trip but it followed me without much guile either because it was lazy or because it was an assassin so confident of its prey that it had no need to exert itself. On Saturday morning I woke, feeling cheerful and randy. I was just as cheerful on Sunday but on Monday I woke in a melancholy so profound that I had to drag myself out of bed and stumble, step by step, into the shower. On Tuesday we took a train to Fondi and a cab through the mountains to Sperlonga, where we stayed with friends. I had two good days there but the bête noire caught up with me on the third and we took the train for Naples at Formia. I had four good days in Naples. Had the bête noire lost track of its victim or was it simply moving in the leisurely way of a practiced murderer? My fifth day in Naples was crushing and we took the afternoon train back to Rome. Here again I had three good days but I woke on the fourth in danger of my life and went out to take a walk, putting one foot in front of the other. On some broad and curving street, the name of which I can't remember, I saw coming towards me a line of motorcycle policemen, moving at such a slow pace that they had to keep putting their feet on the paving to keep the engines upright. Behind them were a few hundred men and women carrying signs that said PACE, SPERANZA and AMORE. It was, I realized, a memorial procession for the communist delegate Mazzacone, who had been shot in his bathtub. All I knew about him was that he had been described as saintly in *L'Unità*. I did not know his opinions and had read none of his speeches but I began to cry. There was no question of drying my tears. They splashed down my face and wet my jacket, they were torrential. I joined the procession and as soon as I began to march I felt the cafarde take off. There were marshals with armbands to keep the parade in order and we were told not to speak so that as we moved through Rome there was no sound but the shuffle and hiss of shoe leather, much of it worn, and because of our numbers, a loud, weird and organic sound, a sighing that someone with his back to the parade might have mistaken for the sea.

We marched through the Venezia to the Colosseum. We walked proudly, men, women and children, in spite of the shuffling sound. This grief which, in my case, we accidentally shared reminded me of how little else there was that we had in common. I felt the strongest love for these strangers for the space of three city blocks. There was a memorial service in the Colosseum—nothing as moving as the procession but when I went back to the hotel I felt well. We flew back to New York soon afterwards and it was sitting on a beach that following summer (I had already seen the picture in the dental journal) that I decided, on the strength of a kite string, that my crazy old mother's plan to crucify a man was sound and that I would settle in Bullet Park and murder Nailles. Sometime later I changed my victim to Tony.

PART THREE

XVI

Nailles asked Hammer to go fishing. It came about this way. Nailles was a member of the Volunteer Fire Department, where he drove the old red LaFrance fire truck. To hell over the hills and dales of Bullet Park late at night, ringing his bell and blowing his siren, seemed to him the climax of his diverse life. Mouthwash, fire trucks, chain saws and touch football! The village seemed upended in the starlight and the only lights that burned burned in bathrooms. It was his finest hour.

The fire company had a meeting and dinner on the first Thursday of the month and Nailles attended this. The red fire truck was parked in front of the building. The garage space had been swept and hosed down and tables covered with sheets had been set up as a buffet and bar. Two apprentice firemen were polishing glasses and Charlie Maddux, the self-appointed firehouse cook, was basting a leg of lamb at a gas range in the corner. Charlie was a used-car dealer. He weighed nearly three hundred pounds. He liked to buy food, cook food, eat food, and he very likely dreamed of joints of meat and buckets of shell-fish. His wife was, predictably, a spare woman devoted to a diet of blackstrap molasses and wheat germ. He seemed, as a firehouse cook, to enjoy a sense of reality that he did not enjoy either with his wife or his used cars and he stirred, basted, seasoned, tasted and served the dinner with absolute absorption and like most amateur cooks he was incurably premature, getting the meal onto the table a half hour before anyone was ready. Nailles went upstairs to the meeting room.

There were thirty members of the fire department at that time. About twenty had gathered. Some part of the atmosphere of the place was that it had been the firemen themselves who had converted it from a loft into a habit-able club room. They had, on Saturdays and Sundays, put down the Vinylite floor, nailed and painted the wall-board and wired the fluorescent lights. They were under-standably proud of their work. The meeting was, of course, stag but it was, excepting the locker room at the club, the last stag gathering in the village and its exclu-siveness had been challenged. Some members of the la-dies' auxiliary had wanted to attend the monthly meeting if only to supervise the cooking. They felt that Charlie Maddux was a usurper and that his grocery bills were probably scandalous. They had been forestalled but the sense that the maleness of the place was embattled gave it the snugness of a tree house. The atmosphere of a tree house extended to the ceremoniousness that followed.

The chief called the meeting to order with a memorial gavel and the secretary then uncovered an American flag made of stiff silk with a thick fringe of gold. The secretary read the minutes of the last meeting, which were approved, and the treasurer reported that there was eighty-three dollars and fourteen cents in the treasury. All of this and all that followed was performed with an immutable solemnity that could not have been explained by the few facts and figures involved. There was a somber discussion reproaching those firemen who came to the car wash and did nothing but drink beer. Had anyone spoken humorously it would have been a misunderstanding of the gravity of these rites. "We have a new application for membership," said the secretary. "Mr. Hammer, will you leave the room please while we discuss your application?"

Nailles turned and saw that Hammer was in the back row. Hammer left the room. "Mr. Hammer," the secretary said, "lives on Powder Hill and seems to be the sort of man who would fit into the company all right but when we asked about his experience he said that he'd been the member of a fire department in a place called Ashburnham. It's outside Cleveland. So we wrote for his papers and the letter was returned. There isn't any fire department in Ashburnham. There never was. I don't like to accuse a man of lying but at the same time we don't want any phonies in the outfit, do we?"

"How do we know there isn't a fire department in Ashburnham," Nailles asked.

"The letter was returned."

"It could have been a slipup in the post office. Why don't we take him in? The roster isn't full and even if he doesn't have any experience he could help with the truck wash."

"Do you want to put that in the form of a motion?"

"I move that Paul Hammer be elected a member of the fire department."

"I second the motion."

"All those in favor say aye."

"Aye."

"Contrary-minded?"

"Everything's been ready for twenty minutes," Charlie Maddux shouted up the stairs, "and if you don't get your arses down here now it will all be spoiled. I don't mind cooking but I don't like to see everything get cold."

The meeting was adjourned. Eliot joined Hammer at the bar and asked if he was a fisherman. He was motivated entirely by kindness. Hammer said that he was. "There's a little stream in Venable that I sometimes go to on Saturday morning," Eliot said. "If you'd like to try it I'll pick you up at around eight o'clock. This time of year I use bait."

On Saturday morning Eliot, with Tessie in the back seat, picked up Hammer and they started north on Route 61. Route 61 was one of the most dangerous and in appearance one of the most inhuman of the new highways. It had basically changed the nature of the Eastern landscape like some seismological disturbance, forcing it to conform, it seemed, to some parts of Montana. At least fifty men and women died on its reaches each year. On a Saturday morning the mixture of domestic and industrial traffic was catastrophic. Trucks as massive and towering as the land castles of the barbarians roared triumphantly downhill and labored uphill at a walking pace. Passing them and repassing them made this simple journey seem warlike. Nailles remembered the roads of his young manhood. They followed the contours of the land. It was cool in the valleys, warm on the hilltops. One could measure distances with one's nose. There was the smell of eucalyptus, maples, sweet grass, manure from a cow barn and, as one got into the mountains, the smell of pine. There were landmarks—abandoned farms—a stone tower and a blue lake. In the windows of the houses one passed one saw a cat, an array of geraniums, the face of a child or an old man. He remembered it all as intimate, human and pleasant, compared to this anxious wasteland through which one raced the barbarians.

They turned off 61 at Venable, bought some bait in the village, and started into the woods. It was a walk of about two miles and Tessie limped along gallantly although it was a struggle for the old bitch. Coming down into a valley they heard the sound of the stream. It was explicitly the sound of laughter—nothing else. Giddy laughter, the laughter of silly girls and nymphs, rang through the bleak spring woods. The stream was shallow —this would account for the asinine and continuous laughter—and they walked upstream until they found a deep pool. "I'll go further up and fish down," Nailles said.

"Why don't we plan to meet here at around noon. I want to get back for lunch." Off he went with Tessie.

When they met at noon Nailles had taken two trout. Hammer had caught nothing. They both carried flasks of bourbon and they sat on the banks of the stream —immersed in the sound of watery laughter—and had a drink. They were about the same weight, height and age, and they both wore a size-eight shoe. Nailles's hair was dark and long enough to fall over his brow. He had a habit of combing it or pushing it up with his fingers. His father had criticized this gesture and he may have clung to it as a sign of rebelliousness and independence. Hammer's hair was brown and cut very short. Nailles's face was the broadest and most open. Hammer's face was thin and he frequently touched it with his fingers—a sort of groping gesture as if he were looking for something he had lost. His right hand moved over his face from time to time as one's hand moves over a shelf in a dark closet where a key has been left. His laughter was sharp—three harsh, explosive sounds. He had a nervous way of shifting his head, setting his teeth and bracing his shoulders as if his thinking consisted of a series of resolves and decisions. I must cut down on my smoking. (Teeth-setting.) Life can be beautiful. (Shoulder bracing.) I am often misunderstood. (A sudden lifting of the head.) Nailles's manner was much more serene.

The force of friendship—a force that Nailles had never seen described—was nearly as important to him as love although there was no resemblance at all between the two. Love with its paraphernalia of sexuality, jealousy, nostalgia and exaltation was easier to recognize than friendship, which seemed to have (excepting athletic equipment) no paraphernalia at all. Nailles had enjoyed a large number of friends for as long as he could remember. Most of his friends were partners in games—skiing, fishing, cards or drinking. He was intensely contented in the company of his friends—in which he would now count Hammer—but it was a contentment in which there was no trace of jealousy, sexuality or nostalgia. He could remember as a boy—and as a man—friends who were both jealous and possessive but he could not honestly recall having experienced this. In the clubs that he belonged to there was some vestigial, adolescent jockeying for popularity—or perhaps love—but Nailles was innocent of this. This was not insensibility. To ski a mountain in tandem with a friend was, for Nailles, close to bliss but his happiness frustrated analysis. He was genuinely delighted to meet an old friend but there was no sorrow when they parted. His friends played a practical role in his dreams but no role at all in his longings. When they were apart he did not correspond—he scarcely remembered them—but his happiness when they were reunited was absolute. Here was an affection, stripped of all the sentiments that make an affection recognizable. Nailles was very happy, drinking bourbon in the woods with Hammer.

That Hammer planned to murder his fishing companion did not, at this point, strike him in any way as unnatural. Looking at his victim Hammer thought that he would like to leach from his indictment all the petulant clichés of complaint. He knew that Nailles merchandised Spang and he had heard the worst of the commercials on TV. (*If you were ashamed of your clothing, wouldn't you change it? If you were ashamed of your house, wouldn't you improve it? If you were ashamed of your car, wouldn't you turn it in? Then why be ashamed of your breath when Spang can offer you breath-charm for periods of up to six hours . . .*) It was infantile to rail at this sort of thing, Hammer thought. It had been the national fare for twenty-five years and it was not likely to improve. He wanted change and newness but he wanted his wants to be mature. Why despise Nailles because he loved the gold cigarette lighter that he now took out of his pocket. The economy was frankly capitalistic and who but a child would be shocked to observe that its principal talisman was gold? The woman who dreamed of a mink coat—Hammer thought—had more common sense than the woman who dreamed of heaven. The nature of man was terrifying and singular and man's environment was chaos. It would be wrong, he thought, to call Nailles's religious observances a sham. He guessed they were vague and perhaps sentimental but since Christ's Church was the only place in Bullet Park where mystery was professed and since there was much that was mysterious in Nailles's life (the thighs of Nellie and his love for his son) there was nothing delinquent in his getting to his knees once a week. Hammer had chosen his victim for his excellence.

"Didn't I see your son directing traffic at the Browns'," Hammer asked.

"Yes," Nailles laughed. "He directs traffic at cocktail parties. He's been terribly sick."

"What was the matter?"

"Mononucleosis."

"Who's your doctor?"

"Well we had Mullin until they shut him down and then we went to old Dr. Feigart but neither of them really cured Tony. It was a very strange thing. He'd been sick for over a month when someone told us about this guru. He calls himself Swami Rutuola. He lives over the funeral parlor on River Street. He came to the house one night and I don't know how he did it but he cured Tony."

"Is he a holy man?"

"I really don't know. I don't know anything about him. I don't even know what he did. I wasn't allowed into the room. But he fixed up Tony. He's fine now. He plays basketball and directs traffic at cocktail parties. I must remind him that the Lewellens are having a party on Friday. Well, shall we go?"

They walked back through the woods, the executioner and his victim, trailed by the old setter. Nailles stowed their tack in the back of the car and then opened the door for Tessie. "Jump in, Tessie," he said, "jump in, girl." Tessie whined. Then she made a lurch for the seat and fell to the ground. "Poor old girl," Nailles said. He picked her up, an awkward armful with her legs sticking out, and laid her on the back seat of the car.

"Why don't you do something about her," Hammer asked.

"Well I've done everything I can or almost everything," Nailles said. "There is a kind of serum you can get, a distillate of Novocain. It's supposed to prolong a dog's life but it costs fifteen dollars a shot and they have to have it once a week."

"I didn't mean that," Hammer said.

"What did you mean?"

"Why don't you shoot her?"

The contemptible callousness of his new companion, the heartless brutality involved in the thought of murdering a beloved and trusting old dog, provoked a rage in Nailles so towering and so pure that for a moment he might have killed Hammer.

He said nothing and they drove back to Bullet Park.

XVII

Have you ever committed a murder? Have you ever known the homicide's sublime feeling of rightness? Conscientious men live like the citizens of some rainy border country, familiar with a dozen national anthems, their passports fat with visas, but they will be incapable of love and allegiance until they break the law. Have you ever waked on a summer morning to realize that this is the day when you will kill a man? The declarative splendor of the morning is unparalleled. Lift up a leaf to find a flaw but there will be none. The shade of every blade of grass is perfect. Hammer mowed his lawns that day. The imposture was thrilling. Look at Mr. Hammer cutting his grass. What a nice man Mr. Hammer must be.

Marietta had gone to Blenville for the weekend. Hammer was kept busy with his lawns until noon when he had a drink. He drove to the supermarket and bought a can of Mace and a loaded truncheon from the Self-Defense counter. Everything was ready, everything but

the gasoline. He shook the can with which he had re-
fueled the lawn mower. It was empty. He had this filled
and then sat on his terrace. At three o'clock the mailman
drove his truck down the street, stopping at the mail-
boxes that stood at the foot of every walk and drive.
There was no mail for Hammer but from every house but
his someone appeared—a cook, a mother-in-law, an in-
valid—and opened their boxes in a way that seemed fur-
tive, intimate, almost sexual. It was a little like undoing
one's trousers. They groped inside for some link to the
tempestuous world—bills, love letters, checks and invitations. Then they returned. It was a cloudless day. The
birds in the trees seemed, to Hammer, to be singing
either an invitation list or the names of a law firm. *Tich-
nor, Cabot, Ewing, Trilling* and *Swope*, they sang. He
went into the pantry, smiling at the bottles. He did this
three times and on his fourth trip to the pantry poured
himself a stiff drink. He drank, he thought, not for courage or stimulation but to make the ecstasy of his lawless-
ness endurable. He drank too much. Hammer was not the
sort of drinker who repeats himself, staggers and drives
dangerously; but the inflammation of his thinking was
hazardous. Towards dusk he wanted to tell someone his
plans; he needed a confidant.

He settled on the holy man over the funeral parlor and
settled on him so decisively that he must, unconsciously,
have made the decision earlier. He drove into the slums
and pounded on the door of the Temple of Light. "Come
in," said Rutuola. He sat in a chair with his right hand
covering his bad eye.

"Are you the holy man?" Hammer asked.

"Oh no, no indeed. I've never claimed to be that. You must excuse me. I am very tired tonight."

"You cure the sick?"

"Sometimes, sometimes. I help with prayers but I am so tired tonight that I cannot help myself. I have said a hundred times that I am sitting in a house by the sea at four o'clock and that it is raining but I know that it is half past five and I am sitting in an old chair over a funeral parlor."

"You remember Tony Nailles?"

"Yes."

"I am going to kill him," Hammer said. "I am going to burn him on the altar of Christ's Church."

"Get out of here," the swami said. "Get out of the Temple of Light."

The Lewellens' guests had been invited for seven thirty. Tommy Lewellen stood on his terrace. His idea of a party was a day and a night he had spent in West Berlin with three Kurfürstendamm whores. That was a party. Things were different in Bullet Park, he thought, as he watched the caterer's waiters set tables for fifty under a tent lighted with paper lanterns. "The Amalgamated Development Corporation and Mr. and Mrs. Thomas Lewellen cordially request the pleasure . . ." The business name on the invitation was put there so Lewellen could claim the party as a tax exemption. If the claim was accepted the party would cost him nothing and he would net a thousand. Lewellen was more interested in the financial arrangements of his wife's parties than in anything else. He sometimes got so bored that he seemed to see straight through the display of elegance to the bills, canceled checks, even the nails in the floor. What was wrong with friendly talk and well-dressed men and women eating ham and chicken? Nothing, nothing, nothing at all except that the blandness of the scene would be offensive. No one would get drunk, no one would fight, no one would likely get screwed, nothing would be celebrated, commemorated or advanced. If the gathering he awaited stood at the brink of anything it stood at the brink of licentiousness. Sheer niceness, he thought, might drive a man to greet his guests wearing nothing but a cockwig. Gross and public indecencies would cure the evening of its timelessness and relate it vigorously to death. The waiters were setting out bowls of flowers. The flowers looked fresh enough but Lewellen guessed they had spent the afternoon at a wedding reception and would, after a night in the refrigerator, wilt during a fund-raising lunch in Greenwich, Connecticut.

The energies of change were almost unknown to Lewellen, but that the scene that was about to begin would claim to be totally innocent of change made it half a scene, half a loaf, half an anything, a picture cut from a magazine and pasted against the evening sky, and what a miserable thing was the sky—thought Lewellen—a boring reach of blue with some thunderclouds stacked up in the west like the towers of an old-fashioned West Side apartment hotel, the last abode of funky Hungarian widows who left their dirty dishes in the hallway. What a bore was the sky! Thunder sounded. The rhythm of thunder, thought Lewellen, was like the rhythm of a large orgasm. He liked that.

He could see against the clear afterglow in the northwest clouds of black smoke rising from the ghetto on the riverbanks. The wind was from the south, and if there had been any shooting he would not have heard it.

Tony Nailles, who would direct traffic, came over the lawn with a flashlight. "Hi Tony," said Lewellen. "You want a drink?" "I'd like a beer," Tony said. "There isn't any beer," said Lewellen, "why don't you have a gin and tonic?" As Tony went over to one of the two bars, a car came up the drive and stopped on the lawn. It was the Wickwires. They were, as always, impeccably dressed and incandescently charming but he wore dark glasses and had a piece of court plaster over one eye. "What a divine idea to have a tent," she exclaimed. She was in a wheelchair.

Nailles, stepping into the bathroom, found Nellie naked and took her in his arms. "If we're going to do it," Nellie said, "let's do it before I take my bath." They did. Then Nailles prepared to dress. Nellie had put his clothes on the bed and, standing naked above them, Nailles felt a powerful reluctance to dress. Having, in his experience with trains, learned something about the mysterious polarities that moved him, he wondered what would happen if his unwillingness to dress turned into a phobia. Would he spend the rest of his life padding naked around the bedroom while poor Nellie tried to conceal his condition from the rest of the world? He did not cherish his nakedness but he detested his suit. Spread out on the bed it seemed to claim a rectitude and a uniformity that was repulsively unlike his nature. Did he want to go to the party in a fig leaf, a tiger skin, nothing at all? Something like that.

Nailles thought about his mother. He had visited her on Tuesday night. "Are you feeling any better, Mother," he had asked. "Would you like Tony to come and see you. Is there anything I can get you." She had not replied for nearly a month. Then from some part of his mind, deeper than memory, he heard singing:

> "The poor soul sat singing by a sycamore tree,
> Sing all a green willow,
> Her hand on her bosom, her head on her knee,
> Sing willow, willow, willow."

Dressed, Nailles began to look for his wallet. It would be in the jacket pocket of the suit he had worn that afternoon. When he reached into the pocket he found it empty. The empty pocket seemed mysteriously portentous, as if he had asked some grave questions about pain and death and had got no answer; had been told there was none. "I came into the house," he said aloud, "and I made a drink and then I went upstairs and undressed and took a shower so it must be in the bedroom somewhere." He must have put the wallet on some surface in the bedroom and now he examined all of these—the dressing table, the chest of drawers, etc. It was nowhere. He could not recall having been in any of the other bedrooms but he examined them. He heard Nellie's heels coming down the hall. "I've lost my wallet," he said. "Oh dear," said Nellie. He had no use for the wallet that night, she knew, but she knew that he would not go to the party without it. The loss of any object was for both of them acute as if their lives rested on some substructure of talismans. "I came into the house," Nailles kept saying, "and I made a drink and then I went upstairs and I undressed and took a shower so it must be here somewhere."

For the next half hour or longer they were upstairs, downstairs, in and out of the living room, opening unused drawers onto collections of Christmas ribbon, feeling under chairs, lifting up newspapers and magazines, shaking out pillows and grabbing under cushions. To look into their faces you would have thought they had lost their grail, their cross, their anchor. Why couldn't Nailles go to the party without his wallet? He couldn't. "I came into the house," he said, "and I made a drink and then I went upstairs and undressed and took a shower." "Oh here it is," cried Nellie. It was the pure voice of an angel, freed from the mortal bonds of grossness and aspiration. "It was in the pantry under the minutes of your last meeting. You must have put it there when you made your drink." "Thank you darling, thank you," said Nailles to his deliverer. They started for the party. Thunder sounded. The noise reminded Nailles again of what it had felt like to be young and easy. "You know I was awfully happy that summer I climbed in the Tirol," he said. "I climbed the Grand Kaiser and the Pengelstein. In the Tirol when there's a thunderstorm they ring all the church bells. All up and down the valley. It's very exciting. I don't know why I tell you all of this. I guess it must be the storm."

Eliot and Nellie got to the party at quarter to eight. Ten minutes later Hammer parked his car at the foot of the driveway. He was very drunk and had not changed his clothes. He wore a sweater. Tony called down to him: "Please bring your car up. There's plenty of room on the lawn. Please bring your car up." When Hammer did not move Tony jogged down the drive. "Please bring your car up the driveway," he said. "There's still plenty of room on the hill."

"I have to leave early," Hammer said, "and I thought that if I parked here it would be easier to get away."

"You won't have any trouble," Tony said. "They're only expecting about thirty cars."

"Well get in then," Hammer said, "and I'll drive you up the hill."

As soon as Tony slipped into the car Hammer flushed the Mace into his eyes. Tony let out a loud, hoarse roar of pain and fell forward, striking his head on the dashboard. Hammer gave him a vicious, a murderer's blow with the truncheon. He drove the short distance to church, where the door was, as usual, unlocked for prayer and meditation.

He was luckier than he knew. Ten minutes earlier Miss Templeton had finished arranging the roses on the altar. He dragged Tony into the narthex and then went back to his car for the gasoline. Then he locked the narthex door, the only door into the church, excepting the door to the vestarium. The only light that burned was the vigil, and in this faint light he dragged Tony down the aisle to the chancel. He found the switch for the chancel lights and was about to pour the gasoline onto Tony when he thought he would first smoke a cigarette. He was tired and winded. He laughed when he noticed how expertly the Lamb of God on the altar hooked its hoof around the wooden standard of Christendom. He heard a stir from the narthex and he thought his heart would explode until he realized that it was nothing. It had begun to rain. That was all.

When Rutuola got out of a taxi at the Lewellens' the headwaiter stopped him. "If it's a delivery," he said, "you'll have to go in the back way."

"I have to see Mr. Nailles," the swami said.

"You can't come in here."

"Mr. Nailles, Mr. Nailles," he shouted. "Mr. Nailles, come here quickly please."

Nailles, who was standing at one of the bars, heard his name called and left the tent. "Go to Christ's Church," Rutuola said. "Don't ask me any questions. Go to Christ's Church now."

Nailles felt, from Rutuola's voice, that Tony was in danger but he did not run to the car and did nothing else hurriedly. His lips were swollen. His nerves were unusually steady. Some cars, coming up from the railroad station where the late train had just arrived, slowed him down but he did not take the risk of trying to pass them. When he got to the church he recognized Hammer's car.

In some way he had expected this. He pounded on the locked door.

"Who is it," Hammer asked.

"Nailles."

"You can't get in. I've locked all the doors."

"What are you doing, what are you going to do?"

"I'm going to kill Tony."

Nailles returned to his car. There was a loud and painful ringing in his ears that seemed like some part of his purposefulness. He was neither frightened nor confused. He drove directly to Chestnut Lane, got the chain saw from the cellar and returned to the church.

"Hammer?"

"Yes."

"Is Tony all right?"

"He's all right now but I'm going to kill him. First I want to finish this cigarette."

Nailles put his foot on the strut of the saw and gave a steady draw to the starting cord. The cylinders made a putting sound and then, as the transmission caught, the chain began its howling. The lancet door was paneled but the interstices were made of thin wood and the chain splintered and cut through them. He made a diagonal slash across the door and broke it easily with his shoulders. Hammer was sitting in a front pew, crying. The red gasoline tank was beside him. Nailles lifted his son off the altar and carried him out into the rain. It was pouring. Water seemed to crowd into the light. The rain fell with such force that it stripped the leaves off the trees and the air smelled of bilge. It was the cold rain that brought

Tony around. "Daddy," he mumbled, "Daddy. Who was that man in the sweater? What did he want?"

"Are you hurt? I mean are you seriously hurt? Do you think we ought to go to the hospital?"

"No I'm all right. I have a headache and my eyes hurt but I'd rather go home."

The papers carried the story. "Chain saw balks bizarre homicide. Eliot Nailles, of Chestnut Lane, Bullet Park, New York, cut his way through the locked door of Christ's Church early last evening with a chain saw and succeeded in saving the life of his son, Anthony. Paul Hammer, also of Bullet Park, confessed to attempted homicide and was remanded to the State Hospital for the Criminally Insane. Hammer confessed to having kidnapped the young man from a dinner party given by Mr. and Mrs. Thomas Lewellen of Marlborough Circle. He carried Nailles to the church with the object of immolating him in the chancel. He intended, he claimed, to awaken the world."

Tony went back to school on Monday and Nailles—drugged—went off to work and everything was as wonderful, wonderful, wonderful, wonderful as it had been.

A NOTE
ON THE TYPE

The text of this book is set in Monticello, a Linotype revival of the original Binny & Ronaldson Roman No. 1, cut by Archibald Binny and cast in 1796 by that Philadelphia type foundry. The face was named Monticello in honor of its use in the monumental fifty-volume *Papers of Thomas Jefferson*, published by Princeton University Press. Monticello is a transitional type design, embodying certain features of Bulmer and Baskerville, but it is a distinguished face in its own right.

Composed, printed, and bound by
the Haddon Craftsmen, Inc., Scranton, Pa.

Typography and binding design by
Kenneth Miyamoto